Thunder in the Mountains

The Story of the Nez Perce War

Written and Illustrated
by
Ronald K. Fisher

Edited by
Dr. Merle Wells, Idaho Historical Society

 Alpha Omega, Coeur d'Alene, Idaho

Library of Congress Catalog Card Number: 91-76063

ISBN: 0-941734-02-1

Cover: "Chief Joseph," an original oil
painting by Nola Mileck.
©1987 by Nola Mileck
Cover design by Kathy Spence, Action Printers.

Published by Alpha Omega, Coeur d'Alene, Idaho.

Printed and bound in the United States of America
by BookCrafters, Chelsea, Michigan
and Action Printers, Coeur d'Alene, Idaho.

Thunder in the Mountains

The Story of the Nez Perce War

Ronald K. Fisher

For my mom, Myrtle A. Fisher, whose patience, interest, and support remains constant through countless rewrites
and
Charlene Wicks, whose encouragement, advice, and opinions I value highly
and
Nancy Williamson, whose friendship, proofreading skill, and enthusiasm for this project were greatly appreciated
and
Dr. Merle Wells, whose willingness to share his wealth of historical knowledge I have come to depend upon.

Table of Contents

Chapter 1
Mother Earth's Chosen People

Long, long ago, before the time of human beings, the earth was inhabited by a race of animal people. These mythical creatures lived much as the Indians who inherited the land from them. They talked, fished, hunted, dug camas, lived in tepees, used sweat lodges, and elected chiefs. Some were giants, some could change from animal to human form at will, others put their fur on and off like a fluffy coat, and still others had mysterious supernatural powers.

The animal people had names like Fox, Beaver, Eagle, Grizzly Bear, Ant, and Spider. The greatest of these was Coyote. With powerful supernatural forces at his command, he enjoyed playing cruel tricks and sometimes caused much trouble. However, just as he could be vain greedy, and foolish, he could also be good and kind. Coyote did much to help his friends among the animal people.

Coyote used his power to look into the future and predict the dawning of a new age when creatures called human beings would struggle to overcome sorrow.

One day a huge monster appeared in the land of the animal people. It satisfied its voracious appetite by devouring every creature it encountered. The terrified animals cried for help. They begged the powerful Coyote to save them from a terrible death. Coyote became angry when he saw his friends fall prey to the savage beast. He devised a clever plan to remove the danger.

Coyote used his magic to make himself appear small and weak. He sought out the monster and placed himself directly in its path. The beast was always hungry and soon Coyote found himself facing its enormous, open jaws. In his present reduced size, Coyote was hardly more than a single bite for the monster who swallowed him whole in one gulp. Once inside, Coyote went to work. Withdrawing a knife concealed in his thick fur, he began stabbing and tearing at the monster's insides. The great beast threw itself violently from side to side and rolled upon the ground. It begged its tormentor to stop. But it was too late. The brave Coyote slashed and hacked even more fiercely until at last the gigantic monster lay dead.

Exhausted, Coyote crawled from the creature's mouth. Once outside, he returned to his normal size. In a short time, he was joined by Fox who was filled with admiration by the brave deed. "Well done!" Fox said to Coyote. "At last our people are free!"

But Coyote's work was not yet complete. Gripping his knife, he cut the monster's body into tiny pieces which he scattered about the land in all directions. As each piece of flesh touched the ground, it was magically transformed into one of the many Indian tribes who now roam the earth. When the last of the pieces was gone, Fox said, "Brother Coyote, you have done a great thing. But you have nothing left to create a tribe for the beautiful valley in which we stand. Surely land such as this deserves a people of its own to watch over and care for it."

2

Coyote was the mythological creator of the animal people.

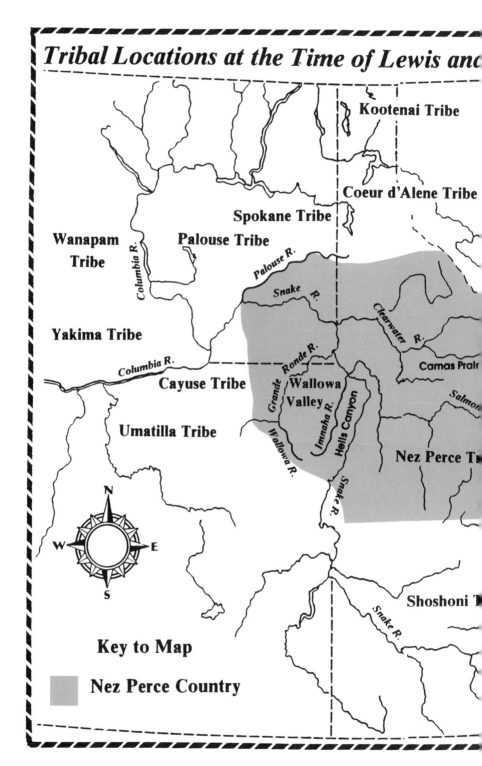

Tribal Locations at the Time of Lewis and

Kootenai Tribe

Coeur d'Alene Tribe

Spokane Tribe

Palouse Tribe

Wanapam
Tribe

Columbia R.

Palouse R.

Snake R.

Clearwater R.

Yakima Tribe

Columbia R.

Camas Prair

Cayuse Tribe

Grande Ronde R.

Wallowa
Valley

Imnaha R.

Hells Canyon

Salmon

Umatilla Tribe

Wallowa R.

Nez Perce T

Snake R.

N
W E
S

Shoshoni

Snake R.

Key to Map

Nez Perce Country

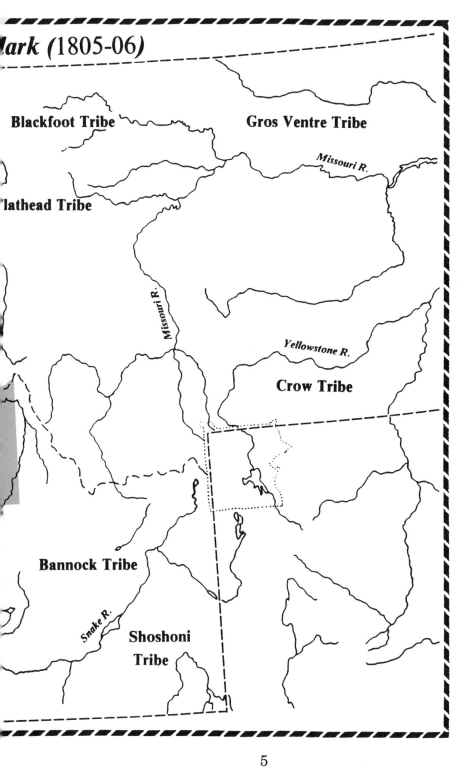

lark (1805-06)

Blackfoot Tribe

Gros Ventre Tribe

Missouri R.

lathead Tribe

Missouri R.

Yellowstone R.

Crow Tribe

Bannock Tribe

Snake R.

Shoshoni
Tribe

"Ah, brother Fox," said Coyote, "I do have something left for this special place. Behold!" So saying, Coyote held up his hands still covered with the rich blood of the monster's heart. Coyote shook his fingers and sprinkled droplets of blood on the fertile earth. In this way, from the most important part of the great beast, its heart, came the most important tribe, Nimipu, We People, also called the Nez Perces.

Such was the legend of the creation of the Nez Perce tribe. It was told to countless, wide-eyed Indian children as they sat transfixed around campfires in the lodges of their people. Nimipu! We People! How proud they were to be among the favored of the great spirits of nature!

From stories such as these, the Nez Perces learned tribal pride, bravery, honor, and a love of nature. They developed a strong protective attitude toward their beloved homeland given to them by the old ones, the animal spirits of long ago at the beginning of time. The earth was their mother from which they sprang as the droplets of blood fell from Coyote's crimson fingers. From the earth they drew strength. It nourished and sustained them. It protected the bones of their ancestors and promised a home for each new generation. Mother Earth was a nurturing parent for her Nez Perce children.

For countless generations the Nez Perces remained secure and unchallenged masters of their ancestral homeland in the Pacific Northwest. This beautiful, fertile area included approximately twenty-seven thousand square miles of land in northcentral Idaho, northeastern Oregon, and southeastern Washington. The mighty Snake River and its tributaries, the Salmon, Clearwater, Imnaha, and Grande Ronde, provided a network of waterways to sustain lush valleys, rich grasslands, and abundant wildlife. These fertile areas included the Camas Prairie in central

Idaho where each year Indians gathered camas, their main winter food, and the Palouse Hills in southeastern Washington where thousands of Indian ponies grazed in fields of bunchgrass.

Rich though their territory was, the wealth of the Nez Perce people was not based on land. It stemmed from their skillful breeding of fine horses.

Horses mysteriously disappeared from the New World during prehistoric times. They were returned in 1519 when Spanish explorers arrived in North America. At first, mounted soldiers terrorized the Indians who fled from the fearsome beasts with their armored riders. Soon, however, fear gave way to curiosity and Indians quickly discovered the many advantages of owning and riding horses. The animal changed their entire way of life. They could travel farther in all directions trading and enriching their culture with information from other tribes. They could hunt better, fight better, and protect their families better. Indians became expert horsemen. Many tribes centered their entire way of life on developing their equestrian skill and increasing their valuable herds.

Between 1710 and 1720, the Nez Perces acquired horses from their neighbors to the south, the Shoshonis. The Nez Perces appeared to have a natural talent for raising horses. By 1750 they were expert horsemen with large magnificent herds. They were one of the few tribes to develop and consistently practice the skills of selective breeding. Their animals, highly valued for endurance, were much sought after as buffalo and war horses. Their beautiful, rugged Appaloosa continues to be bred today by many horse fanciers and used as a symbol for the gem state of Idaho.

The acquisition of horses enabled the Nez Perces to increase their mobility. They traveled from their homeland west across the Columbia River to The Dalles and the land

By 1750, the Nez Perces were expert breeders of horses.

of the Yakima tribe. They traveled east across the Continental Divide to the buffalo country along the headwaters of the Colorado, Missouri, and Yellowstone rivers. They traded with the plains tribes and began to copy their adornment. The long, flowing war bonnet of eagle feathers was proudly worn by Nez Perce leaders for the first time.

The Nez Perces made friends with many tribes they met in their travels. They also made some enemies. The Blackfeet were very territorial and resented the intrusion of anyone upon their land. The Nez Perces quickly learned to fear this fierce tribe and ventured into their area only when they had enough warriors to withstand a sudden attack.

According to tribal history, one such journey into Blackfoot territory occured late in the eighteenth century. The purpose was a buffalo hunt, but the end result was of far greater importance to the Nez Perce people. The hunting party included a young girl called Watkuweis (a name which can roughly be translated "Stray Away"). It is not known if the group located a buffalo herd, but they did encounter a savage Blackfoot war party. During the battle that followed, Watkuweis was captured and carried far away from her people. The frightened girl was taken to Canada where she was sold as a slave from tribe to tribe. Finally, she was purchased by a white man who lived in the eastern Red River settlements. The white people were kind to Watkuweis. Though she still missed her homeland, she found a sense of security among the French-Canadians.

While in the settlement, Watkuweis gave birth to her first child. Soon after, things began to change. The young mother grew increasingly unhappy with her new life. Each day the desire to return home grew stronger and stronger. At last Watkuweis took her baby and ran away. She traveled for months through the harsh wilderness. Undoubtedly she suffered a great deal during this time. The long journey proved far too difficult for her infant child who died along the way. Finally, the exhausted girl reached a group of friendly Salish Indians who helped reunite her with her people. Overjoyed to be home again, Watkuweis eagerly shared stories of her capture and life among the white men. She called them So-ya-po (the Crowned Ones) because of the tall hats they wore. The Nez Perces were fascinated with these stories. Watkuweis was the first of their people to actually meet the strange and powerful men with white skin who they had learned about from other tribes. The stories fired their imaginations and the Nez Perces grew eager to see these new people for themselves.

Chapter 2

The Arrival of the Crowned Ones

Though the Nez Perce tribe had yet to be visited by white explorers, by 1800 they were becoming increasingly aware of their presence on the North American Continent. They saw colorful beads, silver ornaments, and other articles proudly displayed by tribes who had encountered white trappers and traders. They had yet to hear their first explosion of rifle fire, but they were told about the powerful weapons carried by white men. If they had known that these rifle shots would herald the beginning of their fight for survival and end their traditional way of life, perhaps the Nez Perces would not have awaited their deadly arrival with such impatience.

Shortly after the Nez Perces became expert horsemen, the Blackfeet acquired their first guns. They were obtained from Great Britain's Hudson's Bay Company which was slowly extending its trapping westward across Canada. These weapons forever changed the course of intertribal warfare. The Blackfeet became more hostile than ever and claimed the entire buffalo country for themselves. Their defense of the hunting ground was so effective the Nez Perces cancelled their annual trips across the

11

Lolo Trail to the Bitterroot Valley in 1800. Instead, they traveled southeast to the Lemhi Valley and the plains of the Upper Snake River to replenish their supply of meat. Unfortunately, this land had already been claimed by the Shoshoni tribe who would fight to defend it. Wherever they went, it appeared the Nez Perces would have to purchase their right to hunt with the blood of their young warriors.

In 1805, Broken Arm, a great Nez Perce chief, decided it was time to arm his people with the powerful weapons of the white man. The land of the Hidatsa, over a thousand miles away in present-day North Dakota, appeared to be the best place for trading. The chief selected three of the tribe's strongest young warriors to make the long, dangerous journey east over the snow-filled Lolo Pass.

Broken Arm also decided to extend the hand of friendship to the Shoshonis. He thought perhaps the two tribes could join together and drive the Blackfeet away from the buffalo country. He chose three more young men to carry his message and the pipe of peace southward.

Sadly, the Nez Perce envoys were viewed as intruders by the Shoshoni people. Broken Arm's men were killed before they could attempt to accomplish their mission.

When news of the murders reached Broken Arm's village, his people demanded an attack on their Shoshoni enemies. By late summer, a war party was prepared to strike southward.

Their departure was temporarily interrupted by the return of the three men sent to purchase guns from the Hidatsas. Exhausted from their travels, the trio proudly displayed six rifles and a supply of powder and lead. These were the first such weapons to reach Nez Perce hands. The youths also had exciting news about a large group of white men who had spent the previous winter in the Mandan

Horses and guns forever changed the Nez Perce way of life.

Indian villages. Though they had not seen these explorers themselves, they were said to be traveling west directly toward the land of the Nez Perces. They would undoubtedly arrive in the very near future.

Interested though he was in the report of his young men, Broken Arm still had a war to fight with the Shoshonis who had attacked his messengers. On September 14, 1805, the chief departed with a large war party containing all his able-bodied fighting men. He left the camp of women, children, and old people in the care of Tetoharsky, his peace chief, and Twisted Hair, a notable chief who had grown too old to fight.

As the war party made its way south, Tetoharsky and Twisted Hair led the remainder of their people west to the Weippe Prairie to begin their fall harvest of camas roots. It was there, on September 20, they learned of the arrival of the first white men on their land.

Formerly excited by the idea of at last meeting white explorers, the chiefs became alarmed under the present circumstances. Suppose the powerful newcomers were hostile? With the warriors away, who would protect the helpless people left in their care? Tetoharsky and Twisted Hair held a council with the other men to decide what action to take. Some suggested they could successfully defend themselves if they conducted a surprise attack on the white men. Others proposed they welcome the newcomers and take the chance they came in peace and friendship.

While these discussions progressed, an old woman dared to approach the council. Normally, Nez Perce women were not allowed to voice their opinions when the men gathered together. However, this one demanded to be heard. Her name was Watkuweis. She reminded the council that while they had never met a white man, she had lived in a white settlement in Canada. She recounted the many acts of kindness shown to her by the French-Canadians. Now, she asked that her people help her repay her debt by treating these white explorers as the Canadians had treated her. Watkuweis insisted that the hand of friendship be extended to the newcomers.

After much discussion, the chiefs agreed to accept the advice of Watkuweis. They decided to lay aside their fears and welcome the white men into their territory.

The Lewis and Clark Expedition, officially called the Corps of Discovery, entered the Nez Perce homeland about three miles from the present town of Weippe, Idaho. The explorers were weak from starvation having run out of

Watkuweis begged her people to welcome Lewis and Clark.

food as they crossed the rugged Lolo Trail. Twisted Hair and Tetoharsky welcomed them and gave them salmon and camas roots to eat. The hungry white men ate too much too fast and became very ill. It was almost a week before they were recovered enough to travel or work.

During this time they became acquainted with their native hosts, who belonged to one of the largest tribes in the Northwest numbering between four thousand and six thousand individuals. The explorers called them Choppunnish Indians because they thought they heard them use that word in reference to themselves. Clark became friends with Twisted Hair who he described as "a cheerful man of about 65 with apparent sincerity."

Lewis and Clark held a council with the Nez Perce chiefs to explain the purpose of their visit and ask for help when they continued on their way. They said they had been sent by the Great Father in Washington (referring to President Thomas Jefferson) to explore this area and establish a route to the Pacific Ocean. They said the Great Father wanted all Indian tribes to live in peace with each other and with the white men. If friendly relations could be established, other Americans would follow the expedition bringing many wonderful things to trade with the Nez Perces. Lewis and Clark ended the meeting by presenting gifts to those in attendance.

The chiefs listened attentively and agreed to help the white explorers on their journey. Twisted Hair drew a map of the river beyond his camp on a white elk skin. He also offered to send five of his people as guides when the Corps of Discovery left the village.

The explorers learned they could now travel by canoe down the Clearwater and Snake rivers to the Columbia River. They set up camp near the Clearwater and fashioned five dugout canoes for the trip. By October 7, they were ready to continue on their way.

The white men branded their horses and left them in the care of Chief Twisted Hair. The Indians were sorry to see their new friends depart, but they remembered the promise that more Americans would follow bringing many wonderful things to their people.

Lewis and Clark revisited the Nez Perces in May, 1806 on their return trip to St. Louis. Twisted Hair returned the white men's horses in good condition. Once again, the explorers enjoyed the hospitality of the Indians' camp. Council meetings were held during which President Jefferson's plans for the Oregon Country were further explained. The Oregon Country included the present-day

William Clark   **Meriwether Lewis**

states of Washington, Oregon, Idaho, and parts of Montana and Wyoming. It also included a part of Canada. The Nez Perces welcomed the Americans' offer of peace and friendship. One young boy demonstrated his people's good will by presenting a fine mare and her colt as gifts to Lewis and Clark.

The second visit reinforced and cemented feelings of good will between the white men and the Indian people. When it was over, several young warriors agreed to guide the expedition back over the rugged, snow-covered Bitterroot Mountains. The tribe looked forward with greater anticipation to the arrival of more new friends from the East.

In a very short time, the promises of Lewis and Clark began to come true for the Nez Perce people. David Thompson, a member of the British North West Trading Company, began to extend his work toward the Oregon Country. Thompson built a trading post in Canada which he called Kootenai House on the upper part of the Columbia River near the present British Columbia-Montana border.

Eager to begin trading, some Nez Perce and Flathead warriors attempted to visit the new post as soon as they learned about it. However, they were driven away by a hostile group of Blackfoot, Piegan, and Blood Indians. The Nez Perces and Flatheads persisted and finally arrived at Kootenai House in December, 1807.

In 1809, Thompson moved farther south to establish two more posts closer to the land of the Nez Perces. The first of these, Kullyspell House, was located on the northeastern shore of Lake Pend Oreille in northern Idaho. It was the first building constructed by a white man in the Pacific Northwest. The second trading post, Saleesh House, was located on the Clark Fork River near Thompson Falls, Montana. Saleesh House was intended primarily for the Flathead Indians. However, it was conveniently located for Nez Perces to visit on their way to and from the buffalo ground.

The name "Nez Perce" (Pierced Nose) was first applied to the tribe by French-Canadian traders sometime between 1805 and 1835. It is claimed some Frenchmen noticed that these Indians had pierced their noses to insert ornaments made from shells. David Thompson made the first written use of the name when he recorded, ". . . traded a very trifle of provisions from the Nez Perce." Though the Indians deny ever having practiced this custom, the name became attached to their people and has become an accepted means of referring to them.

In 1810, two of Thompson's men, Jaco Finlay and Finan McDonald, at last built a trading post for the Nez Perce Indians. This facility, called Spokane House, was located about ten miles northwest of the present-day city of Spokane, Washington. In addition to the Nez Perce, the post served the Spokane and Kalispel tribes.

As the number of opportunities for trading increased, so did the number of guns owned by Nez Perce warriors. Shortly after the opening of Saleesh House, the tribe possessed enough of these weapons to dramatically alter the course of warfare with their enemies in the buffalo country. In 1810, a group of Nez Perce and Flathead warriors used their new rifles to defeat a Piegan war party on the plains. The Piegans were so enraged they attempted to prevent Thompson from traveling east for supplies to restock his forts in the Northwest.

A gentleman in London by the name of Beau Brummel set the trend for wearing beaver hats. As the fashion spread quickly throughout Europe and America, the demand for beaver greatly increased. The glossy fur became almost as valuable as gold. The abundance of beaver in the Pacific Northwest caused trappers to flock to the area.

Each year after David Thompson extended the fur business into their territory, the Nez Perces saw an increased number of trappers and traders on their land. This continued until the early 1840's when the beaver were almost gone and silk hats replaced those made of fur among fashionably dressed men.

Thompson's work in the Oregon Country soon brought his North West Company into competition with another, older British firm—the Hudson's Bay Company. Established in 1670 to trap in the area around Hudson's Bay in north central Canada, the HBC had slowly extended its operation west across Canada and south into the Oregon Country.

A fierce rivalry between the two firms soon exploded into open warfare. This nearly caused the British government to close down both operations. To remain active, the

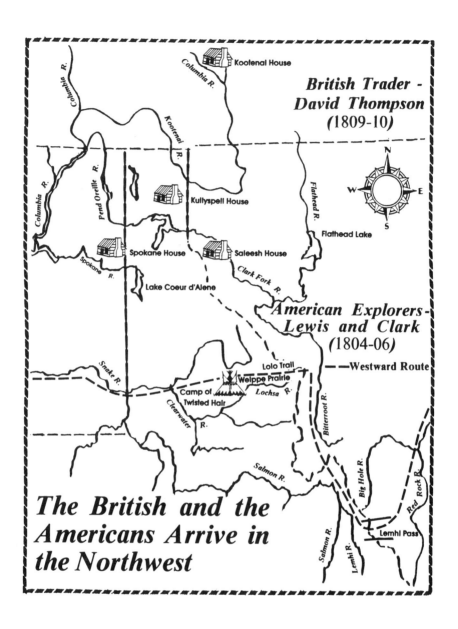

Kootenai House

British Trader - David Thompson (1809-10)

Columbia R.

Columbia R.

Kootenai R.

Pend Oreille R.

Kullyspell House

Flathead R.

Flathead Lake

Columbia R.

Spokane R.

Spokane House

Saleesh House

Clark Fork R.

Lake Coeur d'Alene

American Explorers - Lewis and Clark (1804-06)

Snake R.

Lolo Trail

Weippe Prairie

——**Westward Route**

Camp of Twisted Hair

Lochsa R.

Bitterroot R.

Clearwater R.

Salmon R.

Big Hole R.

Red Rock R.

The British and the Americans Arrive in the Northwest

Salmon R.

Lemhi R.

Lemhi Pass

companies merged in 1821 to create the new Hudson's Bay Company. This powerful organization sought to maintain firm control of the entire Pacific Northwest fur trade and eliminate any possible competition from American trappers.

The United States entered the western fur trade in 1811 with the arrival of John Jacob Astor's Pacific Fur Company. Astor intended to establish a trading post, called Fort Astoria, at the mouth of the Columbia River. This would serve as headquarters for a chain of posts to be built along the route traveled by Lewis and Clark. Astor sent one group of men by ship to begin construction of Fort Astoria while a second group traveled overland to find locations for the other forts.

The overland explorers, known as the Astorians, encountered many problems as they traveled west. Led by Astor's partner, William Price Hunt, the Americans fell victim to poor planning and bad decision making. Their suffering became almost unbearable when they reached Hells Canyon on the Snake River. This is the deepest gorge in North America. The explorers were unable to descend the steep canyon walls to obtain water. They were forced to drink rainwater when it was available from muddy puddles along the way. Food was also scarce and the starving Astorians filled their empty stomachs with strips of leather torn from their clothing. It is a wonder the exhausted group of travelers managed to find their way to the newly constructed Fort Astoria.

Shortly before reaching Hells Canyon, some of the Astorians led by Donald McKenzie left the main group to find a better route to the Columbia. These men arrived in a Nez Perce settlement where they were given food and shelter. The friendly Indians guided the explorers to the Clearwater River where they were able to travel by canoe safely to the lower Columbia and reach Fort Astoria in advance of Hunt and the other Astorians. McKenzie was so impressed with the hospitality of the Nez Perce people he decided to return one day and establish a trading post on their land.

Chapter 3

The Quest for the Book of Heaven

Increased contact with white trappers and traders continued to alter the Nez Perce way of life. Following the immense cultural impact of horses and firearms, was the equally tremendous effect of the white man's religion.

The Nez Perces had been somewhat aware of the white man's way of worshipping God since their first contact with Lewis and Clark. They had observed trappers and traders praying, reading from the Bible, and singing hymns. However, these things were only mildly interesting to them at the time. They had no relevance to the Indians' spiritual beliefs and traditional way of life.

Likewise, white men took little notice of the Indians' religion at first. They were interested in exploring and trading and cared nothing about influencing or changing ancient tribal beliefs.

The Hudson's Bay Company made one of the first organized attempts to convert Northwest tribes to the white man's religion. The company's license from the British Government stipulated that the HBC must provide religious instruction for all natives within its territories. The Columbia River Department ignored this directive until the early 1800's when a religious revival in England focused attention on its lack of compliance. Religious groups put pressure on Hudson's Bay Governor George Simpson to begin the conversion of tribes in the Pacific Northwest.

In 1824, Simpson made a tour of inspection and reorganization throughout the Columbia River District. When he arrived at Spokane House on October 24, he expressed his desire to send two young Indian boys to the Red River Missionary School near present-day Winnipeg in Manitoba, Canada.

At first the Indians were unwilling to send their children so far away to a strange place. Simpson wrote to Alexander Ross, the leader of HBC trapping brigades in the Snake River Valley. He asked Ross to help him convince the chiefs to take advantage of this valuable learning experience.

The Indians had no understanding of the white man's religion, but they were attracted to the power and knowledge which might be available to their people. They finally agreed to send two teen-aged youths to the Canadian mission.

The boys selected were Coutonais Pelly from the Kootenai tribe and Spokane Garry from the Spokane tribe. Residing at the mission from 1825 to 1829, the youths studied the English language and took courses in religion, reading, writing, geography, and farming. They returned home completely transformed by their experiences. Dressed in white man's clothing, they carried leatherbound copies of the King James Version of the Bible and the Book of Common Prayer of the Church of England. Filled with enthusiasm and armed with their newly-acquired knowledge, the young men began spreading the Word of God among the Salish and Shahaptin people.

Spokane Garry was especially impressive to the Indians of the Northwest. His father, Illim-Spokanee, was one of the most influential chiefs of the Spokane tribe. The chief died while his son was away at school. When the eighteen-year-old Garry returned home, his father's authority and respect were transferred to him. This tribal power combined with the knowledge he had acquired at the mission allowed Garry to command attention wherever he went.

Garry spent the winter of 1829–30 teaching the Spokanes and other tribes about the white man's God, Heaven, Hell, and Ten Commandments. He read selections from the Bible and sang religious hymns he had learned from the missionaries.

Many Indians came to hear Spokane Garry speak. Among them was Lawyer, son of Chief Twisted Hair and leader of the Kamiah band of Nez Perces. Lawyer was so named because of his persuasive ability and shrewd bargaining talents. He was joined by Timothy, chief of a Nez Perce band that lived opposite the juncture of the Snake and Clearwater rivers. These two leaders were inspired by Garry's words. They were also somewhat jealous of the Spokanes and wanted this knowledge and power for their own people.

The opportunity to attend missionary school was soon available to the Nez Perces. In 1830, the Hudson's Bay Company decided to send five more young Indian boys to the Red River school. Garry and Pelly also decided to return at this time to further their education. Among the new students chosen were two Nez Perces. One, named Ellis, was the son of Red Grizzly Bear, a powerful war chief who had met Lewis and Clark. The other was a young man named Pitt. The remaining three boys were from the Cayuse, Spokane, and Kootenai tribes.

The youths remained at the mission until the summer of 1833. Like Garry and Pelly, they learned English and much about the white man's religion. However, when they returned home, they failed to create the sensation or achieve the status attained by Spokane Garry. They enjoyed brief periods of influence, but soon faded into the ranks of their tribesmen.

This was not the end of the Nez Perces' quest for an understanding of the white man's religion. At the insistence of Timothy and Lawyer, the Nez Perces joined the Flatheads in 1831 to send representatives east to request missionaries for their people. The tribes also hoped to acquire their own copies of the white man's Book of Heaven (the Bible) which had become a symbol of knowledge and power among many Northwest tribes.

The chiefs chose to send emissaries to the Americans rather than the British at the Red River settlement. The reason for this is unknown. Perhaps they remembered the kindness of Lewis and Clark and thought the United States would be more receptive to their requests.

Four men made the long journey east to St. Louis. One was an older Flathead chief named Man of the Morning. The other three were Nez Perces. They included a prominent 44-year-old warrior named Speaking Eagle and two younger men in their twenties known as Rabbit Skin Leggings and No Horns on His Head.

The Indians did not know how to reach their destination. Their only hope of a successful trip was to join one of the American fur caravans. These would be returning east after attending their yearly rendezvous with Rocky Mountain trappers. The opportunity for travel presented itself in the late summer of 1831 when traders Drips and Fontenelle left Cache Valley with their load of furs. The

Americans permitted the Indians to accompany them to St. Louis.

Overwhelmed by the wonders of the white man's world, the tribesmen stayed close to Fontenelle when they reached the city. The trader took them to see William Clark, the old friend of their people who was now Superintendent of Indian Affairs. Clark extended a warm welcome to his four visitors. They were the first Northwest Indians he had seen since the completion of his expedition in 1806. Though they did not speak English, the warriors managed to communicate the reasons for their visit including their interest in the white man's religion and their desire for missionaries.

Fontenelle next took the Indians to a Catholic church. There, the Right Reverend Joseph Rosati, Bishop of St. Louis, described them as "exceedingly well pleased" with the church. Unfortunately, no one spoke their language and the Indians had a great deal of trouble communicating with the priests.

As their tour of the city continued, Speaking Eagle and Man of the Morning became seriously ill. They were visited by two priests who baptized them and gave them each a crucifix. Bishop Rosati wrote: "The poor Indians seemed delighted with the visit . . . a little cross was presented to them. They took it with eagerness, kissed it repeatedly, and it could be taken from them only after death."

The two Indians died and were buried in the Catholic cemetary. Their younger companions were now left alone to complete their mission. Failing to secure a definite promise of missionaries for their people, Rabbit Skin Leggings and No Horns on His Head decided to return home. They left St. Louis on March 26, 1832 with Fontenelle and his men aboard a steamboat called the Yellowstone.

Rabbit Skin Leggings   **No Horns on His Head**

The journey was to end in tragedy for the young Nez Perces. Indians had no immunity to white man's diseases. Even simple childhood ailments such as measles caused the death of numerous Native Americans. When the travelers reached the mouth of the Yellowstone River, No Horns on His Head became ill with a disease he had contracted in St. Louis. He, like the two older members of his group, died before he could share his knowledge of the white man's culture with his people.

Rabbit Skin Leggings sadly continued his journey home with Fontenelle's pack train. When he reached Pierre's Hole in southeastern Idaho, he joined a band of Nez Perces who were making preparations for a buffalo hunt.

Rabbit Skin Leggings was the center of attention as he shared his recent adventures in the great city of the white man. However, he held the Indians' interest for only a short time. The camp was soon filled with excitement caused by the arrival of a group of traders led by Captain

Benjamin Louis Eulalie de Bonneville. The accomplishments of Rabbit Skin Leggings were temporarily forgotten as the Nez Perces eagerly welcomed the Americans.

Bonneville, a graduate of West Point, was a career army officer of French descent. In 1831, he was granted a leave of absence from the military to enter the Pacific Northwest fur trade. Bonneville's motives remain a mystery. However, it is thought he may have been gathering information about the land, Indians, and activities of the British Hudson's Bay Company for the American Government.

Though Bonneville remained unaware of Rabbit Skin Leggings, he did take note of the pious and honest nature of the Nez Perce people. The captain thought perhaps these Indians had already been visited by missionaries whose influence caused their surprisingly Christian behavior.

When Bonneville departed from the camp on March 15, he left one of his men and a supply of trade goods with the Nez Perces. The trader, a man named Hodgkiss, was instructed to exchange his merchandise for beaver pelts collected by the tribe.

Soon after their parting from the Americans, the Nez Perces discovered a large group of Blackfoot Indians had invaded their territory. Blue John, an important Nez Perce warrior, decided a raid on the enemies' horse herd might help prevent an attack on his people. After consulting his guardian spirit, Blue John said the undertaking would be successful if no rain fell before the Nez Perces reached the Blackfeet. Encouraged by this prediction, many warriors, including Rabbit Skin Leggings, quickly formed a war party.

Clear weather inspired confidence as the Nez Perces departed on their mission. However, before they reached the

Blackfoot camp at the end of a long canyon, the sky filled with clouds and rain began to fall.

Blackfoot scouts were quick to notice the approaching war party. They spread the alarm bringing their main force of 300 warriors to attack the Nez Perces. When the battle was over, Blue John and all his followers lay dead. The only survivor was a Flathead warrior who had joined the raid against his people's Blackfoot enemies. This man carried news of the tragedy back to the Nez Perce people.

With the death of Rabbit Skin Leggings, all four messengers to St. Louis were gone. They died without having had the opportunity to make a complete report to their people. Their quest for missionaries appeared to have been a complete failure. However, the impressions created by these four brave men on the religious population of St. Louis would, in time, cause the churches to take action. Speaking Eagle, Man of the Morning, Rabbit Skin Leggings, and No Horns on His Head had indeed performed well and had opened the door for the arrival of missionaries in their homeland.

Chapter 4
The Bald Chief Visits the Wallowa Valley

In June, 1833, Bonneville returned to southeastern Idaho. Once again he was warmly welcomed by the Nez Perces. However, Hodgkiss reported the Indians were now unwilling to trade their beaver pelts to the Americans. HBC trader Francis Ermatinger had arrived offering higher prices for prime skins. Since it was impossible to outbid the wealthy Hudson's Bay Company, Bonneville decided to move his business to Wyoming and return later to visit other Nez Perce bands who lived farther west.

Bonneville spent the winter of 1833–34 beside the Portneuf River in southeastern Idaho. In the spring, determined to form trade alliances and compete with the HBC, the captain and some of his men journeyed farther into the Nez Perce homeland. The rest of the American traders remained encamped beside the river.

The Wallowa Valley had thus far failed to arouse the interest or attention of the white men. Covering an area of 3,178 square miles, the valley contained some of the deepest, most rugged canyons of the world along with some of the finest natural grazing land on the continent. Throughout the year, the land supported the Nez Perces' large herds of horses. Lush, high meadows provided summer grazing while deep, lava-rimmed canyons were rich in bunchgrass for winter fodder. Drained by the Wallowa River, the beautiful valley was the traditional homeland of the Wallamwatkin band of Nez Perces. These Indians had occupied the area for as long as anyone could remember. Completely content, they had known no other home nor did they desire one.

When Bonneville arrived in the Wallowa Valley in 1834, he was received in grand style by Tuekakas, the principal chief of the Wallamwatkin Nez Perces. This is history's first mention of the chief whose name means The Oldest Grizzly. Tuekakas was the son of a Cayuse chief and a Nez Perce woman. He would later be renamed "Old Joseph" by white men. His son, yet to be born in 1840, would also be called Joseph. This boy grown to manhood would become the famous chief who was the living symbol of the Nez Perces' fight for freedom.

Already in his late forties as he welcomed Bonneville, Tuekakas was a sturdy, muscular, strong-willed man. The entire population of his village turned out to greet the Americans. Dressed in their finest, the Nez Perces slowly approached their guests. Tuekakas arrived first and warmly clasped the hand of Bonneville as a sign of peace and friendship. The chief then introduced each member of his tribal council in order of their importance. These men also shook the captain's hand to reemphasize their leader's pledge of lasting good will. Later, the white men were entertained at a reception and banquet of deer, elk, buffalo, fish, and roots. The Nez Perces were very curious about the United States and kept the Americans busy answering their many questions.

Bonneville was delighted with his reception into the Wallowa Valley. He called the Nez Perces "among the gentlest and the least barbarous people of these remote wildernesses."

The Indians were equally impressed with the Americans who they called the "Big Hearts of the East." They were eager to trade and encouraged Bonneville to establish a fort in their valley.

Bonneville, himself, was of great interest to the Indians. They were fascinated by his stories and descriptions of the white man's world. They were even more surprised and curious when, as he talked, the captain removed his hat. Bonneville was completely bald! The long-haired Nez Perces were unfamiliar with this common hair loss problem of the white man. They immediately wanted to know if the captain had been scalped or born with this strange condition. Bonneville came to be known as the "Bald Chief" among the Indian people.

Encouraged by the friendship of Tuekakas and the Wallamwatkins, Bonneville continued his journey toward Hells Canyon on the Snake River. Near present-day Asotin, Washington, the captain met another band of Nez Perces led by an important buffalo-hunting and war chief. This man, named Apash Wyakaikt (Flint Color or Flint Necklace), was later renamed "Looking Glass" by white men because of a small, round trade mirror he wore braided into his hair. Like Tuekakas, Apash Wyakaikt was also the parent of a famous Nez Perce chief who would carry on his father's name. Young Looking Glass was to earn his place in history as the war chief of the Nez Perces in the great retreat of 1877.

Old Looking Glass welcomed Bonneville with the same courtesy formerly exhibited by the Wallamwatkins. The captain quickly earned the friendship of the Asotins by treating the chief's young daughter who had been suffering from a painful ailment for three days. Bonneville suggested a sweat bath followed by a dose of gunpowder dissolved in cold water. The treatment proved effective and the girl soon felt much better.

Looking Glass showed his appreciation by presenting Bonneville with one of his best horses. In the spirit of the moment, the captain gave the chief a rifle. This began an incident which demonstrates the shrewd trading ability of the Asotin leader. Eager to acquire more from the wealthy Americans, Looking Glass introduced his wife who appeared very sad and close to tears. The chief explained that she had loved the horse which he had just given to Bonneville. After the presentation, she had become extremely upset and he did not know how to comfort her. The captain felt sorry for the woman and gave her a pair of shiny earrings to help lift her spirits.

Looking Glass next introduced his son who he said had always cared for the horse which he loved a great deal. The tender-hearted Bonneville was moved by the sad-faced boy and presented him with a fine hatchet.

Looking Glass expressed his gratitude for the gifts and said his new rifle was a wonderful symbol of power. However, in reality, the weapon would remain useless without the powder and ball necessary to fire it. Bonneville got the message and provided a generous supply of ammunition for the chief's gun. Looking Glass had been well-compensated for the horse. He told Bonneville that each time he brought home meat for his family he would say, "This was killed by the rifle of my friend, the Bald-Headed Chief, to whom I gave that very fine horse." The crafty old chief smiled his approval of the day's exchange of gifts.

Bonneville continued his journey feeling increasingly optimistic about trade opportunities in the Northwest. On March 4, 1834, he reached Fort Walla Walla, an outpost of the Hudson's Bay Company. The clerk in charge, Pierre C.

Looking Glass struck a shrewd bargain with Captain Bonneville.

Pambrun, cordially welcomed the Americans even though they were potential adversaries in the fur trade. Eager to begin work, Bonneville remained at the post only two days. Before leaving, he bought supplies from Pambrun at greatly inflated trading post prices. Pambrun was later reprimanded by HBC Chief Factor Dr. John McLoughlin for selling merchandise to American competitors.

Bonneville returned to the Portneuf River where he had left some of his traders in the spring of 1833. When he arrived, on July 3, he immediately sent a small group of men back to St. Louis with the furs he had collected in his travels. The captain then sent another group of men to begin trapping in Wyoming while he returned to the Columbia River with the 23 remaining men. He intended to begin trading with the Nez Perce and Cayuse Indians as soon as possible.

Bonneville's apparent success was soon turned to failure. The Americans ran out of supplies when they reached the valley of the Grande Ronde River. They continued across the Blue Mountains to the Umatilla River where Bonneville sent messengers to Fort Walla Walla for help. Pambrun refused to aid the Americans in any way. He did not want to anger Chief Factor McLoughlin a second time. Indians in the area also turned their backs on Bonneville's men. They had been influenced by the HBC with whom they wished to maintain friendly trade relations.

Without supplies Bonneville was forced to cancel his plans and return east. He spent the winter with friendly Shoshoni Indians on the Upper Bear River and returned to the United States in the spring of 1835.

Despite his disappointments in the fur trade, Bonneville maintained fond memories of his Indian friends. He described the Northwest tribes as possessing "a considerable degree of civilization." He believed they were ready to accept the teachings of the white man. American farmers would soon show them how to till the soil and American missionaries would instruct them in the practice of Christianity.

Chapter 5
West With the Missionaries

As Bonneville was preparing to make his departure from the Pacific Northwest, the first missionaries were making their way into the land of the Nez Perces. The arrival of Man of the Morning, Speaking Eagle, No Horns on His Head, and Rabbit Skin Leggings in St. Louis had created quite a sensation. William Walker, another visitor in the city at that time, had learned about the four Native Americans from William Clark. Walker did nothing at the time, but he continued to think about the Indians' incredible search for Christian teachers. Finally, when he returned home to Ohio in January, 1833, he wrote to his friend in New York, G. P. Disosway. This man was a Methodist who actively supported missionary work. In the message, Walker mistakenly said all the Indians who visited St. Louis were Flatheads. He went on to describe in detail the process of head flattening and ended by drawing a picture to illustrate the resulting slope of the forehead.

Obviously, Walker's letter is in error. Historians doubt very much that he had ever seen the St. Louis visitors. Though head flattening was a custom of some tribes along the lower Columbia, neither the Nez Perces nor the Flat-

Walker's illustration of a Flathead Indian disturbed the Christian population of the United States.

heads ever engaged in the practice. Inaccurate as it was, the sensationalistic description produced results more quickly than the real Indians had been able to do.

Disosway sent Walker's letter and drawing to the "Christian Advocate" journal which published them on March 1, 1833. The information disturbed the Christian population of the United States who reprinted the material in many of their religious papers.

On March 22, the "Advocate" printed an editorial requesting someone to take action on behalf of the Northwest tribes. The article cried:

> Hear! Hear! Who will respond to the call from beyond the Rocky Mountains? . . . We are for having a mission established there at once . . . All we want is men. Who will go? Who?

The editorial drew responses from churches throughout the East. A spirited race was underway to send missionaries to the tribes of the Pacific Northwest.

The Methodists were first to answer the call for Christian teachers. In 1834, a Methodist minister named Jason Lee traveled west with fur traders Nathaniel J. Wyeth and William L. Sublette. Lee was assigned to establish a mission in the Willamette Valley of Oregon. On his way, he stopped at Fort Hall in present-day Idaho where he was welcomed by Lawyer's band of Nez Perces. Lee conducted the first Christian church service in the Pacific Northwest during his stay at Fort Hall. Eager to reach his destination, the minister was soon on his way again leaving the Nez Perces to wait a while longer for a mission of their own.

In 1835, the American Board for Foreign Missions sent Reverend Samuel Parker, a Presbyterian minister, to locate sites for future missions in the West. The Board permitted Dr. Marcus Whitman, an aspiring missionary, to accompany Parker on this journey. The two men traveled with the American Fur Company caravan which was journeying to the Green River Rendezvous in present-day western Wyoming.

The rendezvous was attended by many Indians. In addition to a group of Utes, there were over 2,000 Shoshonis and forty lodges of Flatheads and Nez Perces. Parker and Whitman took the opportunity to ask these tribes if they were interested in having missions located in their areas. The overwhelmingly positive response encouraged the two men to take immediate action to meet the Indians' needs. Parker decided to continue west alone while Whitman returned east to organize the establishment of a mission for these tribes during the next year.

Before leaving the rendezvous, Whitman asked permission to take a young Nez Perce boy named Tackitootis with him to New York. Whitman said:

> My reason for taking him is that he can speak the English language a little and by being with white people he will soon speak so as to interpret or assist in learning his language.

After some discussion, the boy's father was finally persuaded to entrust his son to Whitman. A few days later, a Nez Perce chief asked that his son, Ais, also be taken to New York to become an interpreter for his people. Whitman agreed and left with the boys on August 22 when the fur caravan began its return trip east.

It was the policy of the American Board for Foreign Missions to send only married couples to distant lands. Before traveling west with Samuel Parker, Marcus Whitman had become engaged to an attractive, 27-year-old schoolteacher named Narcissa Prentiss. This young woman was a strong-willed Presbyterian who, like her fiance', was attracted to the life of a western missionary. When Marcus returned home to Angelica, New York, he and Narcissa were married on February 18, 1836.

The marriage qualified the young couple to return as missionaries to the Pacific Northwest. After granting them permission, the Board decided to select another husband and wife team to accompany Marcus and Narcissa and establish a second mission. Reverend Henry Spalding and his wife, Eliza, were chosen to go. The Spaldings had asked to travel west the year before, but were refused because Eliza was about to have a baby. The Board feared the journey would be much too difficult for such a young child. Unfortunately, the infant was stillborn. The Spaldings were once again available for assignment. Permission was granted and Henry and Eliza prepared to face the hardships of the western wilderness.

From the beginning there was friction between the two missionary couples. Their personalities were very different making it difficult for them to become friends. Eliza and Narcissa were the same age, but had little else in common other than their dedication to missionary life. Narcissa was lovely, blond, and in the best of health. She was popular, outgoing, and enjoyed the challenge of new experiences. Eliza, on the other hand, was tall, thin, plain, rather frail, and often in poor health. Her quiet, practical manner, however, masked a determination to achieve the goals she set for herself. More accomplished intellectually than Narcissa, Eliza was a gifted linguist who mastered Hebrew, Greek, and later, Shahaptin, the Nez Perce language. Different though they were, the ladies shared the distinction of being the first white women to travel west across the Rocky Mountains.

Marcus Whitman and Henry Spalding also found it difficult to establish a close working relationship. At 33 years of age, both men were hard-working but their qualifications varied greatly. Marcus can best be described as a doctor-missionary. He was the first American physician to practice west of the Rocky Mountains. Unlike Spalding, he was not an ordained minister. The muscular, big-boned Whitman has been described as "rather forbidding at first, but makes a good impression soon and is respected." He was constantly at work and took little time to carry on lengthy conversations. This brusqueness sometimes created the impression that he was uncaring and impolite.

Spalding was a somber, straight-laced man who possessed a violent temper. Born out of wedlock, deserted by his mother, and unacknowledged by his father, he had struggled to obtain an education and make a place for himself in society. Spalding had graduated from Western Reserve College at Hudson, Ohio at the age of thirty. Before Whitman, he had met and proposed marriage to the beautiful Narcissa Prentiss. Her refusal of him recalled the misery of his earlier parental rejection. Narcissa's later marriage to Marcus Whitman aroused Spalding's jealousy and drove a permanent wedge between the two couples.

Despite their tenuous relationship, the Whitmans and the Spaldings managed to complete the journey west. They arrived at the Green River Rendezvous on July 6, 1836. The missionaries were welcomed by over a hundred trappers and a large number of Indians from various tribes. In addition to 200 Nez Perces and Flatheads, there were a few Cayuse Indians and several hundred representatives from the Utah, Shoshoni, and various other tribes.

The two Nez Perce boys who had traveled east with Whitman to become interpreters were now reunited with their people. While they were away, they were given white man's names. Tackitootis was called Richard and Ais was renamed John. Narcissa described their homecoming. She wrote:

> It was truly pleasing to see the meeting of Richard and John with their friends. Richard was affected to tears. His father is not here but several of his band and brothers are. When they met, each took off his hat as respectful as in civilized life.

Trappers and Indians alike crowded around the missionaries. Eliza and Narcissa were the first white women the Indians had seen. They became the center of attention as native women satisfied their curiosity about their hair, clothing, and personal belongings. Eliza said the Indian women "were not satisfied, short of saluting Mrs. Whitman and myself with a kiss." Trappers said this was how American ladies greeted each other in the East.

While the women concentrated their attention on Eliza and Narcissa, the Indian men began to argue among themselves about where the missionaries would settle. Narcissa said, "They nearly came to blows" deciding which tribe would provide a home for the Christian teachers. Luckily, violence was avoided when John L. McLloyd arrived with his group of Hudson's Bay Company traders. McLloyd carried a letter from Samuel Parker advising the missionaries to travel to the Columbia with the HBC caravan when it returned west from the rendezvous. The missionaries wanted Parker's advice concerning the best place to establish a settlement. They decided to accept McLloyd's hospitality and travel to Fort Vancouver with the British traders.

Leaving the rendezvous on July 18, the HBC caravan traveled toward Fort Walla Walla on the way to the Columbia River and Fort Vancouver. The missionaries were accompanied by two Nez Perce chiefs, Tackensuatis and Lawyer, and several of their warriors as well as a small group of Flathead Indians. Spalding said the chiefs could not be persuaded to leave even though they were delaying a buffalo hunt and risking the loss of winter food for their people. Tackensuatis said, "I shall go no more with my people, but with you; where you settle I shall settle."

The caravan reached Fort Walla Walla on September 1 and received a cordial welcome from Pierre Pambrun. The missionaries were disappointed to find no message had been left for them by Samuel Parker. Pambrun suggested that perhaps Parker was waiting at Fort Vancouver.

Narcissa Prentiss Whitman   **Dr. Marcus Whitman**

Reverend Samuel Parker

The Nez Perces and Flatheads decided to make camp near the fort while the caravan continued on to the Columbia. After meeting with Parker, the missionaries were to return, meet the Indians, and locate a suitable place to settle.

Six days after leaving Walla Walla, the Whitmans and the Spaldings reached Fort Vancouver. This post, located at the mouth of the Willamette River on the northern bank of the Columbia, was the headquarters of HBC activity in the Northwest. Built and managed by Chief Factor Dr. John McLoughlin, the luxurious fort had become known as the "New York of the Pacific Ocean." Formal dinners were served each night. People dressed in their finest clothing. Vancouver was an island of elegant living in the midst of a vast wilderness.

Dr. McLoughlin was a strict leader known for his explosive temper. The Indians called him the "White Headed Eagle" because of his flowing, white hair. Though considered a tyrant by some, McLoughlin, was generally respected by Indians as a good chief and by settlers as a good doctor.

McLoughlin graciously welcomed the missionaries and gave them comfortable quarters in his own home. They dined on fresh fruits and vegetables and enjoyed the comforts of civilization which had been unavailable to them for a long time.

McLoughlin said that Parker had visited Fort Vancouver, but had departed some time ago. He added that Parker had suggested that the land near the Clearwater and Walla Walla rivers would make good locations for missions. The Chief Factor said the ladies would be safer and more comfortable if they waited at the fort while their husbands explored these sites for themselves.

Eliza and Narcissa decided to accept McLoughlin's hospitality. The Whitmans were about to have their first child and Narcissa wanted it to be born in their new home. However, travel was becoming very difficult for her and she decided there was time before the birth for Marcus to locate a suitable place to live.

When Whitman and Spalding revisited Fort Walla Walla, they discovered the Nez Perces and Flatheads had left to return home. The Indians told Pambrun they would come back for the missionaries at a later time. Eager to locate a place to settle, Henry and Marcus found two Cayuse Indians to lead them up the Walla Walla River. On October 5, Whitman selected a site on the north bank of the river about twenty miles from the Columbia. The place was known to the Indians as Waiilatpu meaning The Place of the Rye Grass. Whitman's new mission would serve the Cayuse Indians who lived in the area.

After Whitman and Spalding arrived back at Fort Walla Walla, they discovered Tackensuatis had returned with twenty or thirty Nez Perces. The chief was upset when he learned the missionaries had selected Waiilatpu as a place to settle. He said the Cayuses were bad and untrustworthy people and the white men might be in danger. Whitman refused to listen, but Spalding agreed to travel with the Nez Perces into their territory. He realized that even if Tackensuatis was incorrect concerning the Cayuse Indians, his family could never share a mission successfully with the Whitmans. The tension between the two couples was too great to permit any type of extended relationship.

Tackensuatis led Spalding up the Clearwater to a place where a small stream flowed into the river from the south. It was called Lapwai which means The Place of the Butterflies. After careful inspection of the area, the missionary chose a site in the valley at the foot of a hill where the soil was good and timber grew along a nearby creek. The location was near the village of Thunder Eyes, a local chief who had already made friends with American trappers in the area. Spalding later gave this leader the Christian name James.

Pleased with the selection of his land, Spalding traveled to Fort Walla Walla and joined Whitman. It was time to return to Vancouver for Eliza and Narcissa. Before leaving, he asked Tackensuatis to meet him at Walla Walla in five weeks to help transport his baggage to Lapwai. The chief agreed and happily bade a temporary farewell to his new friend. With open arms, the chief had welcomed the man who would begin opening the door of civilization for the Nez Perce people and closing the door on their traditional way of life forever.

Chapter 6
A Mission in the Place of the Butterflies

Henry and Eliza Spalding arrived at Lapwai on November 29. Tackensuatis provided a tepee in which they lived for three weeks while the Nez Perces helped them build a log cabin. Changes in tribal behavior were evident immediately as warriors, who had never engaged in physical labor, worked to transport logs to the mission site. Traditionally, it was the job of Indian women to construct and maintain a home for their families. Some tribal members now looked on with contempt as men put aside their masculine pride and began to engage in "women's work." Spalding commented, "I put an axe upon the shoulder of my friend, Tackensuatis, and told the other chiefs to follow me with their men." Though subtle at first, attitudes were already beginning to develop which would eventually grow into sharp divisions of opinion among the Nez Perce people. Tribal cohesiveness began to crumble as one group of Indians watched scornfully as another group labored for the white man in "womanly fashion."

The Spalding mission was completed on December 23, 1836. The log structure measured forty-two by eighteen feet. It was divided into two large rooms. One served as living quarters for the missionaries while the other was used as a classroom and meeting place for the Indians. The roof became an annoying aspect of the building. Constructed of grass and clay, it leaked each time it rained spattering the entire inside of the cabin with droplets of mud.

Many Nez Perces gathered at the Spalding mission. Tuekakas led his people from the Wallowa Valley to settle at Lapwai. He wanted to be among the first to learn to read and write. Along with Chief Yellow Bull and Chief Tamootsin, Tuekakas welcomed the Spaldings to the Nez Perce homeland.

Despite their enthusiastic reception by some Nez Perce leaders, the missionaries were not welcomed by the entire Nez Perce tribe. Toohoolhoolzote, a chief whose band of 183 people lived along the Snake River, became a leader for the opposition. Toohoolhoolzote was a passionate orator known for his intelligence and ability to be sharp and vindictive or smooth and convincing as the situation warranted. A strong man standing five feet ten inches tall with a broad chest, he argued eloquently against the establishment of a mission for the Nez Perce people. He wanted to know why his people should be forced to give up their ancestral ways which had served them so well since earliest times. Why should they stop their traditional buffalo hunts and become farmers who dig in the earth for a living? How could the Nez Perce children dare to carve the breast of their Mother Earth? Surely this would be the beginning of unhappy times for his proud, free people.

Tuekakas and Yellow Bull argued against Toohoolhoolzote. They said the powerful white men were moving west whether the Nez Perces welcomed them or not. Indian people were helpless to stop the Americans who were already in the land of the Cheyenne building homes and fencing land. Whole herds of buffalo had been wiped out by their firearms according to rumors from the Sioux, Cheyenne, and Blackfeet. Tuekakas said he feared that, like the buffalo, his people would also be slaughtered if they failed to find a way to coexist with the white men.

Tuekakas and Yellow Bull also pointed out the beneficial aspects of white settlement in the West. Missions and trading posts would be stocked with medicine, cloth, metal utensils, guns, and other valuable trade goods. Indians could learn reading, writing, and many other things which would enable them to acquire much of the white man's power for themselves. These things, along with an understanding of the Christian religion, would help them survive in the changing world brought about by white occupation of their land. Tuekakas believed his people must accept the newcomers or eventually die by their hand.

The Spaldings opened their mission school for the Nez Perces on January 27, 1837. About 100 students of all ages attended. Henry described the event as follows:

> Here a scene commenced more interesting, if possible, than any we had before witnessed. Nothing but observation can give an idea of the tireless application of old and young, mothers with babes in their arms, grandparents, and grandchildren. Having no books. Mrs. Spalding was obliged to supply the deficiency with her pen, and print her own books.

Because the Spaldings did not speak Shahaptin, the Nez Perce language, work at the mission was difficult at first. Richard and John, the two Nez Perce boys who traveled east with Whitman, separated in order to help both missionary couples. Richard went to Waiilatpu with the Whitmans while John remained at Lapwai to serve as interpreter for the Spaldings.

The Spaldings built their mission at Lapwai in present-day Idaho.

Eliza drew pictures to help in communicating religious stories to her students while she and her husband labored to learn Shahaptin. Meanwhile, the Indians worked hard in class to master the English language.

Teaching at Lapwai became somewhat easier in 1838 with the arrival of another young missionary couple. Asa B. Smith and his wife, Sarah, settled near the Clearwater River about sixty miles above the Spalding mission. Smith, a well-educated 29-year-old man, proved to be an arrogant trouble-maker with a superior attitude toward the other Americans. However, he did master the Nez Perce language with the help of Chief Lawyer who he repaid with food and clothing for his family. Smith used his knowledge to develop a written form of Shahaptin and produce the first Nez Perce dictionary and grammar.

Education at the Spalding mission was further enhanced in 1839 when a church in Hawaii donated a printing press. No longer needed at the American Board Mission in Honolulu, the press became the first such machine to be used in the Pacific Northwest. Henry and Eliza were now able to produce copies of textbooks, hymnbooks, and the Gospel of Matthew for their students.

The Spaldings believed they could improve the Indians' way of life by converting them to Christianity and imposing the white man's culture and values upon them. Desiring their students to remain at the mission on a year-around basis, they condemned tribal traditions of food gathering and hunting. Henry taught Nez Perce men how to till the soil and plant corn, potatoes, peas, and other garden vegetables. He introduced cattle, sheep, and hogs to provide a constant supply of meat and end the necessity for trips to the buffalo country. In this way, the Nez Perces could avoid warfare with plains tribes and lead peaceful, Christian lives under the missionary's firm guidance.

In addition to these changes in daily activities, the Spaldings also worked to instill Christian values in their Nez Perce students. Working on Sunday was prohibited. Families were separated as Indian men were led to abandon their traditional custom of having more than one wife. Henry said each man must select one woman to marry in a Christian ceremony and send all other "wives" and their children back to their parents or other relatives. This was an extremely difficult emotional task for people raised in the security of an extended family whose members displayed a high degree of interdependence.

Many Indians came to love and respect Eliza Spalding who they found to be kind and compassionate. Her gentle manner, however, was in sharp contrast to her husband's sometimes violent outbursts of temper and frustration. Though sincere in his desire to help the Nez Perce people, Henry became angry and impatient when progress seemed slow and opposition arose to his teachings. Though Eliza tried to calm her husband, she was often unsuccessful in preventing his angry tirades.

Spalding learned that Hudson's Bay traders sometimes persuaded Indian leaders to whip tribesmen who broke company rules. Henry threatened to do the same to Nez Perces who interfered with his work at the mission. Occasionally, when warnings were not enough to secure obedience, the missionary carried out his threat of physical punishment.

Nez Perce leaders used reason and persuasion to maintain their positions of authority. Tribal members who refused to obey were never beaten. Spalding had difficulty finding chiefs willing to use the lash on their people. When no one else was available, the missionary administered the punishment himself.

The sometimes harsh discipline at the mission drew more protests from tribal leaders and medicine men. They began to resent the missionaries who disrupted their hereditary traditions and way of life. The medicine men wanted to preserve the old ways—the caring and responsibility for each other, and the love and respect for sacred Mother Earth. Toohoolhoolzote once again voiced his opposition to the white man's religion. He angrily pointed out "to argue about Heaven and Hell, marry in religious ceremonies, and uproot sacred meadows would not add one buffalo to the plain or one shaft of light to the sun."

These conflicts caused some Nez Perce bands to reject the white man's ways. Disillusioned chiefs gathered their people together and left Lapwai determined to return to the old ways. This action shattered the unity of the tribe. Those who left the mission were called non-Christian Nez Perces. They were considered outcasts by the Christian bands who remained loyal to the Spaldings.

After this division, life for both groups of Indians became more difficult. With fewer people, non-Christian Nez Perces found it harder to hunt, gather food, and protect themselves. The Christian group was often confused and upset by the cultural upheaval they were experiencing. Many felt a loss of dignity and identity with their own people. Beggars appeared for the first time in the Nez Perce villages. In their traditional way of life, all tribal members worked and cared for each other. They freely shared whatever they had with others in their camp. At Lapwai, however, some individuals decided it was easier to wait for handouts at the mission than work to provide food for themselves and their families. Small groups of Indians gathered each day to beg for scraps from the white man's table. Their actions brought shame to their people who once relied on no one but themselves.

Despite this situation, Nez Perce leaders such as Tuekakas, Yellow Bull, Tamootsin, and Lawyer continued to support the Spaldings. Tuekakas and Tamootsin were the first two converts to the white man's religion. Both men were baptized and given Christian names. Tuekakas was called Joseph and Tamootsin was renamed Timothy. Spalding performed legal wedding ceremonies for Timothy and his wife, Tamar, and Joseph and his wife, Khapkhapaponimi. The latter woman was given the name Asenoth. A week later, Spalding completed the conversion of the two families by baptizing Timothy's two small children and Joseph's two children, Celia and Elawinonmi.

Timothy displayed his sincerity and devotion to the white man's religion by renaming his village Alpowa which means The Place Where the Sabbath is Observed. This kind, gentle man became a lifelong friend of the Americans.

In December, 1838, Joseph helped the missionaries conduct a Christian service for his people. Spalding praised the chief for speaking to the other Indians "most affectingly, urging all present to give their hearts to Jesus Christ without delay."

On April 12, 1840, Spalding baptized another child for Chief Joseph. This boy, given the name Ephraim, was to become the famous Young Chief Joseph who would one day lead his people through the historic Nez Perce War of 1877.

Old Chief Joseph's fourth child, Ollokot (Frog), was born two or three years after Ephraim. He would grow to become an outstanding war leader who would help his brother in the great conflict ahead.

As young children, Ephraim and Ollokot often attended the Spalding mission school. At five years of age, Ephraim took his father's name and also became known as Joseph. The child grew to resemble his influential parent in many ways. Possessing the old chief's keen insight and mild, tolerant disposition, Young Joseph was quickly identified as a leader among his people.

Ollokot also possessed the qualities of leadership. However, unlike his brother, who tended toward peaceful actions and eloquent speech, Ollokot developed into a daring hunter. His skill with weapons earned him status as a great warrior. Ollokot's impetuous, fun-loving nature made him a favorite of his people. Despite the age differ-

Chief Tuekakas was one of the Spaldings' first converts to Christianity.

ence, physically he resembled Young Joseph so closely the boys could be mistaken for twins.

From their earliest days, Young Joseph and Ollokot were caught in a whirlwind of cultural conflicts. Traditional Indian values were struggling to survive in the flood of changes introduced by the white man. Each day the Nez Perces grappled with an existence that was neither white nor Indian but an uneasy combination of both.

Chapter 7
"A Night That Will Have No Morning"

In December, 1842, Dr. Elijah White, Subagent of Indian Affairs West of the Rockies, called a council at Lapwai for all Nez Perce bands. Dr. White made two proposals he believed would help establish and maintain peaceful relations between Indians and whites. The first was a system of laws listing eleven criminal offenses and their punishments. These regulations ranged from murder and burning someone's home, both punishable by hanging, to stealing and damaging property, which were punishable by fines, lashes, or both. The Indians readily agreed to accept these rules and White reported they seemed "greatly pleased with all proposed."

Dr. White's second request involved a basic change in the Nez Perce system of leadership. Chiefs traditionally governed their people by reason and persuasion. Rule by majority vote was never part of their decision-making. Tribal members listened to the recommendations of their leaders and decided for themselves whether or not to comply. There was no punishment for disagreement and dissenters maintained their tribal status and respect. Dr. White thought it would be much easier for the United

States Government to deal with the tribe as a whole if one leader could be designated head chief of the Nez Perces. This man would be given full authority to speak for his people and thus eliminate the cumbersome council and independent decision-making process. White secretly sponsored Ellis for this position. This chief had been educated in the Red River Missionary School and tended to look with favor upon the white man. The Nez Perces finally agreed to allow the selection of a head chief. At the time they could not have realized the dangerous situation they had created for themselves. This mistake in judgement became a leading cause of the Nez Perce War of 1877. The tribe elected Ellis to be their head chief. They also selected twelve sub-chiefs, including Old Joseph, to assist Ellis in his duties as liaison between whites and Indians.

The new system of criminal justice remained in force until 1845 when Dr. White was relieved of his post and returned east. Without the subagent's continued vigilance, the Nez Perces gradually reverted to their old ways. When Ellis died of measles on a trip to the buffalo country in 1848, some of the bands elected Lawyer, son of Chief Twisted Hair, to replace him as head chief. However, they placed little value upon this position and regarded the title as an honor awarded to a popular leader. It is unfortunate that the United States Government did not understand the head chief's lack of real authority. Such an understanding might have helped maintain a peaceful relationship between white and Indian people.

By 1845, the missionaries were also plunged into dangerous situations as they struggled to maintain their influence and authority. The situation at Waiilatpu was especially grim as the Cayuse Indians became increasingly hostile toward Marcus and Narcissa Whitman.

White settlers had begun to arrive in large numbers. Each year the wagon trains grew in size bringing an endless stream of new families onto tribal land. Over 3,000 arrived in 1845 and more than 1,500 in 1846. Also in 1846, the United States and Great Britain signed a treaty establishing America's northwest boundary at the 49th-parallel. Land in the Oregon Country was now officially American and westward expansion could be fully undertaken.

In September, 1845, the Cayuses decided to stop white immigration into the Grande Ronde Valley. Whitman learned about their plans from friendly Indians and hurried to warn the wagon train before it was attacked. The Cayuses were surprised to find Whitman accompanying the heavily guarded wagons when they arrived in the Grande Ronde. Whitman argued with the angry chiefs and finally persuaded them to let the settlers pass unharmed into the valley.

After this incident, the Indians began to question the missionary's loyalty to their people. They felt that somehow Whitman was responsible for the white occupation of their land.

These feelings of anger and mistrust spread to other tribes. Christian bands were harassed and lost much of their influence in tribal matters. Non-Christian Nez Perces threatened Chief Timothy and destroyed many improvements he had made on his land. More Indians returned to the old ways and life at the missions became increasingly unpleasant.

One evening, a group of Nez Perce warriors decided to demonstrate their growing disrespect for the missionaries at Lapwai. The Indians tore cedar rails from the mission fence to build a fire and proceeded to gamble, shout, and sing as loudly as they could. When Spalding attempted to

Thousands of Americans traveled over the Oregon Trail to the Pacific Northwest.

stop the destruction of his fence, he was seized and thrown into the blaze. Fortunately, the missionary wore a heavy buffalo coat which prevented him from being seriously burned. The Indians appeared to be satisfied with Spalding's loss of dignity and allowed him to return home without further injury.

The situation at Waiilatpu reached its terrible climax in 1847. That year the Cayuses became infected with a virulent form of measles contracted from settlers in the area. Almost every member of the tribe became ill and nearly half died from the disease.

Whitman attempted to treat the Cayuses, but often found them unwilling to follow his advice. The Indians believed that use of their traditional sweat lodge would help combat the disease. After becoming very warm in the lodge, the Cayuses dove into the icy water of a nearby stream. Far from helping, this increased the severity of the illness and large numbers of Indians continued to die.

Matters for Whitman were made worse when Joe Lewis, a halfbreed from Maine, arrived at Waiilatpu. Lewis hated the white settlers and circulated the rumor that Whitman and Spalding were out to steal Indian land. Lewis claimed he had overheard the missionaries plotting to eliminate the Cayuses as quickly as possible by poisoning them. The terrified Indians were ready to believe anything. They thought this story could be true. Their people did continue to weaken and die while white settlers treated by Whitman grew stronger and recovered. The time was near when Cayuse warriors, their minds clouded by hatred and disease, would seek terrible vengeance on their imagined enemy at the mission.

Unaware of the danger, Henry Spalding traveled to Waiilatpu in November. He planned to enroll his ten-year-old daughter, Eliza, in the mission school.

Whitman explained about the measles epidemic and asked Spalding to help treat his Cayuse patients. Marcus was on his way to the Umatilla River to visit several families and Henry agreed to accompany him. On the way, Spalding's horse fell and the missionary injured his leg. Whitman helped him reach the lodge of a friendly Cayuse chief named Stickus. The chief allowed Spalding to recover in his village while Whitman saw his patients on the Umatilla and then returned home.

On November 29, 1847, while Spalding recuperated in the home of Chief Stickus, angry Cayuse Indians attacked the Whitman mission. Sixteen people, including Marcus and Narcissa, were killed. The warriors took forty-seven prisoners among whom they discovered Spalding's daughter, Eliza. The rest of the people at the mission escaped or, like Joe Lewis, were set free because the Indians numbered them among their friends.

The massacre at the Whitman mission was discovered on November 30 by Father Brouillet. The priest had traveled to Waiilatpu from a Catholic mission on the Umatilla River. Fearing for the safety of the Spaldings, Father Brouillet set out at once to warn the missionaries at Lapwai.

Meanwhile, Spalding had recovered enough to leave the Indian village and return to Waiilatpu. On the way, he encountered the terrified Father Brouillet who informed him of the horrible events at the Whitman mission. Henry decided to return home immediately to protect his family and save Lapwai if he could.

The journey was very dangerous. Spalding knew he would be killed if Cayuse warriors discovered him along the way. He was forced to hide during the day and travel only at night. During a brief rest, the missionary's horse strayed away leaving him to travel on foot over the rocky ground. With little food or rest, Spalding limped painfully in the direction of the Snake River and the village of his friend, Chief Timothy.

After four days, Henry arrived near Alpowa and cautiously crept toward the lodge of Chief Timothy. A heavy rain fell confining the people of the village to their homes. As he passed among the tepees, Spalding heard warriors discussing the Whitman massacre. Unable to tell if the Nez Perces were in agreement with the Cayuse attacks, Henry was afraid to make his presence known in the camp. The missionary silently made his way to the river and crossed in a canoe he found near the shore. After another day of travel, he located a dugout, crossed the Clearwater, and arrived on a hill overlooking Lapwai.

The scene below filled the missionary with despair. The mission site was filled with Indians moving about among the buildings. Spalding feared he was too late to save Eliza and his children. However, on closer inspection, he discovered the warriors were not Cayuse. Instead, they were friendly Nez Perces who had come to protect the missionaries from attack.

Though many Nez Perces had also begun to hate and mistrust the missionaries, others were still loyal. They were willing to fight anyone who threatened the safety of the Spaldings.

The Indians said they had learned about the massacre two days before from William Canfield, a survivor who had made his way to Lapwai. Mrs. Spalding and her three small children were safe at the home of William Craig, a mountain man who had offered them protection.

The Hudson's Bay Company learned about the Whitman massacre a week after it occurred. Chief Factor James Douglas immediately sent veteran trader Peter Skene Ogden and sixteen HBC men on a mission to rescue the hostages. Ogden met with Cayuse chiefs Tauitau and Tilokaikt on December 23. Reminding the Indians they had traded peacefully with the HBC for thirty years, Ogden offered to ransom the prisoners and do what he could to prevent a war between the Americans and the Cayuse tribe. The chiefs finally agreed to accept the ransom which consisted of 62 blankets, 63 cotton shirts, 12 guns, 600 loads of ammunition, 37 pounds of tobacco, and 12 flints. Six days later the Indians released the captives and promised them safe conduct out of their territory.

The Spaldings were soon reunited with their daughter who they found in poor health as a result of her terrifying ordeal. Henry said she was ". . . too weak to stand, a mere skeleton, and her mind as much impaired as her health by the events she had been through."

Lapwai was now considered far too dangerous for the continuance of the mission. On January 1, 1848, the Spaldings and other whites in the area were escorted to Fort Walla Walla by a solemn group of fifty Nez Perces who still remained loyal to the missionaries.

The Spaldings were met at the fort by a nervous Peter Skene Ogden and the ransomed captives from Waiilatpu. Ogden had heard rumors that the Cayuse Indians continued to threaten the safety of the missionaries. On January 2, he ushered the refugees into three boats and left Walla Walla for the safety of the Willamette Valley. Their departure was none too soon. A few hours later, an angry group of fifty Cayuse warriors arrived at the fort to complete their vengeance by killing Spalding and his family.

Not everyone was happy to see the Spaldings abandon their mission at Lapwai. Chief Timothy, who remained supportive of the missionaries throughout their stay with his people, sadly said good-by with these words:

> Now, my beloved teacher, you are passing over my country for the last time. You are leaving us forever and my people, oh my people, will see no more light. We shall meet no more in the classroom and my children, oh my children, will live only in a night that will have no morning.

When the Spalding mission closed in 1847, Young Joseph and Ollokot were still very small children. At seven years of age, Joseph had not attended school long enough to learn to read and write much English. Most of his education came from the traditional heritage of his people. His father taught him how to hunt, ride a pony, and defend himself with spears, knives, bows and arrows, and guns. In addition, Old Joseph molded his son's value

Chief Timothy remained a loyal friend of the missionaries.

system with his own special combination of Christian and Indian morality. In later life, Young Joseph commented on his education:

> Our fathers gave us many laws, which they had learned from their fathers. These laws were good. They told us to treat all men as they treated us; that we should never be first to break a bargain; that it was a disgrace to tell a lie; that we should speak only the truth.... We were taught that the Great Spirit sees and hears everything, and that he never forgets; that hereafter he will give every man a spirit-home according to his deserts: if he has been a good man, he will have a good home; if he had been a bad man, he will have a bad home. This I believe, and all my people believe the same.

Even after becoming a devout Christian, Old Joseph clung to many of his ancient tribal beliefs. One of these was the need for his children to participate in the traditional Sacred Vigil of Nez Perce boys and girls.

From earliest times, the Nez Perces believed their world was filled with spirits representing animals or powerful forces of nature such as thunder and lightning. These spirits were capable of helping Indian people they liked or harming those they disliked. Sometime between the ages of nine and fifteen, Nez Perce boys and girls sought to establish a personal relationship with one or more of these spirits of nature. Once contacted, the spirits became an individual's Wyakin or guardian spirit. Indian people believed they could call upon their Wyakins to help them with earthly problems and protect them in times of danger.

Acquiring a Wyakin was one of the most sacred experiences for Nez Perce boys and girls. They received instruction for several years from tribal elders to prepare them for this solemn event which they called a Sacred Vigil. When they were ready, each young person departed alone without food or water to seek a guardian spirit. After locating a quiet solitary place, the youth remained waiting day and night for a vision to reveal the identity of his Wyakin. Finally, thirst, hunger, and anticipation usually combined to produce the desired state of mind and the quest for spiritual contact was completed.

The exact identity of a Wyakin was a closely guarded secret. Each child was left to interpret his own vision and the power of his guardian spirit. Failure to receive a Wyakin was dealt with honestly. The Nez Perces feared to anger the forces of nature by falsifying this sacred event. Though forbidden to reveal the exact nature of their Wyakins, youths could hint about their guardian spirits. Each year a Guardian Spirit Dance was held during which young men and women formed a circle to chant informa-

During his Sacred Vigil, Young Joseph saw himself as a great chief.

tion about their Wyakins. After their Sacred Vigil, many young people took names associated with some aspect of the spiritual guardian.

Sometime after 1849, Young Joseph was ready for his Sacred Vigil. His father had carefully prepared him for this momentous event which, according to tradition, determined the boy's future greatness or obscurity according to the plans of the spirits. Joseph's search for his Wyakin followed the pattern established by countless generations of Nez Perce boys and girls. Yet, his solitary quest produced a vision of greatness which set the youth forever apart and placed his feet upon the path that led him into history.

In his vision, Joseph saw himself as a great chief leading his people through a violent thunder storm. With powerful forces of nature as his Wyakin, the young man took the tribal name Hin-mut-too-yah-lat-kekht which can be translated "Thunder Rolling in the Mountains." Joseph would find numerous occasions to test the strength of his guardian spirit in the many conflicts ahead for the young chief and his people.

Chapter 8

The Great Treaty Council of 1855

The Nez Perces lived in peace for several years after the Whitman massacre. The explosion of violence frightened white trespassers away from tribal land and Indian people were free to roam about as they pleased.

Old Joseph and his band of Wallamwatkin Nez Perces left Lapwai and returned to their ancestral home in the Wallowa Valley. They continued to practice the Christian religion and became prosperous by farming and trading.

Fifteen or twenty miles from Old Joseph's home was the valley of the Grande Ronde River. This became a favorite trading place for the Nez Perces and white emigrants on the Oregon Trail. The Wallamwatkins brought ponies to the valley which they offered to the settlers in exchange for weapons and supplies. One good pony could be traded for one good rifle and a supply of ammunition. The Americans were eager to acquire fine Nez Perce horses which the Indians bred in large numbers. The animals represented great wealth for tribal members who possessed the largest herds. Some chiefs claimed ownership of over 2,000 horses.

Meanwhile, the United States Congress encouraged Americans to settle the land in the Pacific Northwest whether or not it was claimed by Indian tribes. Oregon Territory was established on August 14, 1848. This huge section of land included all of present-day Washington, Oregon, Idaho, and parts of Montana and Wyoming. In 1853, the land north of the Columbia River, encompassing present-day Washington, northern Idaho, and northwestern Montana, was separated from Oregon to become Washington Territory. Territorial governments were organized to protect settlers and encourage further development of these areas toward statehood.

President Franklin Pierce appointed Isaac Ingalls Stevens as the first governor of Washington Territory. Stevens, who was then thirty-four years old, has been described as an energetic, aggressive, ambitious politician. Born in Andover, Massachusetts, the new governor graduated from West Point and served with distinction in the Engineer Corps during the Mexican War.

In addition to his territorial office, Stevens was selected by the War Department to lead one of the four Pacific Railroad survey groups who were looking for the best route for a railroad stretching west to the Pacific Ocean. Stevens saw this as an excellent opportunity to bring people and prosperity to Washington Territory. However, in order to have his path selected, he must prove it would be less expensive, more feasible, and safer from Indians than any route further to the south.

Included among Stevens' duties as governor was becoming Superintendent of Indian Affairs for his territory. In this capacity, he immediately organized an Indian service and appointed agents for the tribes in Washington. Stevens decided the best way to maintain peace with the Indians was to place them on reservations away from white settlers and land he needed for a railroad. He decided to begin meeting with the tribes as he surveyed the land on

72

his way to Olympia, the territorial capital at the southern end of Puget Sound.

Stevens had little difficulty reaching agreements with the Indians west of the Cascades. Many white people had already settled on their land. Though numerous, the tribes were small and somewhat intimidated by the Americans. The Indians had already settled in areas where they could find food and did not feel the need to travel about. They generally agreed to accept these areas as reservations and leave the remaining land to the whites.

East of the Cascades, however, was a very different situation. Stevens knew the tribes living there were the largest and most powerful in the Pacific Northwest. They were not afraid of the white people and refused to be intimidated by them. The governor must face a multitude of proud, well-armed warriors and impress them with the strength of the American Government. He must be prepared to deal effectively with the Cayuse, Yakima, Umatilla, and Nez Perce tribes. Stevens saw an immediate need to establish reservations for these Indians to keep them away from settlers flocking into the Columbia Basin. Failure to do so, he thought, would surely result in war and threaten the future security of Washington Territory. The largest, most powerful tribe, the Nez Perce, was considered friendly to whites. However, the other tribes were generally unfriendly and, at times, openly hostile.

Governor Stevens made careful preparations for what has been called the greatest peace gathering of Indians ever held in the West. Aided by Joel Palmer, Superintendent of Indian Affairs for Oregon Territory, Stevens made contact with the tribes and expressed his desire to meet with them.

Chief Kamiakin of the Yakimas suggested the gathering be held on ancient tribal council ground in the Walla

Isaac Ingalls Stevens   **Joel Palmer**

Walla Valley. Stevens agreed and traveled with Palmer and his men to the place which was located about six miles north of the abandoned Whitman mission.

The date set for the council was May 21, 1855. Before that time, the governor had much to do. Stevens selected a place near a creek at the foot of the Blue Mountains as the council grounds. He directed construction of a large shelter facing the mountains. This structure of stout poles supporting a roof covered with boughs would provide shade for Indian leaders seated on the ground within. Stevens and his men pitched their tents near the creek. There the soldiers also constructed a log cabin to safely hold supplies and gifts for the Indians. The governor brought in beef cattle and a large supply of potatoes, sugar, coffee, bacon, and flour to provide a banquet for his guests and to be used as gifts for Indian families. To aid in communication, Stevens hired six interpreters. He also asked the Christian

Chief Timothy to make a written record of the proceedings in the language of his people for future reference.

By May 21, all was in readiness for the council, but Indians were nowhere to be seen. The council ground was occupied by approximately one hundred white men. Forty-seven of these were soldiers brought for protection from The Dalles. In addition to Stevens and Palmer, the others included settlers, interpreters, and two Catholic priests (Father Chirouse, missionary to the Wallawallas, and Father Pandosy, missionary to the Yakimas). The Americans nervously waited for the arrival of the tribes and hoped their invitation had not been ignored.

The waiting ceased on May 24 with the impressive entrance of the Nez Perces to the council. The Americans gazed in wonder as 2,500 tribesmen mounted on their finest ponies approached the assembly. The main body of Indians stopped about a mile from the white men. From their ranks, the chiefs, dressed in their best ceremonial clothing, rode forward to welcome the governor. One by one, in order of importance, they dismounted and shook hands with Stevens and Palmer. Then they proudly took their places beside the territorial officials as their people advanced in a powerful display of tribal strength and superiority.

A thousand warriors, fully adorned for battle, charged forward to circle the assembly wildly beating drums, clashing shields, chanting songs, and sounding loud whoops. When they reached the council, they wheeled their ponies around and around and dashed off to return again in a repetition of their mock attack. Having done this several times, the warriors dismounted and performed a dance accompanied by the thunderous beating of tribal drums.

This display was carefully staged as a welcome for the governor. However, the Nez Perces also wanted to impress Stevens and his men with the cultural richness and power of their people and present their demand to be treated with fairness and dignity.

At the conclusion of the welcoming ceremony, the warriors withdrew and encamped with their families a half mile from the council site. The chiefs remained a while longer to smoke the pipe of peace with the white officials. Among those present were Old Joseph, Utsinmalikin, Metat Waptass, Red Wolf, Old James, and Lawyer, the tribe's head chief who Stevens considered to be "wise, enlightened, and magnanimous." Other important Nez Perce leaders were not present. Most noteworthy among these was the influential war chief, Looking Glass, who was away on a long trip to the buffalo country.

Once the Nez Perces were settled, Stevens issued supplies. He presented each person with one and a half pounds of beef, two pounds of potatoes, and a half pound of corn. The governor hoped that full stomachs would help the Indians maintain a feeling of good will throughout the council.

Shortly after the spectacular entrance of the Nez Perces, the other tribes made their appearance at the meeting. The Cayuses, Wallawallas, Umatillas, and Yakimas arrived without fanfare and went directly into camp about a mile from the council ground. These Indians appeared much less friendly and refused to accept any food or gifts from the governor.

On May 30, Stevens delivered the opening speech for the council. The governor explained how the "Great Father" in Washington loved his red children and wished to protect and care for them. He said this could best be accomplished by assigning the various tribes to reservations where they would remain separated from white settlers who represented a possible threat to their peace and safety. Stevens said that twenty years ago a Great Father named Andrew Jackson had taken similar precautions to care for the Indian tribes in the East. He had escorted them out of the dangerous white settlements west across a great river onto land where no Americans would bother them. The governor expressed his desire to create similar havens of security for the tribes of the Northwest. He said the council had been called with this purpose in mind.

The chiefs, sitting in a circle around the territorial officials, listened patiently to the governor's words. The speech progressed very slowly as interpreters carefully repeated each phrase so the assembly of over a thousand Indians could understand the proceedings.

Stevens did not realize how well-informed the chiefs were concerning the treatment of other Native Americans. Because of this, he made a poor choice of examples to illustrate the United States' "humane" treatment of the eastern tribes. The incident he referred to concerning Andrew Jackson was far from an action in the best interests of a threatened people. In actuality, it was the forcible removal of the Cherokee and other tribes to Indian Territory (Oklahoma) in the 1830's. It has become known as the tragic Trail of Tears in which fully a quarter of the Indians involved died along the way from mistreatment and neglect. The tribes of the Pacific Northwest had known about this horrible event for at least fifteen years. It had been described to them in graphic detail by plains Indians they encountered in the buffalo country. Stevens' misuse of this information lessened his credibility and put the tribes assembled on their guard.

On May 31, Stevens continued to describe the ways in which the United States Government wished to help the tribes of the Northwest. After reminding the Indians how they had already benefitted from the white man's horses, cattle, wheat, potatoes, grain, and other crops, the governor promised to furnish them with clothing and tools for blacksmiths, tinsmiths, and wheelwrights. He also said the Americans were prepared to negotiate peace between the Nez Perces and their enemies, the Blackfeet. This would enable Northwest tribes to hunt buffalo without fear of attack on the Great Plains.

Superintendent Palmer also spoke to the assembly. He prepared the way for a discussion of reservations by describing the history of conflict that existed between white and Indian people. He said the two races could not live peacefully together. They needed their own areas separated by clear, well-defined boundaries.

Having concluded their speeches, the white officials adjourned the council session. Stevens gave the Indians the next day off to rest and talk among themselves.

The council resumed on Saturday, June 2. Palmer addressed the tribes saying:

> This land was not made for you alone . . . The fish that come up the rivers, the beasts that roam through the forests and plains, and the fowls of the air, were made alike for the white man and the red man . . . Now while there is room to select for you a home where there are no white men living let us do so.

Stevens outlined his plans to establish two reservations for the northwestern tribes. One would be located in Nez Perce country. It would be bordered on the east and west by the Bitterroot and Blue mountains and on the north and south by the Palouse, Grande Ronde and Salmon rivers. This area would become home for the Spokane, Cayuse, Wallawalla, Umatilla, and Nez Perce tribes. The

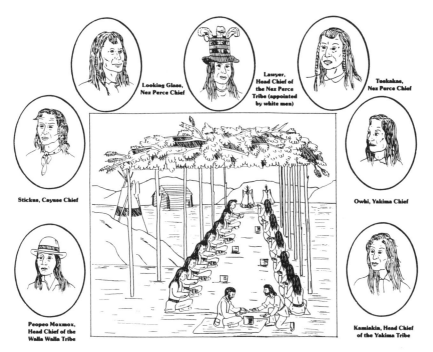

Looking Glass,
Nez Perce Chief

Lawyer,
Head Chief of
the Nez Perce
Tribe (appointed
by white men)

Tuekakas,
Nez Perce Chief

Stickus, Cayuse Chief

Owhi, Yakima Chief

Peopeo Moxmox,
Head Chief of the
Walla Walla Tribe

Kamiakin, Head Chief
of the Yakima Tribe

In 1855, Stevens organized the greatest peace gathering of Indians ever held in the West.

second reservation would be located in Yakima country between the Yakima and Columbia rivers. This land would house all the tribes along the Columbia River from The Dalles to the Okanogan and Colville valleys to the north.

The Indians sat in silence listening to the proposals of the white officials. They did not want to give up their land. They did not want to be herded onto reservations where different tribes would be forced to live together. When their time to speak arrived, Peopeo Moxmox (Yellow Bird) of the Wallawallas angrily stepped forward. This chief's son had been killed by a white man who was never punished for the crime. Expressing the Indians' general mistrust of agreements and the tribes' confusion about selling land, the Wallawalla leader said:

79

> Goods and the Earth are not equal; goods are for using on the Earth. I do not know where they have given lands for goods.

The other chiefs nodded in agreement and the governor could sense an increasing hostility in the council. Wishing to avoid an open debate, Stevens hurried to adjourn the meeting and allow the tribes to return to their camps. The Indians slowly dispersed grumbling angrily and leaving a worried governor who now fully realized the difficulty of the task he had set for himself.

Lawyer had said little during the council. Aware of the hostility of Peopeo Moxmox, Young Chief, and Kamiakin, the Nez Perce head chief had preferred to watch, listen and remain detached from controversy. However, in the evening after the meeting, Lawyer visited the governor's tent to deliver a warning. The chief said that while he personally approved of the treaty, many other leaders were angry and confused. They didn't understand the concept of selling land. Through his spies, he had learned that Peopeo Moxmox, Kamiakin, and others were planning to attack the white officials and murder them. Lawyer said:

> I will come with my family and pitch my lodge in the midst of your camp so that those Cayuses may see that you and your party are under the protection of the head chief of the Nez Perces.

The attack never came and historians speculate on the validity of the rumor. Some say Lawyer may have invented it to enhance his status with the governor. Others say that Lawyer may have feared for his own safety when his support of Stevens became known. The chief may have felt safer surrounded by the soldiers in the white man's camp. Whatever motivated Lawyer to relate this information, it was believed by the governor. Stevens ordered his men to remain alert and stationed guards about the area. He also informed the other tribes that the white officials were under the protection of the Nez Perces.

Despite threats of violence, the meetings progressed peacefully. On June 4, Eagle From the Light, a Nez Perce chief, expressed his confusion with the white man's requests. He said:

> I have been talked to by the French and by the Americans, and one says to me, go this way, and the other says, go another way; and that is the reason I am lost between them.
>
> A long time ago they hung my brother for no offense . . . Spalding sent my father to the East—the States—and he went. His body was never returned. He was sent to learn a good counsel and friendship and many things.

On June 5, Stickus, a Cayuse chief, angrily spoke against the governor's proposals. The land of his birth would not be included in either of the two reservations. Stickus did not wish to leave his homeland and argued:

> How is it that I have been troubled in mind? If your mother were here in this country who gave you birth, and suckled you, and while you were sucking some person came and took away your mother and left you alone and sold your mother, how would you feel then? This is our mother, this country, as if we drew our living from her . . .

The governor assured the tribes they would be compensated for their losses with thousands of dollars in tools, clothing, supplies, equipment, and houses. They would receive annuities for head chiefs, schools, teachers, and be allowed to leave the reservation to trade, pasture their animals, gather roots, and hunt on land that was unoccupied by white men. The discussion went on with both sides failing to completely understand the other's point of view.

On June 7, Lawyer made a long speech supporting the governor's position. He reminded his people of their long, friendly association with the Americans starting with the arrival of Lewis and Clark. Lawyer pointed out that since most of the Nez Perces' land was included within the boundaries of the reservation, acceptance of the treaty was in the best interests of the tribe.

Old Joseph requested that the Wallowa Valley be added to the reservation lands. Stevens agreed, wishing to gain more support from the powerful Nez Perce leaders.

The territorial officials also agreed to create a third reservation centering on the Umatilla Valley. This would accommodate the Umatillas, Cayuses and Wallawallas. It would allow for more separation of the tribes assigned to the Nez Perce reservation. This proposal was agreed to by all except Kamiakin who remained silent. Father Pandosy explained that Kamiakin was reluctant to speak for his people who were second only to the Nez Perces in power and number. The Yakimas were a loose confederation of fourteen bands who did not recognize a head chief. Kamiakin, generally considered unfriendly to whites, hesitated to express his views as those of his entire tribe.

On June 8, just as Stevens felt some progress was being made toward a favorable treaty agreement, council proceedings were abruptly stopped by the unexpected arrival of Old Looking Glass, war chief of the Nez Perces. News of the council had reached the chief in the buffalo country where he had been on an extended hunt for the last three years. Fearing his land would be lost in treaty negotiations, the seventy-year-old leader had left his band and hurried across the mountains with three buffalo-hunting chiefs and some twenty warriors. In an amazing feat of endurance, the old man had ridden a distance of three hundred miles in only seven days.

Old Looking Glass and his followers stormed into the council grounds clothed in buffalo robes and fully painted for war. A Blackfoot scalp dangled from the lance of one of the warriors. All eyes were fixed on the spirited old man as he angrily addressed the assembly. He shouted:

> My people, what have you done? While I was gone you have sold my country. I have come home, and there is not left me a place on which to pitch my lodge. Go home to your lodges. I will talk to you.

Turning to Stevens, Looking Glass added sharply, "I am head chief of the Nez Perces, not Lawyer. The boys talked yesterday. Now I will talk."

Stevens was upset by the presence of the war chief who he considered to be "old, irascible, and treacherous." However, since Looking Glass was very influential among the Nez Perces, the governor did not wish to further upset him. Fearing all hope for a treaty was lost, Stevens immediately adjourned the council and sent the tribes back to their camps.

That evening Lawyer visited Stevens. He said the governor should have stated that Old Looking Glass was neither head chief nor official spokesman for his people. The war chief had overstepped his authority by ordering the Nez Perces back to their lodges. Stevens assured Lawyer that there was no threat to his position. Looking Glass was an "angry and excited old man, whose heart would become all right if left to himself for awhile."

To help repair Lawyer's damaged ego, the governor presented him with a paper certifying his position as head chief of the Nez Perces. However, Stevens reminded the chief he could retain the office only as long as he carried out his duties to the satisfaction of the agent on the reservation.

Stevens met privately with Kamiakin, Peopeo Moxmox, and the other chiefs and persuaded them to sign the treaty.

Old Looking Glass hurried to the council from the buffalo country.

The Nez Perces also met privately to settle the matter of head chief and listen to the arguments of their leaders. Looking Glass wanted all Nez Perce land included in the reservation. Lawyer said this was unreasonable and supported the governor's proposal as outlined in the treaty. After a heated discussion, the leaders voted to support Lawyer and Looking Glass was forced to accept the position of second in authority.

On Monday, June 11, Stevens met with Lawyer and said:

> We are now ready to go into council. I shall call upon your people to keep their word, and upon you as head chief to sign first. We want no speeches. This will be the last day of the council.

Chief Lawyer followed his orders. He was the first to sign the treaty Stevens placed before his tribe. Then, one by one as their names were called, each of the other fifty-seven Nez Perce chiefs touched the tip of the pen as a secretary wrote their names on the document. Looking Glass and Old Joseph were second and third to sign. They were somewhat reluctant but agreed under pressure from the other tribal leaders.

A second treaty was signed by the thirty-six chiefs of the Umatilla Confederated Tribes (the Cayuses, Wallawallas, and Umatillas). Peopeo Moxmox led the way following the same procedure used by the Nez Perce leaders. Finally, a third treaty was signed by Chief Kamiakin and the Yakima tribe.

Stevens was delighted with the results of his negotiations. The Nez Perces had ceded approximately 24,138 square miles of land to the United States Government. Added to the 6,270 square miles ceded by the Umatilla Confederation, the governor had acquired 30,408 square miles of Indian land in his "great council."

Few Nez Perces would remain completely happy with the new treaty. It would take the U.S. Congress four years to ratify the document during which time the Indians began to mistrust the white man's promises. Old Joseph, Looking Glass, Eagle From the Light, Red Heart, and White Bird would become increasingly vocal in their criticism of the delay.

Young Joseph expressed his people's confusion and impatience with white man's law when he said:

> The white people have too many chiefs. They do not understand each other. They do not all talk alike . . . I can not understand why so many chiefs are allowed to talk so many different ways and promise so many different things.

Chapter 9
Kamiakin Confronts the Whirlwind

While surveying the land for his proposed railroad on the way to Olympia in 1853, the newly-appointed Governor Stevens met with the Blackfoot Indians. According to the Fort Laramie treaty council of 1851, this warlike tribe was given a large section of the northwestern Great Plains. The Blackfeet were fiercely protective of this area and attacked white men and Indians alike who trespassed there. They frequently fought with the Sioux, Crow, Shoshoni, Nez Perce, Flathead, Kootenai, Pend Oreille, Coeur d'Alene, and other tribes who periodically traveled onto Blackfoot land to replenish their supply of buffalo meat. In his council with the Blackfoot chiefs, Stevens got the impression the tribal leaders might be willing to negotiate a peace treaty with their western enemies. The governor had used this possibility in his Walla Walla council of 1855. He had said the Americans would be willing to help the Nez Perces and their allies make an agreement with the Blackfeet to assure safe trips to and from the buffalo country if the western tribes signed the proposed treaties. After the successful council, Stevens decided to return to Blackfoot territory and make good his promise to the Nez Perces.

Stevens left the Walla Walla Valley on June 16 to begin a six hundred mile trip northeast into Blackfoot country. The governor met with various bands of Indians along the way and persuaded them to send delegations to the Blackfoot council.

Though he was in a hurry, Stevens took time to arrange a short council with the Flathead, Kootenai, and Pend Oreille tribes. These Indians had always been friendly to the white man. Many had been baptized by Father DeSmet and were strongly influenced by Christianity. Stevens wanted these tribes to move onto a single reservation and release more land for white settlement. The Indians disliked the governor's proposal and could not decide on a reservation that was acceptable to all three tribes. The chiefs argued for eight days. Finally, the impatient Stevens began to browbeat and shame them into acceptance. He accused Victor, proud head chief of the Flatheads, of being "an old woman . . . dumb as a dog." At last the chiefs weakened and agreed to accept whatever reservation the government chose for them. They reluctantly ceded some twenty-five thousand square miles of land to the United States in exchange for a reservation one-tenth that size. For the first time the Flatheads, Kootenais, and Pend Oreilles were filled with bitterness against the white man. Stevens was pleased with his acquisition which included the Hellgate-Missoula region and Clark Fork Valley trade route, both of which areas were necessary for his proposed railroad.

Stevens chose a place at the confluence of the Missouri and Judith rivers as the site for the Blackfoot council. The meeting was attended by some 3,500 Indians representing the Gros Ventre, Piegan, Blood, Blackfoot, Nez Perce, Pend Oreille, Kootenai, and Flathead tribes. Nez Perce chiefs present were Old Looking Glass, Eagle From the Light,

Metat Waptass, Spotted Eagle, White Bird, Plenty Bears, Stabbing Man, and Jason. These leaders were accompanied by William Craig, special agent for the Nez Perces.

Stevens suggested the area currently claimed by the Blackfeet be divided in two parts. The land south of the Missouri River would become a common hunting ground for all tribes signing the new treaty. The land north of the Missouri would remain the exclusive domain of the Blackfeet. In return for their acceptance of these terms, the Blackfeet would receive annuities, schools, teachers, farm equipment, trading posts, and other benefits much the same as the Walla Walla treaties of 1855.

In only three days the assembly approved the terms of the new treaty. Relations between the Blackfeet and the western tribes was much improved.

Stevens had good reason to be proud of himself. However, the governor had little time to enjoy the feeling of accomplishment for even as his party prepared to cross the Continental Divide on their way home, a breathless messenger was riding in their direction carrying news of the outbreak of war. The Cayuses, Wallawallas, Umatillas, Palouses, and Yakimas, dissatisfied after the treaty council of 1855, had begun attacking settlers and miners in the Northwest.

There were several reasons for the outbreak of violence. The Yakimas were upset with Kamiakin. They said he should not have signed the treaty and had no authority to speak for the entire tribe. Kamiakin, embarrassed by the criticism, made many warlike statements that helped fire the emotions of his own people and those of many neighboring tribes.

News of the Walla Walla treaties traveled quickly. White men heard that land in the Northwest had been opened for settlement. They began to arrive in large numbers long

Stevens held a council with the Blackfeet and their allies.

before the treaties were ratified and the tribes received any benefits. The problem was compounded when gold was discovered in the Colville Valley. Prospectors poured into the area pushing the Indians aside and saying they no longer owned the land. The tribes begged for help, but Superintendent of Indian Affairs B. F. Kendall said, "To attempt to restrain miners would be, to my mind, like attempting to restrain the whirlwind . . ."

Finally, three months after the council, a group of five angry Yakima warriors, led by Qualchin, son of Chief Owhi, decided to strike back. They attacked and killed a group of six white men traveling down the Yakima River. Other murders followed. These included A. J. Bolon, special agent for the Yakimas, who had threatened to call in troops if the Indians did not calm down.

When news of Bolon's murder reached Olympia, Acting Governor Charles H. Mason sent troops from Forts Vancouver and Steilacoom to protect white travelers on the eastern side of the Cascades. Major Haller was sent from The Dalles with one hundred men and a howitzer to deal with the situation.

The arrival of armed troops was, to the Indians, the final violation of the Walla Walla treaties. Kamiakin and the other chiefs spoke against killing, but angry warriors refused to listen to their words.

The chiefs at last gave in and the first battle of the Yakima War was fought on October 5, 1855 near the Toppenish River north of the Columbia. Over 500 warriors, mostly Yakimas, led by Kamiakin and Qualchin, attacked Major Haller and his soldiers. The Indians were victorious after two hours of fighting. Haller was forced to bury his howitzer and burn all his baggage and supplies to keep them away from the hostiles. He then retreated to The Dalles. Five soldiers had been killed and seventeen wounded. The Indians claimed only two warriors killed and four wounded. News of the victory encouraged more tribes to join with Kamiakin and the settlers began to fear a coordinated general uprising throughout the Northwest.

A new force of soldiers was quickly organized at The Dalles led by Major Gabriel Rains. This included 335 men armed with three howitzers, a unit of regulars from Fort Steilacoom, and a group of 19 dragoons from Fort Vancouver. Volunteer units were also organized to help combat the hostiles. Acting Governor Mason sent some volunteers to escort Governor Stevens back to Olympia from the Blackfoot council.

When Stevens learned of the uprising in the Northwest, he decided to return to Olympia immediately. He managed to overtake William Craig, Old Looking Glass, and the other Nez Perce chiefs as they traveled home from the council. These Indians agreed to accompany the governor across the mountains to help ensure his safety.

Stevens wanted to know which tribes supported the hostiles and which remained loyal to the United States. On November 23, he passed through the territory of the Coeur d'Alenes on his way to Olympia. He visited the principal village of this tribe near the Mission of the Sacred Heart at present-day Cataldo, Idaho. William Craig, Looking Glass, and three other chiefs galloped into the midst of the Coeur d'Alenes waving their rifles in a threatening manner. Craig and the Nez Perces shouted at the startled villagers, "Are you friends or enemies? Do you want peace or war?" The Coeur d'Alenes insisted they were peaceful and had not been involved in the current violence. This same procedure was repeated when Stevens reached the principal Spokane village and this tribe also professed their friendly feelings toward the territorial government.

Despite their verbal reassurances, the governor remained concerned about the loyalty of the Coeur d'Alene and Spokane tribes. On December 3, Stevens held a council for them at Colville. He later described the event, which lasted three days, as, "One of the most stormy councils . . . that ever occurred in my whole Indian experience."

The Indians expressed their true feelings which were in complete sympathy with the Yakima and other hostile tribes. They resented the miners who had invaded their land. They also lived in fear of being herded onto the Nez Perce reservation against their will. As these feelings of anger and fear grew, so did the possibility of war with the Americans.

Stevens' men charged into the Coeur d'Alene village near the Mission of the Sacred Heart.

Spokane Garry took this opportunity to address the council as spokesman for his people. At 44 years of age, the once powerful Garry had lost much of his energy and influence in the struggle between white and Indian cultures. Some Spokanes still considered him to be a leader, but others looked down upon him as a collaborator with their American enemies. Garry felt compelled to reaffirm his tribal loyalty by addressing the governor on behalf of the Spokanes. Facing the assembly, he said:

> . . . I think the difference between us and you Americans is in the clothing; the blood and body are the same . . . If you take those Indians for men, treat them so now. The Indians are proud, they are not poor. If you talk truth to the Indians to make a peace, the Indians will do the same for you . . . The Indians are not satisfied with the land you gave them . . . I

could fix it by giving them a little more land . . . Those Indians have gone to war, and I don't know how myself to fix it up again. That is your business.

Stevens was upset at being blamed for the war. He said the tribes had appeared satisfied at the end of the Walla Walla council. He did not understand why the Yakimas, Wallawallas, Cayuses, and Umatillas were angry. The boundaries of the reservations could not be the cause of the trouble.

The Spokanes informed the governor they had been visited by messengers from the hostile tribes. According to all information available, land was indeed the cause of the outbreak of war. Even some Nez Perce bands were upset and close to joining the rebellion.

Alarmed by this revelation, Stevens adjourned the council and immediately headed for Nez Perce country. The governor feared the consequences if the powerful Nez Perces allied themselves with the hostiles to attack their former American friends.

Stevens' feelings of uneasiness increased when he heard the rumor that Looking Glass was merely pretending to be a friend of the white man. In reality the old war chief supposedly intended to trap the governor when they reached Nez Perce country and turn him over to the hostiles.

Stevens' fear of Looking Glass and his concerns about the Nez Perce people were greatly relieved when he arrived at Lapwai on December 11. The governor was met by Chief Lawyer and some 2,000 warriors who expressed their friendship and offered to protect the white official as he traveled home through Wallawalla and Cayuse country. Looking Glass was among those who pledged to protect the governor with their lives.

The Nez Perces concealed a deep division of their people from Governor Stevens. The tribe had been under great pressure to join Kamiakin and the warring forces. Many Nez Perces were in agreement with the hostiles and wanted to actively support them. So far, Lawyer and several other chiefs had managed to control their people and keep them peaceful. However, each day events occurred that brought the tribe closer to declaring war on the Americans. White men accused a Nez Perce warrior of being a spy for the hostiles in the Walla Walla Valley. Though they had no proof, and the Indian denied the charges, the settlers pronounced him guilty and punished him by hanging. Though Federal officials were horrified and condemned the actions of the settlers, the tolerance of the Nez Perce people was strained to the extreme limit.

Old Joseph was especially pressured to enter the war. His Wallowa Valley and the Grande Ronde country bordered the land of the hostiles. Old Joseph's father was a Cayuse chief. The Wallamwatkins were linked to the warring tribes by marriage and friendship and felt a sense of loyalty to them. Despite this, Old Joseph valued the safety of his people above all things. He worked hard to maintain peace and keep American troops out of the Nez Perce homeland.

The Oregon volunteers continued to do battle with the hostiles. During a four-day encounter in the Walla Walla Valley, Peopeo Moxmox, head chief of the Wallawallas, was killed and his followers scattered.

In March, 1856, Colonel George H. Wright arrived at The Dalles from San Francisco to take command of the troops in the Northwest. Governor Stevens blamed Kamiakin for all the trouble and urged Wright to direct his efforts toward defeating the Yakima leader.

William Craig wrote letters to Stevens from Lapwai describing the increasingly warlike attitude of the Nez Perce tribe. Treaty promises had not been kept and Craig feared he would soon have to leave the reservation for his own safety.

Stevens traveled to the Dalles to enlist volunteers to help transport supplies to the Nez Perces in a desperate attempt to pacify the tribe and reestablish feelings of good will.

Meanwhile, Captain John, a Nez Perce friend of Chief Lawyer, led a group of Oregon volunteers under Colonel B. F. Shaw into the Grande Ronde Valley. They traveled into territory set aside for Old Joseph's Wallamwatkin band under the terms of the Walla Walla treaty. The volunteers soon discovered a large camp of Cayuse and Wallawalla Indians. Most of the warriors were away and the camp was inhabited by women, children, and old people protected by a few young men. Shaw sent Captain John to arrange a meeting with the hostiles. The Nez Perce quickly returned saying a Cayuse had threatened to shoot him as he approached the encampment. Shaw immediately ordered an attack. The terrified Indians fled in all directions. The volunteers cut them down as they sought safety in caves and bushes along the river. The white men destroyed the village and everything in it. At least 27 Cayuse and Wallawalla Indians lost their lives in what has been called the Battle of the Grande Ronde. An accurate death count was impossible because the bodies were scattered about the area. Colonel Shaw lost five men killed and four wounded.

News of the battle so enraged the Nez Perce leaders they refused to accept the supplies sent to them by Governor

Stevens. Furthermore, they ordered all white men, including Craig, to leave their territory immediately. Like Looking Glass, Old Joseph began to openly express his growing dislike for the white men.

In August, 1856, Lieutenant Colonel Edward J. Steptoe was sent from Fort Vancouver to replace the Oregon volunteers with regular soldiers in the Walla Walla Valley and build a permanent military post there. When the troops arrived, Governor Stevens decided to hold a council with the hostile tribes and attempt to end the war.

The meeting was attended by a large number of Nez Perces, Cayuses, Umatillas, and Wallawallas. The Spokanes and Coeur d'Alenes refused Stevens' invitation as did Looking Glass and his band of Nez Perces. The Yakimas also failed to arrive although Kamiakin was rumored to be in the area.

The council, which was held in the Walla Walla Valley and lasted four days, was an awkward affair. The governor delivered a long speech concerning the importance and fairness of his treaties and the threat posed by Indians who rebelled against them. The Indians insisted their lands be returned to them and threatened to fight if necessary.

Stevens began to fear for his safety. He decided to move the meeting closer to Steptoe's soldiers who were encamped eight miles from the council grounds. On the way, the governor encountered Kamiakin, Owhi, and Qualchin near the Touchet River. Stevens considered these chiefs to be among the most dangerous in the area. However, they made no threatening moves and let the white men pass unharmed.

The unproductive council continued near Steptoe's camp. Only Lawyer and his followers remained loyal to the governor. All others present called for a rejection of the

Walla Walla treaties. The meeting ended on September 7 with a frustrated Stevens saying to the Indians, "Follow your hearts; those who wish to go into war go."

The governor now considered the area unsafe. He ordered William Craig to move from Lapwai to a place near Steptoe's camp in the Walla Walla Valley.

On September 19, a group of 50 Nez Perces led by Spotted Eagle, a friend of Lawyer, set out to accompany Stevens to The Dalles. As they departed, a group of hostiles set fire to the grass where Steptoe's men grazed their horses. The angry warriors then followed the governor's party shouting threats and insults.

About three miles from Steptoe's camp, the warriors, who Stevens claimed included 450 Yakimas, Palouses, Wallawallas, and Nez Perces, opened fire. The governor sent a messenger back to Steptoe for help and held off his attackers until the soldiers arrived and drove the Indians away with a mountain howitzer.

Discouraged by this incident, Steptoe accompanied Governor Stevens to The Dalles and asked Colonel Wright to personally handle the situation.

Wright traveled to Walla Walla and attempted to call a second council. Few Indians were willing to attend. Only five important chiefs arrived. Among these were two Nez Perces, Red Wolf and Eagle From the Light, and three Cayuses. Colonel Wright won the respect of these leaders by listening to their complaints against Stevens and demonstrating an understanding of their situation. He promised the treaties would be ratified and troops kept out of Indian lands. This simple act of understanding provided the reassurance needed by the tribes. Word of the successful council spread rapidly and by November, 1856, the violence in the Northwest had subsided.

Colonel George Wright

**Lieutenant
Edward J. Steptoe**

Colonel Steptoe built a permanent military post called Fort Walla Walla on Mill Creek six miles from its confluence with the Walla Walla River. The site chosen was 30 miles east of old Fort Walla Walla which once had been an outpost of the Hudson's Bay Company. The new fort and the presence of eighteen hundred regular troops in Washington and Oregon helped discourage future outbreaks of war. Steptoe was given the authority to issue a proclamation declaring the country east of the Cascades off limits to all whites except missionaries, Hudson's Bay employees, and prospectors traveling to the northern mining areas.

Stevens violently disagreed with Steptoe's proclamation. He wanted nothing to discourage white settlement of the Washington Territory. However, no active opposition to Steptoe was taken by the governor. In 1857, Stevens was elected as a delegate to Congress and moved with his family to Washington D.C. There he worked for ratification of his Walla Walla treaties which were signed by the President in 1859, four years after the council. Stevens next served as a Union officer in the Civil War in which he was killed at the Battle of Chantilly on September 1, 1862 at the age of forty-four.

Colonel Wright was determined to maintain peace in the Northwest. In 1858, a combined force of Spokanes, Coeur d'Alenes, Palouses, and a few Yakimas made one last attempt to drive the white men from their lands. Wright crushed the rebellion in the Battle of Four Lakes and the Battle of Spokane Plains. The defeated tribes lost heart and finally realized the impossibility of preventing white settlement of their native homeland. They signed treaties with the Americans and promised to end the hostilities forever.

Colonel Wright was pleased with the new agreements. However, he wanted to impress the tribes with the finality of these treaties and inspire fear of the consequences if they were broken. In a show of force, the soldiers killed 800 of the Spokanes' best war horses. They captured Chief Owhi of the Yakimas and later shot him. They also captured Owhi's son, Qualchin, and hanged him as a war criminal.

Kamiakin learned about the deaths of Owhi and Qualchin as he recovered from injuries he received in the Battle of Spokane Plains. Fearing he was next on Colonel Wright's list of executions, the Yakima chief immediately fled to Canada. He later returned to the United States and lived on the Great Plains for a time with the Crow Indians. In 1861, he secretly returned to the Northwest and took up residence in Palouse country. There he died in poverty and obscurity in about 1878.

In 1858, the Walla Walla Valley was officially opened for settlement. Powerless to launch a protest, the defeated tribes watched helplessly as white families moved onto Indian land. By April of 1859, over 2,000 settlers had arrived and laid claim to the valley.

Chapter 10

The Thief Treaty

As the Coeur d'Alenes, Spokanes, Yakimas, and Palouses were fighting the last battles in their war, the life of
the Nez Perces was settling into a semblance of peace. The
Wallowa Valley remained undisturbed and Old Joseph's
people resumed their traditional pattern of life. The Wallamwatkins spent their winters in sheltered mountain
valleys and canyons where they were protected from fierce
seasonal cold and storms. In the spring, they moved to
higher slopes where kouse roots, an important part of the
Nez Perce diet, were ready to harvest in April. Summers
were spent in the lush Wallowa Valley with its beautiful
lake and swift-flowing river where salmon could be caught
from July to September. Before returning to their winter
home in the canyons, Old Joseph's people made their annual trip to the wet mountain meadows where they dug
camas roots, their main winter source of food. There they
also hunted for deer, elk, and bear. Sometimes they traveled to the Umatilla Valley to visit friends and relatives
among the Cayuse and Umatilla tribes. At other times,
they went to Montana where they hunted buffalo.

The revival of the old ways, the peaceful security of living undisturbed in their beautiful valley was, in reality, only a brief respite for the Nez Perces. By 1863, conditions had once again reached the point where Old Joseph's people felt the pressure of white encroachment on their land and sensed a renewed threat to their way of life.

The years directly preceding 1863 had seen a growing uneasiness among many Nez Perces concerning the treaty agreement of 1855. Promises made by the Americans had not been kept, buildings had not been constructed, Lawyer's salary as head chief had not been received, horses purchased by the soldiers during the Yakima War had not been paid for, and the land was being overrun by miners, stockmen, and settlers. One by one angry chiefs turned away from Lawyer who continued to advocate loyalty to the Federal Government.

In response to the growing unrest, Fort Lapwai was established in 1862 several miles north of the Nez Perce agency buildings. The new army post was manned by four companies of the First Oregon Cavalry.

In January, 1863, Old Looking Glass, fiery war chief of the Nez Perces, died. This silenced forever one of the strongest patriotic voices of the tribe. The old chief's thirty-one-year-old son inherited his father's name, position, and the small trade mirror he always wore. Hanging his father's mirror from a thong around his neck like a badge of office, the six-foot-tall, heavily muscled Young Chief Looking Glass assumed his father's duties as leader of the Asotin band of Nez Perces. The young man possessed the qualities of a natural leader. He had distinguished himself as both a warrior and a buffalo hunter. He had often traveled over the Lolo Trail to the buffalo country where he had many influential friends among the Flathead, Bannock, and Crow tribes. Young Looking Glass had inherited much of his father's aggressiveness along with his decisiveness and persuasive abilities. However, he did not share the old chief's war-like tendencies and preferred instead to direct his people toward peaceful coexistence with the white men.

The year 1863, which began with the loss of a great tribal leader, was to bring many more changes for the Nez Perce people. It marks the beginning of events leading directly to the major confrontation between the United States Government and the Nez Perce tribe in the war of 1877.

When gold was discovered on the Nez Perce reservation in 1860, Americans began to regret allowing the Indians to control such a large section of land. Finally, in 1863, Calvin H. Hale, Superintendent of Indian Affairs for Washington Territory, was assigned to renegotiate the boundaries of the reservation. In the spring of that year, Hale called a council meeting near Fort Lapwai presided over by himself and agents Charles Hutchins and S. D. Howe. Also present were William Craig and Robert Newell, both friends of the Nez Perce people. The Indians requested that Perrin Whitman, nephew of Dr. Marcus Whitman, serve as interpreter. He was one of the few white men they trusted to accurately communicate their ideas and translate the words of the territorial officials for them.

Over 3,000 Nez Perces gathered near the fort to attend the meeting. Old Joseph, who now suffered from vision problems and failing health, was escorted to the council by his sons, Young Joseph and Ollokot.

Hale asked the chiefs to cede about 10,000 square miles of land to the United States Government. This included mining areas as well as rich agricultural areas in Oregon and Washington, a large area in Idaho, and Oregon's Wallowa Valley. This would reduce the size of the reservation to five or six hundred square miles of land near the South Fork of the Clearwater River. The Indians were offered the usual annuities in goods and implements in exchange for their agreement.

It took only a short time for the chiefs to unanimously reject this first proposal. The new reservation would be far too small to house the large, migratory Nez Perce tribe. Hale agreed to double the land offering if the leaders would continue to negotiate.

The Nez Perce bands were sharply divided over acceptance of this treaty. Those whose lands were included in the new proposal spoke in favor of agreement. They were led by Lawyer who said the chiefs who disagreed had "no respect for the laws of God and the American Government and were bad leaders."

Spokesmen for those in opposition to the treaty were Old Joseph, Eagle From the Light, Big Thunder, White Bird, Coolcoolselina, and Toohoolhoolzote. Except for Big Thunder, whose home was in the Lapwai area, all of these chiefs were being asked to give up their ancestral homelands. They accused Lawyer of causing much of the trouble with his pro-white attitude which was not in the best interests of the tribe. They said the head chief had no right to speak for them and claimed the right to express their own opinions concerning the disposition of their lands.

The agents reminded the dissenters that their disagreement would not release them from the terms of the treaty they had signed in 1855. Old Joseph and the others scoffed at the idea they were still bound by an agreement that had already been broken many times by the white men.

Unable to reach a satisfactory agreement, the dissenting bands left the council grounds on July 7. Their anger frightened the white officials who asked for protection

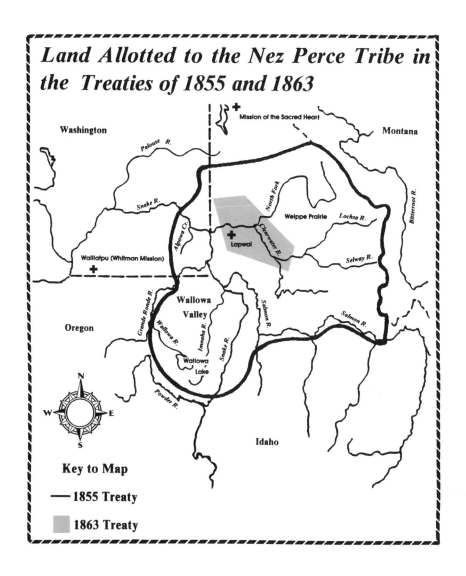

Land Allotted to the Nez Perce Tribe in the Treaties of 1855 and 1863

Mission of the Sacred Heart

Washington

Montana

Palouse R.

Snake R.

North Fork

Weippe Prairie

Lochsa R.

Bitterroot R.

Clearwater R.

Alpowa Cr.

Lapwai

Waiilatpu (Whitman Mission)

Selway R.

Grande Ronde R.

Wallowa Valley

Wallowa R.

Imnaha R.

Snake R.

Salmon R.

Salmon R.

Oregon

Wallowa Lake

Powder R.

Idaho

N W E S

Key to Map

— 1855 Treaty

1863 Treaty

from Fort Lapwai. A detachment of cavalry was sent to protect Hale and the others from possible harm.

The Americans called those who left the council "non-treaty Indians." They were now considered to be trouble-makers who could become a threat to peace in the Washington Territory. The remaining Nez Perce bands, who tended to support the current negotiations, were called "treaty Indians." They were hailed as friends of the white man and supporters of peace in their homeland.

After the departure of the nontreaty bands, the new agreement was signed by Lawyer and his followers on June 9, 1863. It transferred ownership of 6,932,270 acres of land to the U.S. Government and reduced the size of the reservation to 784,996 acres. The treaty stipulated that all Indians must vacate land ceded to the government within one year. This included the bands occupying the Wallowa, Imnaha, and Grande Ronde country of Oregon, the Snake and Salmon river valleys, the Camas Prairie, and the land of the Upper Clearwater and its tributaries including the trails to the Bitterroot Valley.

Old Joseph assumed his refusal to sign the new treaty meant that, for his people, the Treaty of 1855 was still in effect. That agreement allowed the Wallamwatkins to retain possession of the Wallowa Valley. The aging chief was horrified to learn the American Government considered the entire Nez Perce tribe to be bound by the Treaty of 1863. The Americans identified Lawyer as head chief and spokesman for all Nez Perce people. To them, his signature represented compliance of the entire tribe. Old Joseph was now expected to remove his people from their beloved valley forever.

As his father grew older and less active, Young Joseph took more responsibility for the leadership of his people. At the age of 23, he had grown into a strong, handsome young man who possessed his father's dignity, tolerance, and compassion. A gifted orator, he spoke eloquently and displayed keen insight and great intelligence. Standing six-feet-two-inches tall and weighing two-hundred pounds, Young Joseph towered over most of his people. Yet, his imposing appearance, which could be intimidating, contrasted sharply with the quiet, polite manner in which he expressed himself. Recognized as a leader and patriot from childhood, Young Joseph became a strong advocate for peace who, like his father, valued tribal survival above all things.

Sharing his father's outrage over the Treaty of 1863, Young Joseph attempted to explain his people's reaction to the loss of their valley. He told the agents at Lapwai:

> . . . The white man had no right to come here and take our country. We have never accepted presents from the Government. Neither Lawyer nor any other chief had authority to sell this land. It had always belonged to my people. It came unclouded to them from our fathers, and we will defend this land as long as a drop of Indian blood warms the hearts of our men.

Despite their logic, the protests of the Wallamwatkins were ignored by the U.S. Government. Angry and frustrated, Old Joseph destroyed his precious New Testament which he had cherished since his conversion to Christianity. He also tore to pieces a copy of the Treaty of 1863. He grudgingly called it a "Thief Treaty" and vowed his people would never honor it. Finally the disillusioned old man turned his back on all white men and swore to never again have any dealings with them. He set up a series of poles along Wallowa Hill overlooking the Wallowa River. Standing three to four feet tall and anchored in piles of rocks, these markers indicated the boundary of Nez Perce land which Old Joseph warned the Americans not to cross.

As Old Joseph and the nontreaty Indians launched their protest against the Treaty of 1863, Lawyer and the treaty Nez Perces were discovering that compliance had not made them immune from problems with the white men.

On March 4, 1863, Congress established the Territory of Idaho. This huge section of land included all of the present

Old Joseph tore up a copy of the "Thief Treaty."

states of Idaho and Montana as well as most of Wyoming. William H. Wallace was appointed to be the first territorial governor. However, his term in office was short. After less than seven months, Wallace was elected to serve as Idaho's Congressional delegate. He was replaced as governor by a rascal named Caleb Lyon, who has been called ". . . a conspicuous and dangerous failure as an executive."

Governor Lyon also held the office of Superintendent of Indian Affairs for Idaho Territory. He met with Lawyer on August 21, 1864 and listened patiently to the chief's concerns about unfulfilled treaty promises. Lyon feigned sympathy for the tribe and counseled patience. He promised to do everything in his power to secure fair treatment for the Indians in his territory. Actually, the governor had no intention of helping the Nez Perce people. Quite the contrary, the extremely unpopular Lyon fled from his office two years later taking the entire Nez Perce Indian fund of $46,418.40 with him.

Other Americans also cheated and stole from the treaty Nez Perces. James O'Neill, agent from 1864–68, got away with $10,000 in agency money. Other agents were also accused of misusing Indian funds. White men caused problems on the reservation by selling whiskey to the Indians and removing timber without paying for it.

It took four years for Congress to ratify the Treaty of 1863. The document was finally signed by President Andrew Johnson on April 20, 1867. By that time, many of the treaty Nez Perces, including Lawyer, had become anxious and discouraged about the promises made to them by the Americans.

Lawyer decided the only way to make the President aware of the Indians' problems was to carry the message to Washington himself. In November, 1867, he petitioned the government through Agent O'Neil saying:

> Myself the Lawyer am anxious to visit Washington with an interpreter and one or more of my chiefs. Have pity on me and give me permission to do so at the expense of the government.

By the time Lawyer's petition reached Washington, the government was already interested in amending the Treaty of 1863 to acquire more reservation land near the agency at Lapwai. Realizing the Nez Perces' need to be pacified before they would give more property to the Americans, the Commissioner of Indian Affairs granted the chief's request.

Agent O'Neill was authorized to bring Lawyer, two interpreters, and three other chiefs to Washington. Robert Newell and Perrin Whitman were chosen as interpreters. The chiefs selected were Timothy, Jason, and Utsinmalikin. The Indians were extremely excited. They were the first Nez Perces ever to visit the "Great Father" in Washington.

The travelers headed east in March, 1868. Going by way of Portland, San Francisco, Panama, and New York, they reached Washington in May. Their visit got off to a poor start when Utsinmalikin contracted Typhoid Fever on May 22 and died three days later.

The Nez Perce delegation remained in Washington throughout the summer. Robert Newell expressed his wish to become agent for the tribe when O'Neill ended his term. The chiefs formally petitioned President Johnson on Newell's behalf on July 9 and received approval on July 22. The chiefs also signed amendments to the Treaty of 1863 giving land to the government near Lapwai for another military post. In return, the Nez Perces were promised money for schools, protection for timber, and additional agricultural land off the reservation. Feeling they had accomplished their mission. Lawyer and his chiefs left Washington to return home on August 22.

When the delegation returned from Washington, things were somewhat better on the reservation. Money was finally received and schools were opened.

Robert Newell became agent for the Nez Perces in June, 1869. However, his work at Lapwai was cut short by his death the following November. Two months later, the Nez Perces lost another old friend when William Craig died after a paralytic stroke. The government had difficulty finding replacements for these men on the reservation.

After President Johnson signed the Treaty of 1863, the Federal Government believed the Wallamwatkins had given up the Wallowa Valley. On May 28, 1867, the U. S. General Land Office sent a team of men to survey the valley in preparation for white settlement. William H. Odell, the leader of these men, wrote in his official report:

> ... A large part of the valley is well adapted to agriculture while the low grassy hills to the N. and E. furnish extensive range for stock ... This Valley should be surveyed as soon as possible, for the wigwam of the savage will soon give way to the whites. Instead of the hunting and fishing grounds of the red man, the valley will teem with a thriving and busy population.

Chapter 11

Dreams and Promises

By 1869, the surveyors had done their work and agents were attempting to persuade the Wallamwatkins to move. Though still in favor of maintaining peaceful relations with the Americans, Old Joseph firmly refused to leave his home.

The chief found it increasingly difficult to control his young warriors and prevent them from taking up arms against the white men. A major confrontation between the Nez Perces and the American Government was building. Fearing for his people, Old Joseph wanted to postpone open warfare as long as possible. However, he knew that war would eventually come. The white men were determined to take the land and the Indians were equally determined to keep it. The Wallamwatkins and their valley were one. How could the Nez Perces survive without the nurturing of their sacred Mother Earth? As their way of life died, so would the Indian people. The chief clung tightly to more than a piece of land. He desperately sought to preserve the existence of his people.

Many nontreaty Indians shared Old Joseph's fear and desperation. They longed for a miracle to help save their dying way of life. Some believed they had found their solution in the Dreamer religion. The leader of this group was Smohalla, a Wanapum shaman and prophet from the Upper Columbia River. Smohalla was a short, stocky hunchback who was subject to fits of catalepsy. General Oliver Otis Howard described him as ". . . a large-headed, hump-shouldered, odd little wizard of an Indian." However, despite his appearance, Smohalla was an impressive orator whose words transcended his physical deformaties and won him respect and a loyal following.

Smohalla left his people for five years for an extended vision quest. When he returned in about 1850, he began preaching a strange new religion based on traditional Indian mythology combined with elements of Catholic and Mormon ceremony.

Smohalla taught that the Great Spirit communicated with his Indian people through dreams. He explained his fits of catalepsy, during which he lie unconscious and his body became rigid, as visible evidence of his contact with the spirit world. He asked his followers to abandon the customs and clothing of the white man and return to a traditional way of life. This would earn them the favor of the Great Spirit who would then allow all their ancestors to return to life. The living and the newly reborn Indians could then join together and drive the white men from their lands forever.

Smohalla preached against farming and stock raising because they required time that could better be spent in dreaming. He said:

> My young men shall never work. Men who work cannot dream; and wisdom comes to us in dreams . . . You ask me to plow the ground. Shall I take a knife and tear my mother's bosom? You ask me to dig for stone. Shall I dig under her skin for her bones? You ask me to cut grass and make hay and sell

Smohalla spread the Dreamer religion among the Northwest tribes.

it and be rich like white men. But how dare I cut off my mother's hair?

The Dreamer faith did not travel beyond a limited area in the Northwest. However, within that area it spread rapidly and gained hundreds of followers. Many nontreaty Nez Perces were attracted to the belief which inspired patriotism and counseled passive resistance to the white man. The Dreamers dressed in traditional clothing. They also refused to cut their hair which they styled in braids with a roll or high pompadour over the forehead. Their new faith renewed their reverance for Mother Earth and caused them to hold tighter than ever to their ancient homeland.

While Smohalla was spreading word of his Dreamer faith among the Northwest tribes, Christian missionaries were increasing their efforts to convert the Indians to the white man's religion. Churches in the East became concerned that the United States Government had adopted a policy to exterminate the western tribes. Religious leaders put pressure on President Grant to place reservations under church rather than military control. Missionaries could then use peaceful means to break down tribal bonds and turn the Indians into Christian farmers.

The President decided to accept the churches' proposal and assign each reservation to a religious denomination. The Catholics wanted control of the Nez Perce reservation but Grant awarded the tribe to the Presbyterians because their missionaries had been the first to reach it.

During the years following the Treaty of 1855, the Nez Perces had nine different agents. Of these, only William Craig and Robert Newell had truly understood and respected the Indian way of life. On February 8, 1871, the Presbyterian Church selected John B. Monteith as the new agent for the Nez Perce tribe. Monteith, the son of a Presbyterian minister, was strict, determined, and opinionated. Though he was an honest man, he had no respect for traditional Native American values and wanted to assimilate the Nez Perces into the white man's culture as quickly as possible. He attempted to confine young Indians in reservation boarding schools to keep them away from tribal influences that might undermine his control. Monteith sought to make the treaty Nez Perces ashamed of their native heritage and customs. He wanted them to reject the old ways and adopt the "civilized" lifestyle of the white man.

Agent Monteith resented the fact he had little or no control over the nontreaty bands. He feared they might stir up trouble and interfere with his work at Lapwai. He wanted the nontreaties to discontinue their trips to the buffalo country. He feared a war with the plains tribes might develop and spread to include the treaty bands on the reservation. Monteith asked the commander at Fort Lapwai for military aid to block all trails leading east over the mountains. When his request was refused, the agent sought to accomplish his goal by issuing a warning to the Nez Perces. He announced that those bands who moved to new places gave up all rights to their former campsites. In order to lay claim to any specific area, Indians must reside there year-around. In practice, this idea was not as effective as Monteith would have hoped. The agent could only control the treaty Indians on reservation lands. These bands were by now quite sedentary and did not care to travel about. The nontreaties lived mostly off the reservation where Monteith had no authority to say who owned or did not own the land.

Agent Monteith also disliked the nontreaty Indians because of their participation in the Dreamer religion. He considered this to be a "heathen" belief that posed a direct threat to the accomplishment of his goals for the Nez Perce tribe. Though the effect of the Dreamers was not as strong as the agent believed, Monteith continued to blame them for many of his problems.

Actually, most of the agency problems were caused by white men rather than Indians on or off the reservation. Settlers continued to illegally remove timber from tribal lands. Lacking an effective means for policing the boundaries of the reservation, agency officials were unable to control trespassers. Cattle wandered onto Nez Perce land from nearby ranches. These animals destroyed valuable grazing areas and camas fields. As pasture land in the Grande Ronde Valley became exhausted and overcrowded, the open fields of the Wallowa became increasingly more attractive to settlers.

In 1872, the first stockmen began moving their herds into the Wallamwatkins' homeland. These violations continued to upset and anger the Indians who looked to the government to honor its promise to protect them. The situation was becoming extremely complicated and difficult to manage by even the most well-intentioned agent.

Lawyer remained a friend of the white men at Lapwai. However, the chief, though still powerful, was becoming very old and lacked the energy necessary to carry out his duties as head chief. Many young people considered his ideas outdated and refused to follow his advice. Lawyer's followers urged him to step down from his position and allow a younger man, who commanded the respect of the youth, to take his place. Lawyer finally agreed. On April 18, 1870, the tribal council elected Jacob as the new head chief of the Nez Perces.

Monteith found it difficult to work with Jacob who lacked enthusiasm for the Christian religion. The agent continued to find the support he needed in Lawyer who was always willing to help when needed. In this way, the aging chief managed to maintain his tribal influence through his relationship with Agent Monteith.

In the summer of 1871, the Wallamwatkins traveled south in their valley and camped near the juncture of the Lostine and Wallowa rivers. Their chief was Young Joseph who had gradually assumed full responsibility for the band as his aging father became completely blind and less able to lead. Young Joseph was now 31 years of age. He was married to Toma Alwawinmi (Springtime), the daughter of Chief Whisk-Tasket, who lived near Lapwai. The couple had met at the Treaty Council of 1863 and married shortly thereafter. Their first child, a daughter named Walking in Crushed Snow, was born in 1865.

As summer drew to a close, so did the life of Old Joseph, venerable patriot and long-time guardian of his people. In August, the dying chief gathered his family about him as he rested in his lodge beside the river. Though his eyes were blind to sights in this world, his vision for his people remained sharp and clear. Old Joseph saw future generations of Nez Perce children living, growing, and prospering in the land of their ancestors—their beloved Wallowa Valley, their sacred Mother Earth. These thoughts filled the chief's mind during his final hours. Grasping the hand of Young Joseph, he made this last request:

> My son, my body is returning to my mother earth and my spirit is going very soon to see the Great Spirit Chief . . . Always remember that your father never sold his country . . . A few years more, and white men will be all around you. They have their eyes on this land. My son, never forget my dying words. This country holds your father's body. Never sell the bones of your father and your mother.

Young Joseph promised his father to protect their Wallowa homeland with his life. The old man was reassured and peacefully began his journey to the spirit land.

"Old Joseph is dead! Tuekakas, the Oldest Grizzly, great chief of the Wallamwatkin Nez Perces is dead!" The cry went through the village bringing sorrow to the Indian people.

Funeral preparations were begun immediately. The body of the chief was washed, dressed in fine clothing, and decorated with face paint and beautiful ornaments. It was then ready for viewing by family and friends who wished to pay their last respects. Old Joseph's female relatives openly displayed their grief. They cut off their long braids and threw them into the fire. Then, dressed in their most unattractive clothing, they began the traditional death

As a last request, Old Joseph begged his son to protect the Wallowa Valley.

wail that filled the air and proclaimed the passing of a great chief.

After two days, Old Joseph was carefully wrapped in deerskin and carried to his place of burial. This was located at the base of a hill near Wallowa Lake. The body was gently lowered into the grave with its head toward the east as a medicine man praised the brave deeds of the chief. The corpse was then covered with sticks of wood and heaped with stones. Sharp stakes were thrust into the rocks points upward to protect the body from coyotes and other wild animals. Finally, the grave was filled with earth as women wailed and mourners tossed in trinkets as gifts to the departing spirit of their leader.

The sealed grave was fenced and marked with a tall pole that had been painted red. From the top of the pole, a small bell rang in the wind to signify an event of great importance in the Dreamer religion.

Before leaving, the mourners killed a horse and placed its body near the grave of their chief. Old Joseph would need proper transportation on his journey to the afterlife. Each summer, for the next few years, a new horse would be sacrificed for the spirit of the chief.

After the burial, friends moved the lodge of Old Joseph's family to a new location. This prevented the ghost of the dead from bringing madness to the living. Family members were not allowed to reenter their home until a medicine man had rid the dwelling of any lingering spirits. This he did by blowing smoke from a pipe into all corners of the lodge. An additional precaution was taken by those who actually touched the body of the chief. They spent a full week in a sweat lodge to purify their blood of any harmful effects of contact with the dead.

The funeral ceremony officially ended a month later when Old Joseph's family hosted a banquet in his honor. Attended by all the chief's friends and relatives, the event was an opportunity to distribute his possessions as cherished mementos to those who knew and loved him best.

Chapter 12
Confusion and Conflict in the Wallowa

Before Old Joseph's death in 1871, white settlers had begun to arrive in the Wallowa Valley. There were only a few at first. They seemed peaceful and posed little threat to tribal life. Some of them wanted nothing to do with Indians, but others were friendly and enjoyed meeting Nez Perce families. In 1872, Young Joseph visited several of these early settlers. They were impressed with the polite, dignified chief who spoke kindly to them and even played games with their children.

Though Joseph conducted himself in a peaceful, friendly manner in his dealings with the settlers in his valley, the chief could not help being concerned about the future security of his people. The white men claimed their government had purchased the Wallowa in the Treaty of 1863. This gave them every legal right to claim the land for settlement. Joseph said they had been misinformed. His father had never signed the treaty and the valley remained the property of his people. The settlers refused to listen to this argument. They continued to build their homes, plant their crops, and prepare the way for more Americans to follow them.

By August, 1872, the number of white men in the Wallowa Valley had reached alarming proportions. Joseph decided the time had come for him to take formal steps to remove them. He called a council with the settlers to attempt to solve the problem. Between forty and fifty white men attended the meeting. They selected Joseph Johnson as their spokesman because he spoke the Nez Perce language. Chief Joseph was supported by Eagle From the Light and several other nontreaty chiefs.

Once again, Chief Joseph explained the misunderstandings associated with the Treaty of 1863. He said his people wanted no trouble with the white men. However, he could not promise the settlers would not be attacked if they continued to trespass on Indian land. It was becoming increasingly difficult for him to control his young warriors, who viewed the Americans as a threat to their families. Joseph asked the settlers to consider their safety and leave the Wallowa Valley.

Johnson said the white men had no intention of leaving their newly-established homes at this time. He suggested taking the problem to Lapwai for a solution. Perhaps Agent John B. Monteith could help with an exact interpretation of the 1863 treaty.

Joseph said he needed no further explanation of the white man's "Thief Treaty." He was certain beyond doubt the Wallowa Valley rightfully belonged to his people. However, if the settlers wanted to visit Monteith, they were free to do so. He would remain at home and let the white men discover for themselves the truth of his statements.

Settlers A. C. Smith and J. H. Stevens traveled to Lapwai with news of the trouble in the Wallowa Valley. Agent Monteith insisted on meeting with both parties involved and set out immediately for the village of Chief Joseph.

At first, Monteith was inclined to agree with the settlers. He had also been led to believe the Wallamwatkins had given up their valley. Monteith was eager to move the nontreaty bands onto the reservation where he could have better control over them. This outbreak of hostility could help bring about the move.

However, after listening to Joseph's eloquent presentation of the Indian side of the issue, the agent began to believe the Nez Perces may be correct. This confusion prevented Monteith from taking sides and led him to suggest a compromise. He explained that white man had claimed only a small part of the Wallowa Valley. As agent for the Nez Perces, he had no authority to evict settlers from their homes which were outside the boundaries of the reservation. Monteith asked Joseph to remain patient and attempt to coexist with the Americans until an official verdict on the matter could be reached.

Still hoping to settle the disputes peacefully, Joseph agree to the agent's request. Allowing the settlers to remain in the valley, the chief led his people into winter camp and trusted the situation would be improved by spring.

Monteith returned to Lapwai and sent a report of the incident to the Commissioner of Indian Affairs in Washington. The agent wrote: ". . . If there is any way by which the Wallowa Valley could be kept for the Indians, I would recommend that it be done."

After receiving Monteith's report and recommendation, the Indian Bureau in Washington became concerned about the possibility of war in the Wallowa Valley. Officials ordered Agent Monteith and T. B. Odeneal, Superintendent of Indian Affairs in Oregon, to meet with the Wallamwatkins. They wanted the Indians to move onto the Nez Perce or Umatilla reservation. If the nontreaties

Young Chief Joseph made friendly visits to settlers in the Wallowa Valley.

refused, the agent was authorized to offer them a reservation in whatever part of the Wallowa Valley they chose to live. This in return for allowing white settlement of the remainder of the valley.

Agent Monteith and Superintendent Odeneal met with Joseph and the Wallamwatkins on March 27, 1873. As usual, the chief was called upon to explain why his people should be allowed to remain in their valley. Joseph's intelligence and sincerity impressed the white men and led them to believe there had indeed been a misinterpretation of the Treaty of 1863.

Joseph flatly refused to move his people to either the Nez Perce or the Umatilla reservation. In answer to the request to move, he clearly stated:

I will not . . . We have plenty, and we are contented and happy if the white man will let us alone. The reservation is too small for so many people with all their stock . . . Our fathers were born here. Here they lived, here they died, here are their graves. We will never leave them.

The chief was more receptive to Monteith and Odeneal's second proposal. They said the Nez Perces could remain in the Wallowa and continue to claim ownership of the upper valley and lake area. White men would be allowed to settle in the lower part of the valley and be kept away from the Indian land which would now become part of the reservation. Joseph disliked giving up any part of the Wallowa Valley, but was willing to consider this compromise.

Monteith and Odeneal acted quickly to preserve peace in the Wallowa. They immediately sent the compromise proposal to Washington. Their recommendation included the suggestion that all whites forced to move from the upper Wallowa Valley be paid by the government for any improvements they had made on the land.

On May 10, 1873 Commissioner W. W. Curtis of the General Land Office ordered the United States Surveyor General in Oregon to stop further white encroachment on the Wallowa Valley. On June 9, an executive order to establish a reservation for the Nez Perces in the valley was sent to President Grant for his signature.

At this point a mistake in the Bureau of Indian Affairs further complicated the Wallowa Valley issue. The executive order sent to President Grant mixed up the sections of land assigned to whites and Indians. The Indians were given the lower Wallowa Valley where most of the settlers currently lived. The settlers were assigned to the upper part of the valley and lake area where Joseph had been promised a home for his people. How this error occurred is unknown. It remained undetected and the flawed executive order was signed by Grant on June 16.

In the spring of 1873, the Nez Perces returned to the valley from their winter camp in the canyons. They discovered the number of white settlers in the area had continued to grow throughout the winter. Problems arose almost immediately. Some of the young warriors began to argue with the white men over grazing and the ownership of straying cattle. Joseph ordered his people to remain in the upper part of the Wallowa which he believed the government now officially recognized as Indian land.

The open hostility of Joseph's warriors frightened some of the settlers. They held an emergency meeting to organize a volunteer militia to protect themselves from possible attacks. Some families moved back to the Grande Ronde Valley where they warned others of the growing danger in the Wallowa. The threat of violence caused more settlers to begin to fear and hate the Indians.

On May 31, news of President Grant's executive order regarding the Wallowa reached the Northwest. The document, which mistakenly gave the lower part of the valley to the Indians, drew cries of protest from American settlers in the area. Some grudgingly packed up their families and moved to the Grande Ronde. Others refused to leave and wrote angry letters to governmental representatives. These settlers began to put pressure on their elected officials to rescind the executive order. Since Indians could not vote and had no political power whatever, politicians tended to support their white electorate and ignore the Nez Perce point of view.

The settler's arguments gained credibility when Oregon's Governor Lafayette F. Grover joined in the controversy. Grover said that, while the Wallamwatkins had not signed the Treaty of 1863, they had signed the Treaty of

1855. That earlier document had established the Wallowa Valley as part of the Nez Perce reservation and the property of the entire tribe. This gave Lawyer, as head chief, full authority to sign away the valley in 1863. The governor sent this information to President Grant and demanded the cancellation of the executive order. It must be remembered that Lawyer's ability to give away Wallowa land was all imaginary. United States officials had given him this power when they invented the title of "head chief." Nez Perce leaders never recognized the authority of a head chief.

The protests of Governor Grover and Oregon's congressional delegation were received in Washington by the Department of the Interior. Wishing to appease his strong Oregon supporters, the Secretary of the Interior decided to reconsider the situation in the Wallowa Valley.

Agent Monteith had recommended the Indians be allowed to remain in their traditional homeland. He felt his authority was threatened when he learned the Wallowa issue had been reopened. He also felt pressured by Lawyer and his followers who disliked the nontreaty bands and wanted them moved to the reservation. Monteith suddenly found himself in an uncomfortable position with his superiors in Washington and the Indians at Lapwai. In response to this situation, the agent changed his point of view and called Joseph and the nontreaty bands troublemakers. He said they belonged on the reservation and should be forced to move there as soon as possible.

Joseph was angry at the white man's apparent indecisiveness. Lacking an understanding of the political system, the chief marveled at how quickly governmental officials changed their minds and points of view. Monteith had seemed to understand and respect the Nez Perces' right to claim the valley. Now, seemingly without reason, the agent had shifted sides and called for their removal.

Joseph visited the agency to argue on behalf of his people. When his protests were ignored, he asked permission to visit Washington and present his case to President Grant. Without offering an explanation, Monteith flatly refused the chief's request.

On May 18, 1874, Edwin P. Smith, Commissioner of Indian Affairs, announced the entire Wallowa Valley was open for white settlement. This action, in response to public pressure, was a violation of Grant's executive order which still remained in effect. Settlers now entered the upper Wallowa area which Joseph still believed was Indian land. The chief was not informed of Smith's announcement until a year later. During that time, Joseph blamed Agent Monteith for failing to remove settlers from his land.

In July, 1874, the angry nontreaty bands held a council at Tepahlewam (Split Rocks), a place on Camas Prairie near present-day Grangeville, Idaho. Among the leaders present were Joseph, Ollokot, White Bird, Young Looking Glass, and Toohoolhoolzote. There appeared to be a wide variety of Indian responses to white encroachment on their land. The chiefs decided a formal council represented the best way to decide what action, if any, should be taken. Many young men cried for war. The assembly asked for advice from the three most respected Nez Perce warriors: Rainbow, Five Wounds, and Grizzly Bear Ferocious. All three men counseled against open warfare at this time. They were still hopeful the situation could be resolved without risking the lives of their people. To them, bloodshed was a last resort when all attempts at peace had failed. The council decided to accept this recommendation and continue to be patient a while longer. Joseph breathed a sight of relief. Like his father, he believed that open warfare against so formidable an enemy as the United States Army could only bring tragedy to his people.

On September 1, 1874, General Oliver Otis Howard became the new Commander of the Department of the Columbia. Howard was a dignified, deeply religious man who white men called the "Christian General." The Indians called him the "One-Armed Soldier Chief" because he had lost his right arm in the Civil War Battle of Fair Oaks. Howard was considered to be an honest, fair-minded man who was always willing to believe the best of anyone. One of his soldiers described him by saying:

> ... I remember him most for his ever-friendly speech and his quiet manner. I don't believe I ever saw or heard of his being in a controversy ... General Howard was always as courteous to a corporal or a sergeant as he was to a major or a colonel, and those under him liked and respected him for it. Always kind and thoughtful, he was everything a man and an officer could be.

After the Civil War, General Howard gained experience dealing with Indians in the campaign against Cochise and the Apaches in the Southwest. He first met Chief Joseph while on a tour of inspection the year after he arrived in the Pacific Northwest. The encounter took place at the Umatilla reservation where Joseph was visiting his friend, Young Chief.

Joseph had recently learned that on June 10, 1875, President Grant had issued a new proclamation concerning the Wallowa Valley. Responding to political pressure, the President had declared the entire valley open for white settlement. Joseph was angry and confused. He welcomed

General Oliver Otis Howard

the opportunity to meet General Howard. He hoped that the new "soldier chief" would be able to explain the President's change of heart.

Howard took an immediate liking to the personable Nez Perce chief. He later wrote of this first meeting:

> ... I thought he was trying to open the windows of his heart to me, and at the same time endeavoring to read my disposition and character ... I think that Joseph and I became then quite good friends.

Like other white officials who met and talked with Joseph, Howard was impressed with the chief's polite manner and outstanding verbal ability. After listening to the Indian side of the Wallowa issue, the general found himself in agreement with the Nez Perces. He wrote to the Secretary of War:

> ... I think it a great mistake to take from Joseph and his band of Nez Perce Indians that valley. The white people really do not want it. They wish to be bought out. I think gradually this valley will be abandoned by white people, and possibly Congress can be induced to let these really peaceable Indians have this poor valley for their own.

Chapter 13

Mother Earth is Bathed in Blood

While Joseph and the other chiefs were diligently trying to prevent war with the Americans, events in the Wallowa were forcing the Nez Perces closer to the outbreak of hostility.

Nez Perce leaders were attempting to coexist with white men in their valley. Eagle Robe, an old, much respected chief, lived alone on a section of land near the Salmon River. Retired from active leadership, Eagle Robe spent his time peacefully tending his garden. In 1875, a settler named Larry Ott arrived in the valley looking for a place to live. Eagle Robe welcomed the newcomer and gave him some of his land on which to build. The old chief asked only that his lodge and garden remain undisturbed. One day, while Eagle Robe was away visiting a nearby village, the greedy Ott decided to claim more of the Indian's land. He extended his fence to include a large section of the chief's precious garden. Eagle Robe was furious when he returned and saw what his neighbor had done. The old man immediately began to reclaim his stolen property by tearing down the settler's fence posts. The chief's actions soon drew the attention of Larry Ott who seized his revolver and fired upon the old man.

Eagle Robe was discovered mortally wounded by his son, Wahlitis. With his dying words, the chief made the young man promise not to seek revenge. Settlers had committed other crimes against the Nez Perce people. Each time, the white man's law seemed to contain a reason not to punish the offender. Indians were always blamed for provoking acts of violence. Lodging complaints against the settlers often made the situation worse. Protests enraged the white men who took their anger out on tribal members. Eagle Robe did not want his death to create more problems for his people. Though burning to avenge the murder of his father, Wahlitis could not refuse this last request. However, the fires of hatred and revenge refused to be extinguished in the young warrior. They would continue to smolder deep within his heart and burst into flame to change the destiny of the Nez Perce tribe.

In 1876, as the cry for war gained strength among the nontreaty Nez Perces, the opposing struggle for peace was weakened at Lapwai by the death of Chief Lawyer. The old head chief, staunch supporter of white authority, died at Kamiah on January 3. He was about 82 years old. Lawyer was mourned by the treaty bands and many white settlers. They considered him a great leader and true friend who shielded them from the more violent members of his tribe. However, the Dreamers and the nontreaty Indians refused to grieve for the old chief. They called him a traitor who had forsaken the cultural pride and heritage of his people. Whatever their point of view, both Indians and settlers recognized the death of Lawyer as a significant event in tribal history. His passing deprived the treaty bands at Lapwai of much of their ability to influence Agent Monteith and other white officials. This weakened their posi-

**Eagle Robe begged his son not to seek revenge for
Larry Ott's crime.**

tion and placed them at the mercy of the Americans. The
nontreaty Indians now become the last to oppose white
domination of the land. Like the diminutive, Biblical David, Joseph's people bravely challenged their formidable
United States' Goliath.

Each fall the Wallamwatkins retired to their winter
camp hoping their situation would be improved by spring;
however each spring they were disappointed when they returned to the valley. The year 1876 was no exception to
this pattern. That year, before Joseph's people had even
returned to their summer home, settlers had unjustly accused them of making threats and driving off cattle.
Agent Monteith urged the Department of the Columbia to
force the nontreaties onto the reservation.

Matters in the Wallowa became worse when A. B. Findley, an honest man who the Indians generally liked and respected, discovered some of his horses were missing. Findley's neighbor, Wells McNall, volunteered to help track the animals down. This was to prove unfortunate since McNall was a known Indian-hater with a quick temper.

The horses were easy to follow because, unlike Indian ponies, they had been shod. The tracks led Findley and McNall near the hunting camp of some Wallamwatkin warriors. The hunters were away so the two settlers decided to explore their campsite. The Indians had left many of their most prized possessions scattered about the area in plain sight. The Nez Perces viewed stealing from an enemy as an act of bravery; however they had extremely high standards of honesty within their own tribe. Robbing one's own people was severely punished as a shameful act. Thus, even the most precious articles could be left unattended in a Nez Perce village.

Findley and McNall noticed several valuable rifles the Indians had not taken with them. Since McNall was certain these hunters had stolen Findley's horses, he decided to collect and hide their weapons. This might prevent a fight when he confronted them with their crime.

As the two white men were gathering up the rifles, four or five warriors returned to the camp. Among them was Wilhautyah (Wind Blowing), a young friend of Chief Joseph. As soon as McNall noticed the Indians, be began questioning them about the missing horses. The hunters denied any knowledge of the animals and tried to be friendly at first. However, the white man's insulting accusations soon caused temperatures to rise.

During the conversation, Wilhautyah noticed that McNall had taken his rifle. The young warrior quickly pointed out that all thieves were not Indians. He angrily demanded the return of his property. The settler refused and Wilhautyah approached to take the weapon away from him.

McNall had no intention of testing his strength against the angry Nez Perce. Losing control of his own hot temper, he aimed the rifle and shot Wilhautyah in the leg. The painful injury failed to stop the warrior. Though unarmed, he continued to advance on the now frightened white man. McNall cried out for help from his companion. With little time to think, Findley seized a gun and fired upon Wilhautyah killing him instantly.

Findley immediately regretted his senseless crime; however the deed was done and trouble was sure to follow. Adding to the severity of the issue, the missing horses were discovered three days later peacefully grazing near the Findley ranch. Wilhautyah and the other Nez Perces had been innocent of the charges made against them.

Joseph's people cried out for vengeance. Monteith called the killing "a willful, deliberate murder." He advised the chief to leave the matter in the hands of territorial officials.

Lacking confidence in the white man's justice, the Wallamwatkins held a council to determine a course of action. The young warriors wanted immediate revenge. However, their point of view met opposition from Wilhautyah's daughter. Though deeply grieved by the death of her father, she spoke for her family and pleaded with the warriors. She said, "My friends, we do not wish other people or our other friends to be killed for the killing of one person, so let us drop the matter."

Like Eagle Robe, Wilhautyah's young daughter found the strength to place the welfare of her tribe above a personal desire for vengeance. Her remarkable self-control helped to calm the others. The council decided to wait and see if Indians could hope to receive justice in the white man's courts.

About this time, General Howard decided to gather information on the situation in the Wallowa Valley. The complex issue had caused a great deal of confusion among territorial officials. No one appeared to know exactly what action should be taken. Howard was determined to learn the facts and deal with the problem before more lives were lost. The general sent his assistant, Major Henry Clay Wood, to study the situation in the Wallowa. Wood's report stated that the nontreaty bands could not be bound by the Treaty of 1863. The Indians' claim to the valley was valid and must be dealt with before white occupation. Wood recommended immediate action to prevent the outbreak of war.

Howard's decisions were also influenced by Reverend A. L. Lindsley, an important Presbyterian minister in Portland, Oregon. Lindsley was a friend of Agent Monteith and considered himself well-informed concerning matters in the Wallowa Valley. The minister also recognized the Indians' right to claim the land. However, he favored white settlement and said these claims should be "rightfully extinguished" as soon as possible. Lindsley suggested that the government should attempt to purchase the land from the Nez Perces. If that failed, he saw justification for using "harsher methods" to remove the Indians.

The recommendations of Wood and Lindsley reinforced by pressure from white settlers in the area helped formulate Howard's plan of action. Setting aside his personal beliefs in Joseph's cause, the general decided to use whatever means he needed to move the nontreaties onto the reservation. He wanted to open the entire Wallowa Valley for white settlement.

General Howard now became Joseph's leading antagonist in the battle for the Wallowa Valley. The Christian General would also fight a continuous battle with his own conscience which refused to ignore the injustice being done.

Howard recommended that the Secretary of the Interior in Washington appoint a five man commission to meet with Joseph and settle matters in the valley. The general then told Major Wood to arrange a council with the chief to prepare the way for negotiations.

Joseph, Ollokot, and some forty Nez Perces traveled to Lapwai for the meeting. Wood was deeply moved by Joseph who managed to remain dignified and nonthreatening while declaring his grievances against the Americans. The discussion soon turned to the recent murder of Wilhautyah. Joseph described the brutal killing and demanded justice on behalf of his people. The chief said that Wilhautyah's death had strengthened his resolve to keep the valley. The land had been bathed in Nez Perce blood making it more sacred to his tribe than ever before. He said the white men should have to forfeit their claim to the valley as punishment for the crimes they had committed against the Indian people.

Major Wood assured Joseph that General Howard had immediate plans to settle the Wallowa Valley issue. He promised the chief that soon a five man commission would arrive from Washington to end the dispute forever. Like Agent Monteith, the major suggested that Findley and McNall could best be punished in the white man's court. Joseph and Ollokot agreed to wait a while longer for the resolution of their many problems.

The Nez Perces remained patient for two more months. At the end of that time, white officials had still taken no action against Findley and McNall for the murder of

Wilhautyah. Joseph was angry and frustrated. He decided to take matters into his own hands and let the settlers feel the anger of his people.

On Sunday, September 2, 1876, Joseph called the settlers together for a council meeting. The chief specifically asked that Findley and McNall be among those present. The settlers agreed to attend, but told Findley and McNall to stay away in case the Indians planned to harm them.

Joseph was angry when Wilhautyah's murderers failed to attend the council. The chief said that if an Indian committed a crime against a settler, the case should be handled in white man's court. Likewise, if a settler committed a crime against an Indian, the case should be handled in tribal court. Joseph demanded that Findley and McNall be turned over to him for punishment according to Nez Perce law. The angry chief further demanded that all white families vacate their homes in the Wallowa Valley within the next week.

The settlers were outraged by Joseph's order to evacuate the valley. They refused to leave their homes. They also refused to give up Findley and McNall for tribal punishment. The council soon adjourned with both Indians and whites too angry to continue. However, before they left, they all agreed to meet the following day at Ephriam McNall's cabin to discuss the matter further.

The settlers gathered at McNall's cabin on Monday to await the arrival of the Wallamwatkins. Joseph decided a show of strength might help convince the white men to meet his demands of the previous day. To accomplish this, the chief and his brother, Ollokot, led sixty or seventy armed and painted warriors to encircle the cabin filled with settlers. Terrified though they were, the white men still refused to meet the Indian's demands. Joseph said that if they did not comply with his wishes by the following Sunday, he would burn their houses and drive them from his valley.

Joseph's warnings frightened the settlers. It was hard for them to believe this was the same cordial chief who only a short while ago had visited their families and played with their children. What a terrible change had taken place in this once-peaceful man! The settlers were surprised and stunned by Joseph's threat of violence. Those at the council hurried to warn other families in the valley. The entire white population of the Wallowa cried for help from the soldiers at Fort Walla Walla. A troop of 48 cavalrymen was sent along with a citizens' volunteer militia organized in the Grande Ronde.

The soldiers and volunteers arrived in the valley by Saturday, the day before Joseph's deadline for evacuation. This militia was reinforced by some 40 settlers who hated the Indians for endangering their families. One angry man said he would personally kill and scalp Joseph of the chief did not settle down and remain peaceful. Other volunteers bragged they would exterminate all the nontreaty Indians if they tried to evict settlers from the valley.

When Joseph learned about these threats to himself and his people, he decided to pay another visit to the white men. On Saturday evening, he led a large war party and surrounded a meeting of settlers at a cabin near present-day Enterprise, Oregon. Joseph said he and his people were aware of the threats made against them. The Nez Perces were not afraid and the chief's order to leave remained in force. He reminded the settlers that they had just one more day to vacate their homes in the valley. This was their last chance to avoid an attack by his warriors.

The stubborn settlers were still unwilling to leave their homes. They immediately sought help from the military. Lieutenant G. Forse led a group of soldiers to the Wal-

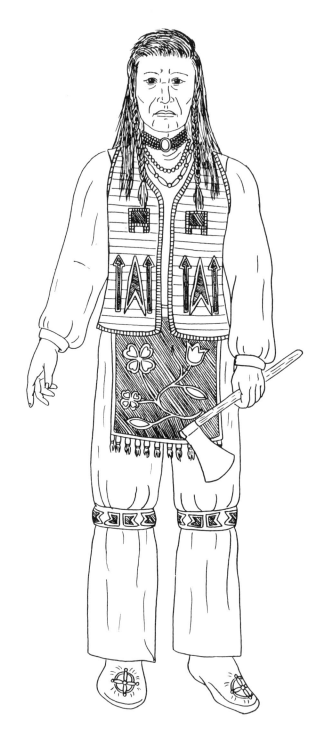

Joseph ordered all white men to leave the Wallowa Valley.

lamwatkins' camp and managed to arrange a meeting with Joseph. The chief described the slaying of his friend, Wilhautyah. He said the Nez Perce people were outraged by the injustice of the white men who had failed to punish the murderers. Joseph refused to cancel his attack unless Findley and McNall were arrested and given a fair trial. Forse agreed to this request. He then suggested that future violence could be avoided if the nontreaty bands moved onto the Nez Perce reservation. Joseph said this was not necessary. General Howard's five man commission would arrive soon to determine proper ownership of the valley. The chief was certain his people would at last gain legal possession of their homeland. Forse said he would see that Findley and McNall were brought to justice; however Joseph must keep his warriors away from other settlers in the valley. The chief agreed and allowed the white men to remain in their homes until the commission had completed its work.

Lieutenant Forse kept his word to Chief Joseph. On his recommendation, Findley and McNall gave themselves up to the authorities in Union, Oregon. No charges were brought against McNall. His actions were considered to be in self-defense. Findley was brought to trial on September 14, 1876. He too was found to have acted in self-defense. Both men were released. The Indians had received their "justice" in the white man's court.

Chapter 14

"If Ever We Owned the Land"

On October 3, 1876, Secretary of the Interior Zachary Chandlier appointed Howard's commission for the Nez Perces. Three of the men selected were easterners who knew nothing about Indians or events in the Wallowa Valley. The other two were General Howard and Major Wood. Howard assumed leadership of the commission and established its goals. He said it would meet with the nontreaty Indians "with a view to secure their permanent settlement on the reservation."

The commission arrived at Lapwai on November 7, 1876 and arranged a council with the Nez Perces six days later. Joseph attended the meeting in the old mission church along with Ollokot, several medicine men, and some sixty warriors. The occasion was a happy one for the chief who believed he was about to receive official ownership of his beloved homeland. Unfortunately, Joseph's smile was soon replaced by a frown of disappointment as he listened to the white men speak.

The commissioners, led by General Howard, asked Joseph to give up the Wallowa Valley and move at once to the Nez Perce reservation. They explained that part of the land had already been surveyed and occupied by white families. Even if these settlers could be persuaded to leave, others would quickly arrive to take their place. Howard said that the President wanted to protect the Indians just as he protected the white people in the Northwest. This could best be done by separating the races and eliminating the chances for conflict. The Nez Perce people would be safer at Lapwai away from the settlers in the valley.

Joseph insisted he would not give up the ancient tribal home of his forefathers. He said he wanted nothing from the President including a reservation in the Wallowa Valley. The Nez Perces were proud of their freedom and independence. They wanted nothing from the white man that would make them dependent on others for their survival. All they desired was to be left alone in their peaceful valley.

The council continued for two more days. During that time, the commissioners learned about the Dreamer religion from Reverend James H. Wilbur of the Yakima reservation. Wilbur believed that Joseph was a member of the Dreamer faith and a participant in a dangerous intertribal conspiracy against the white man. The minister succeeded in convincing all of the commissioners except Major Wood that Joseph was a disciple of Smohalla and a direct threat to peace in the Northwest. This made the white officials even more determined to place the nontreaties on the reservation.

Joseph had no chance to defend himself against Wilbur's accusations against him. Smohalla had no authority over the Nez Perce chief who was not involved in any tribal conspiracy. In fact, Joseph disagreed with the Dreamers on many things including the resurrection of dead Indians for an alliance against the white man. In vain, the chief attempted to make the commissioners understand his point of view regarding ownership of the land. In response to the persistent claim that Lawyer had sold the valley to the Americans, Joseph explained:

> If ever we owned the land, we own it still. Suppose a white man comes to me and says, "Joseph, I want to buy your horses." I say, "No, I will not sell them." Then the white man goes to my neighbor and says, "I want to buy Joseph's horses, but he will not sell." My neighbor says, "Pay me the money and I will sell you Joseph's horses." The white man returns to me and says, "Your neighbor sold me your horses." Do you think I would give them up? If we sold our lands to the government, this is the way they were bought.

Though these arguments were impressive, they did not persuade the commissioners to change their minds. The council ended on November 15 without reaching an agreement. The meeting served only to convince the white officials that debating with the "stubborn" Chief Joseph was useless. Howard and the others decided that the only way to deal with the Indians was by direct order and force if necessary. In their report to Washington, they recommended that the Dreamer teachers be confined to agencies or exiled to Indian Territory in Oklahoma. This would stop their disruptive effect on the Northwest tribes. The commissioners also suggested immediate military occupation of the Wallowa Valley to force the nontreaties onto the reservation unless they moved voluntarily "within a reasonable time." The report concluded with the statement that any acts of violence committed by Indians should be met with immediate, forceful military retaliation. The officials extended these recommendations to include all Nez Perce, Yakima, Palouse, Umatilla, and other Northwest tribes who had refused to sign treaties with the government.

Major Wood was the only member of the commission who refused to sign the report. He felt the recommendations were too harsh and did not want force used against the Indians "until Joseph commits some overt act of hostility." Wood filed his own minority report stating this opinion.

After receiving the reports of General Howard and the commissioners, the Indian Bureau ordered Agent Monteith to move the nontreaties onto the reservation. Monteith was pleased with this opportunity to crush the "heathen Dreamers" who had interfered with his efforts to "civilize" the Nez Perces.

The agent thought force would be necessary to remove the Indians from the valley. However, the government wanted to attempt a peaceful transfer if that were at all possible. On June 25, 1876, General Custer and his men had been massacred by Sioux Indians in the Battle at the Little Bighorn River in Montana Territory. Wishing to avoid further embarrassment, the government now approached hostile tribes with extreme caution. Force could still be used, but only after all peaceful solutions had been tried. Monteith was asked to make one more attempt to persuade the Nez Perces to move voluntarily.

Monteith decided that Indians might have a better chance of winning a debate with other Indians. In early February, 1877, the agent sent a delegation of treaty Nez Perces to convince Joseph to leave the valley. These messengers warned the chief that force would be used if the nontreaty bands continued their stubborn refusals to obey the white man's law.

Joseph considered his situation throughout the night. In the morning he said to the reservation Indians:

I have been talking to the whites many years about the land in question, and it is strange they cannot understand me. The country they claim belonged to my father, and when he died it was given to me and my people, and I will not leave it until I am compelled to.

The treaty Nez Perces carried Joseph's message to Lapwai. Frustrated in his attempt at persuasion, Monteith delivered an ultimatum. The nontreaty bands must move to the reservation by April 1 or be forced from their homes by the U.S. military.

Joseph was upset when he received Montieth's order to leave the Wallowa Valley. He immediately requested a council with General Howard. The general agreed to the meeting but sent Lieutenant William H. Boyle to negotiate in his place. Joseph became ill and also failed to attend the council. The chief sent his brother, Ollokot, to represent the Nez Perce people.

Boyle and Ollokot met at Umatilla for what became a short, unfriendly meeting. Ollokot had drawn a remarkably accurate map of the land claimed by his people. He presented this to Boyle while protesting Monteith's order to move.

Ollokot said that the Wallamwatkins did not want to be placed on any reservation. However, if they were forced to leave the valley, they would choose to live on the Umatilla rather than the Nez Perce reservation. This was because his people shared the same religious beliefs as the Umatillas. They had also intermarried with them and established family bonds. Boyle said the Wallamwatkins no longer had a choice of where to live. They must move to Lapwai and live with the treaty Nez Perces. Ollokot resented Boyle's authoritarian attitude and manner. He angrily left the meeting after requesting that General Howard meet Joseph and the other nontreaty chiefs in the near future.

Agent John B. Monteith

A formal council of the Nez Perces with General Howard was held at Fort Lapwai on May 2, 1877. In addition to Joseph, the chiefs attending were Looking Glass, Toohoolhoolzote, and White Bird, who arrived a day late. Young Chief of the Cayuses was also present as an observer as was Husishusis Kute of the Palouse tribe. About fifty Wallamwatkins accompanied Chief Joseph. They made their camp in the valley near the fort.

The Indians made elaborate preparations before meeting the important "One-Armed-Soldier-Chief." They dressed in their finest beaded ceremonial clothing which they had whitened by rubbing chalk into the leather. Both men and women braided their long, black hair; some adding ornaments made of beads, feathers, animal fur, or shells. The women also decorated themselves with colorful shawls, blankets, and high-topped moccasins; while the men carefully painted their faces and donned feathered headdresses. Thus attired, the warriors rode their best ponies to encircle the fort accompanied by ancient tribal chanting.

The meeting was held in a hospital tent inside the fort. General Howard welcomed each chief by shaking his hand and seating him within the council circle on the floor of the tent. The Indians were also greeted by Agent Monteith and interpreters Perrin Whitman and James Reuben. Father Cataldo opened the session by reciting a prayer in Shahaptin, the Nez Perce language.

Joseph asked if the meeting could be delayed until the arrival of White Bird. Howard refused the chief's request by saying:

> Mr. Monteith's instructions and mine are directly to your people; if you decide to comply with the wishes of the government, you can have first pick of vacant land. We will not wait for White Bird; instructions to him are the same; he can take his turn.

155

In spite of the general's wishes, Joseph managed to postpone the meeting. After Agent Monteith read his orders to move the nontreaty Indians onto the reservation, Joseph refused to comment until he had conferred with White Bird. Reluctantly, Howard adjourned the council until the chiefs had met.

White Bird arrived on Friday, May 3. The stately old man, now over seventy years of age, was the oldest of the nontreaty chiefs. He was welcomed by the other Nez Perce leaders who immediately began to organize for the next council session.

The chiefs selected Toohoolhoolzote as their official spokesman. The fiery old man, who had long opposed white encroachment on tribal land and had spoken out against establishment of the Spalding mission, was happy to speak for his people.

Toohoolhoolzote, though highly respected by the Nez Perces, was not popular with the white men. Agent Monteith warned General Howard that the old chief was one of the most dangerous members of the Dreamer faith. Toohoolhoolzote was unafraid of the Americans and contemptuous of the Christian Nez Perces. He resented being ordered onto a reservation and did not hesitate to speak his mind.

When the council resumed, Howard repeated his orders to move the nontreaties from the valley. Toohoolhoolzote immediately expressed opposition. He described his people's love for the land in terms of the Dreamer religion and said that only the Great Spirit could tell each race of men where to live. The Americans had no right to order his people to leave their precious Mother Earth.

The chief's eloquent speech aroused the emotions of the Indians at the council. Howard became uneasy as he watched them nod in agreement and begin whispering among themselves. Joseph sat quietly observing the faces of the white men. He looked for signs of fear to indicate a weakening of the government's position. White Bird also sat silently watching the proceedings.

Howard managed to appear calm. However, he was very upset by Toohoolhoolzote's discourse and attitude. The general feared the old chief might incite violence if he continued speaking long enough. Howard stopped the proceedings as quickly as possible. He suggested that the council be adjourned until the following Monday. He gave the excuse that this would allow the Indians time to think and talk among themselves. The general failed to say that he would use the delay to alert his men and order more troops in case the council should become a battleground.

Howard's concern grew over the weekend as the Indians met and discussed their situation. Young warriors, fired by the outspoken Toohoolhoolzote, made angry speeches favoring war to protect their land.

By Monday, May 6, both sides were armed to defend themselves. Soldiers, prepared for battle, waited nervously in their barracks; while Indians carried weapons concealed in their blankets. Joseph opened the council proceedings with a bold declaration of his position. He said:

> I am ready to talk today . . . I do not believe that the great Spirit gave one kind of men the right to tell another kind of men what they must do.

The tension of the situation had its effect on General Howard. Seeing his authority challenged by the once-friendly chief, he angrily shouted, "You deny my authority, do you? You want to dictate to me, do you?"

Unable to remain silent, Toohoolhoolzote spoke next. Directing his piercing gaze at the general, he said:

> The Great Spirit Chief made the world as it is . . . I do not see where you get your authority to say that we shall not live where he placed us.

Howard was alarmed at the direction this discussion was taking. Each speech brought the participants closer to the outbreak of violence. He threatened to arrest Toohoolhoolzote if the chief continued with his inflamatory remarks.

Toohoolhoolzote refused to be silenced. The general's threat only served to increase his anger. His statements now became insulting as he said:

> Who are you that you ask us to talk and then tell me I shan't talk? Has Howard created the mountains? Filled the river? Has he made the sun, the plains, the animals? What, indeed, really belongs to General Howard, who doesn't even know the Wallowa Valley is Nez Perce land.

Agent Monteith tried to calm the chief by telling him that Howard was only doing his job. The order to move came from Washington, not from the general himself. Howard added that the reservation was good and would protect the Nez Perces from harm.

With an air of superiority, Toohoolhoolzote inquired, "What person pretended to divide the land and put me on it?"

Sensing he was losing control of the council, Howard decided it was time for a forceful statement of his intentions. Facing the defiant Toohoolhoolzote, the general firmly announced:

> I am that man. I stand here for the President, and there is no spirit, good or bad, that will hinder me. My orders are

plain, and will be executed. I hoped the Indians had good sense enough to make me their friend and not their enemy... Will the Indians come peaceably on the reservation or do they want me to put them there by force?

Toohoolhoolzote failed to conceal the rage within him as he replied, "The Indians can do what they like, but I am not going on the reservation."

Howard lost all patience with Toohoolhoolzote. There appeared to be no way to persuade or force agreement from the old man who the general later described as a "cross-grained growler" and a "large, thick-necked, ugly, obstinate savage of the worst type." Howard decided the only way he could be successful at the council was to remove the defiant chief whose determination to prevail was equal to his own. The general arrested Toohoolhoolzote and ordered Captain Perry to escort him to the guardhouse.

The chief allowed himself to be led from the council. However, before leaving, he could not resist making a final statement to General Howard. He said regarding his arrest:

Is that your order? I do not care. I have expressed my heart to you. I have nothing to take back ... You can arrest me, but you cannot change me or make me take back what I have said.

Expressions of shock and disapproval clouded the faces of the other chiefs as in silence they watched the arrest of Toohoolhoolzote. Seeing the reaction of those around him, Howard thought he may have pushed the Indians too far. His impulsive actions may now replace Toohoolhoolzote's inflamatory words in causing the violence he hoped to avoid.

Joseph also sensed the danger in the situation. He now realized that this meeting had not been called to discuss

Toohoolhoolzote angrily insulted General Howard.

possible solutions to problems in the Wallowa Valley. General Howard had already made all the decisions. The Indians were not here to provide information and opinions. They were here to receive orders. The only choices left to them were to obey or to disobey. Fearing what the powerful white men might do if the Nez Perces continued to defy them, Joseph attempted to calm tempers on both sides. Addressing the council, he said:

> I am going to talk now. I don't care whether you arrest me or not . . . The arrest of Toohoolhoolzote was wrong, but we will not resent the insult. We were invited to this council to express our hearts, and we have done so.

Joseph added that while his people wanted to remain in their native homeland, they were at least willing to look

160

at land on the reservation. The chief hoped this temporary compromise would help prevent an outbreak of violence at the council.

On May 8, General Howard escorted White Bird, Looking Glass, and Joseph on a tour of the Nez Perce reservation. The chiefs asked that Toohoolhoolzote be released and allowed to join them. The general refused saying that the old man had already caused too much trouble and must now remain in the guardhouse until matters were settled with the tribe.

Howard promised the nontreaty bands would have schools, teachers, houses, churches, and gardens if they moved to the reservation. Joseph attempted to explain that his people did not need or want these things. He said:

> . . . The Earth is our mother, and do you think we want to dig and break it? No, indeed! We want to hunt buffalo and fish for salmon, not plow and use the hoe. We do not plant; we harvest only the grain and berries that Mother Earth willingly gives us.

Despite the differences of opinion, the chiefs knew it was senseless to argue against the powerful United States Government. The Indians were not being asked to choose a home on the reservation; they were being ordered to move. Better to select a place that was at least marginally acceptable to their people than be forced as defeated prisoners of war onto land that may be totally useless. White Bird selected a place near Kamiah as a home for his band. Looking Glass chose some land farther down the Clearwater Valley and Joseph said the Wallamwatkins would move to an area above Kamiah on the Clearwater River.

The group returned to Lapwai on May 11. General Howard told the chiefs they would now have just thirty days to move to their new homes. The Indians protested the short amount of time. How could they be expected to pack all their possessions, round up thousands of horses, and move all their people in such a few days? Besides, rain and water from the spring thaw had filled the rivers to overflowing. Crossing the Snake River to the reservation at this time of year would be extremely dangerous. Joseph had the greatest distance to travel. He begged for more time to insure the safety of his people.

Howard believed that the longer the Nez Perces remained in the valley the greater the chances of war with the Americans. Settlers who lived near White Bird's village had recently written to the general complaining about "unruly" Indians near their homes. Howard read these letters to the chiefs hoping to increase their desire to move as soon as possible. However, the messages only made the Nez Perce leaders angrier at the settlers for making them leave their homeland. Howard said that under the present conditions he could not grant the Indians more time in which to move. The nontreaties must be out of the valley in thirty days. He ended the council with a warning that, "If you let time run over one day, the soldiers will be there to drive you on the reservation."

The chiefs sadly left Lapwai to begin the difficult task of moving their people away from the land they loved.

On May 14, Howard released Toohoolhoolzote from prison. The chief had not mellowed during his confinement. He returned to his people filled with thoughts of hatred and revenge. He wanted the white men to pay for his humiliation and loss of freedom.

Chapter 15
Wahlitis' Trail of Vengeance

The Nez Perce chiefs returned home from Lapwai with differing points of view concerning the outcome of the council. Joseph and Looking Glass were determined to avoid war by obeying General Howard's ultimatum. Toohoolhoolzote and White Bird, on the other hand, continued to express defiance of the white man's authority and discussed using the thirty day moving time as a chance to prepare for war.

Joseph became worried about the influence Toohoolhoolzote had on the young men of his band. He later expressed this when he said:

> Toohoolhoolzote, who felt outraged by his imprisonment, talked for war, and made many of my young men willing to fight rather than be driven like dogs from the land where they were born. He declared that blood alone would wash out the disgrace General Howard had put upon him.

Joseph discussed his concerns with Ollokot and they decided to hold a council to reaffirm their determination to avoid war. When the leaders and warriors of the Wallamwatkins were assembled, Joseph said:

163

... rather than have war, I would give up my country. I would give up my father's grave. I would give up everything rather than have the blood of white men upon the hands of my people.

The chief then ordered everyone to pack their possessions, gather their horses and cattle, and prepare to move as quickly as possible.

Despite feelings of anger and resentment, most of the Nez Perce people hurried to obey their chief. However, some young men became rebellious and threatened to commit acts of violence against their white enemies.

Joseph's first priority was the welfare of his people. When he learned what these warriors were saying, he realized how quickly all chances for peace could be lost. His authority in this matter must not be challenged. Joseph armed himself with a pistol and rode through the village. He repeated his order to begin packing and said he would shoot anyone who disobeyed him.

With only about sixty warriors in their band, the Wallamwatkins had a great deal of difficulty rounding up their horses and cattle. The large herds had been allowed to graze freely over many miles of canyons, prairies, forests, and meadows. They had become so widely dispersed it was impossible to collect them all within the short period of time allowed. The Indians were forced to leave many of their best animals behind.

By the end of May, Joseph's people had rounded up nearly 6,000 head of livestock. They were now ready to begin the hundred-mile journey to their new home on the reservation.

General Howard had remained fully informed of the Indians' activities. In early May, he had sent Captain Stephen G. Whipple with five officers, ninety-seven soldiers, and a Gatling gun into the Wallowa Valley to make sure Joseph obeyed his orders. Captain Whipple commented on the dangerous weather and difficult traveling that spring when he reported:

> During the entire month the weather has been most unpropitious for field operations, there having been long rain storms—with some snow—or frequent hard showers. The ground was made very soft by the excess of moisture ... the horses sinking at nearly every step. .... there is no other road than an Indian trail, upon which no labor has ever been done and over which no wheeled vehicle has been ...

Joseph's people traveled to the Snake River which had become a raging torrent in the inclement spring weather. They prepared to cross at a place called Big Eddy located upstream from Lewiston, Idaho.

The Indians were accustomed to crossing rivers. They immediately set to work constructing rafts from logs and the buffalo hide coverings of their tepees. Onto these they loaded their possessions along with the women, children, and old people. These passengers clung tightly to the ropes which tied their bundles onto the rafts. Next, mounted warriors attached their ponies to each of the raft's four corners. They swam the precious cargo across the quarter mile of raging water from the Oregon to the Idaho side of the river.

Incredibly, not one person was lost in this dangerous crossing. However, the Indians' livestock was not so fortunate. When the last raft had been hauled to safety on the north-east bank of the river, the warriors returned to begin herding their horses and cattle across. They took precautions to preserve the safety of their animals. Young colts and calves, who were obviously too weak to survive, were left behind with their mothers. In spite of this, large numbers of animals were lost. During the crossing, a fierce storm suddenly arose increasing the danger with a cloudburst of rain. In the confusion caused by the downpour, many horses and cattle were swept to their death by the powerful current of the river. This loss brought further grief to their owners who, having been stripped of their beloved homeland, must now witness their prized possessions being destroyed by the raging water. It seemed that even Mother Nature had turned her back on the Nez Perce people.

By June 2, the Wallamwatkins had completed their crossing of the Snake River. They next journeyed up a rocky canyon to an ancient tribal meeting place called Tepahlewam (Spilt Rocks). Located beside Tolo Lake about six miles west of Grangeville, Idaho, the area contained a camas meadow where the Indians gathered much of their winter food.

With only twelve days left before their deadline, the Wallamwatkins were soon joined by the other nontreaty Indians. Chief White Bird arrived with his band which contained about fifty warriors. This group from the upper Salmon was second in size to that of Joseph. The third Nez Perce band was led by Looking Glass. This leader of nearly forty men had, like his father, earned a reputation as a great war chief. Toohoolhoolzote led the fourth group of nontreaty Indians. With some thirty fighting men, this chief was known as "a fighter from hell." Though well past his prime, Toohoolhoolzote still possessed great physical strength and commanded the respect of all in council. A small number of Palouse Indians joined the other nontreaty bands. Led by chiefs Hahtalekin and Husishusis Kute, the group contained only sixteen warriors who had persisted in their opposition to white encroachment on their land. Altogether, the gathering at Tepahlewam in-

Crossing the Snake River was extremely dangerous for the Nez Perce people.

cluded about six hundred individuals. Only about 155 of these were fighting men.

The mood was melancholy as the various nontreaty Indians met for one last council as free, independent people. The women went about their usual tasks of digging camas and caring for their families. The men gambled, raced their horses, hunted, and fished. These common everyday activities created the appearance of business as usual in the Indian camp. Yet, try as they might, the Nez Perces could not escape the fact that things were very different now. A touch of finality and desperation colored even the most insignificant events. It was as if things were being done for the last time. The Indians felt compelled to savor each remaining moment of their lives as free people. Soon, white men's rules and customs would reshape their existence and destroy the security they derived from generations of predictable habits and traditions.

The warriors often discussed the sad times that the white man had brought upon their tribe. Toohoolhoolzote continued to excite the young men with descriptions of war and the glories of battle. White Bird also tended to support war as did his followers who remembered the insulting messages the settlers had sent to General Howard. Joseph, who continued to counsel peace, was labeled a coward by the Dreamer medicine men who made brave speeches in favor of war. Looking Glass became alarmed and warned the other chiefs to watch their young men closely.

Despite the growing tension in the camp, the Nez Perces managed to remain in control of their actions. They continued to plan the last stages of their move to the reservation.

The tribal gathering lasted for ten days. On June 12, two days before the final move, a group of young warriors staged a parade through the camp as a last salute to their traditional way of life. At the end of the procession, two young men from White Bird's band rode double on a decorated war horse. One of these was Wahlitis, whose father, Eagle Robe, had been killed in 1875 by Larry Ott. The other rider was Wahlitis' cousin, Red Moccasin Top, the son of Yellow Bull, a sub-chief of White Bird.

As the youths wound their way through the crowded campsite shouting their defiance of the white man, Wahlitis' horse accidentally stepped on a spread canvas covered with a woman's supply of kouse roots drying in the sun. The woman's husband, Yellow Grizzly Bear, saw the incident and became angry. He shouted insults at Wahlitis saying, "See what you do! Playing brave, you ride over my woman's hard-worked food! If you are so brave, why do you not go kill the white man who killed your father?"

Wahlitis defensively shouted back, "You will be sorry for your words!"

Yellow Grizzly Bear's cutting remarks pierced Wahlitis like a knife and revived the old emotions of hatred and vengeance he had buried in his heart. Before his death, Eagle Robe had begged his son not to seek revenge on Larry Ott. Such an act could provide an excuse for other white men to harm Nez Perce people. Wahlitis had promised out of respect for his father even though his failure to strike back made him feel like a coward. Now, others were taunting him for pretending to be brave instead of displaying the courage of a warrior. Wahlitis brooded all night. By morning, he had decided to take action.

Wahlitis asked Red Moccasin Top to accompany him on a raid to avenge his father's death. He also took his 17-year-old nephew, Swan Necklace, along to hold the horses when they dismounted to approach Ott's cabin.

The three young men rode toward Slate Creek, a tributary of the Salmon River about 100 miles from Fort Lapwai. They located the home of Larry Ott, but, though they searched all day, the settler was nowhere to be found. Some say the large gathering of Indians in the area caused Ott to fear for his safety. He fled to Florence, a mining town in Idaho, and disguised himself as a Chinese miner. He remained in hiding until the Nez Perces moved on and thus escaped the vengeance of Wahlitis and his companions.

Failing to locate the object of their hatred, the three warriors spent their anger on other settlers who had wronged their people.

Eight miles above the mouth of Slate Creek lived Richard Devine, a retired English sailor. Devine was a known Indian-hater who had killed a crippled Nez Perce woman when she chased his horse away from her garden. Devine

Wahlitis led the first attacks on white settlers.

also had vicious dogs which he released on Indian pass-
ersby while threatening to shoot anyone who returned.

Leaving their horses with Swan Necklace, Wahlitis and
Red Moccasin Top burst into Devine's cabin and seized his
gun before he could resist. Killed with his own rifle, the
old sailor became the first victim on Wahlitis' trail of
vengeance.

Fired by their brief taste of victory, the young warriors
adorned themselves with paint and feathers. They continued to search out enemies of their people as they rode toward John Day Creek along the Salmon River. Three more
settlers who had been openly hostile to the Nez Perce people soon paid for their hatred with their lives. Before moving on, Wahlitis and the others took their victims' horses,
guns, and ammunition.

The last settler to fall prey to the tiny war party was Samuel Benedict, a store owner who was known for cheating and selling whiskey to the Indians. Benedict had killed a drunken Indian in 1875 and wounded two others. Wahlitis and his men fired at Benedict, but only succeeded in wounding him. The terrified settler fled from his shop and concealed himself in some nearby bushes. He managed to escape from his attackers who were eager to return to their people with news of their brave deeds.

Unaware of the explosive situation that had developed, Joseph had withdrawn from the gathering to attend to family matters. His wife was about to have a baby. According to Nez Perce custom, her tepee had been moved to a private location away from the main campsite. While awaiting the birth of his child, Joseph had taken his older daughter and gone with Ollokot and his wife, Wetatonmi, to butcher some cattle before leaving Tepahlewam. Thus, the chief was not present when Wahlitis, Red Moccasin Top, and Swan Necklace returned from their raid and proudly displayed their trophies of war.

With only a single day left before moving to the reservation, the leaders in the Nez Perce camp were gathered in council. They were still not certain they had made the correct decision. Some continued to demand war. Others said there was no way to defeat the white man. The only way to survive was to obey General Howard's orders. Someone said that every nontreaty band had a right to express an opinion in this time of crisis. Some groups were away hunting buffalo. They were completely unaware of the terrible problem now facing their tribe. No final decision for war or peace should be made until all the bands had returned home and had a chance to meet.

The men were completely absorbed in their important conversation when they were interrupted by the sounds of

Swan Necklace

shouting and confusion outside the council lodge. Yellow Bull recognized the voice of his brother, Big Dawn, calling out:

> Now you will have to go to war! See! Wahlitis has killed men and stolen horses! Now the soldiers will be after us! Prepare for war! Prepare for war!

In contrast to the noise and disturbance outside, a stunned silence settled over the inside of the lodge as the men attempted to comprehend what they were hearing. Then, suddenly, the leather covering of the tepee door was thrown back and a breathless young man informed the assembly:

> You poor people are talking for nothing! Three boys have already started war! They have killed a white man on the Salmon and brought his horse to this camp. It is already war!

The chiefs emerged from the lodge to discover their people in a state of near panic. Fearing that General Howard and his soldiers would attack at any moment, the Indians were frantically gathering their possessions, tearing down their tepees, and preparing to flee.

Taking immediate action, the chiefs hurried throughout the camp ordering everyone to calm down and wait for directions from their leaders. This was not a time to increase the danger by running mindlessly away in all directions. This was a time for the Nez Perces to stand together and draw strength from their unity. The chiefs persuaded their people to remain encamped during the night and allow them time to plan the best defensive actions. A warrior named Two Moons set out to locate Joseph and bring him back to camp.

Joseph's infant daughter represented hope for the future of the Nez Perce people.

While most of the Nez Perce leaders worked to calm their people and avoid further violence, some chiefs seized the opportunity to satisfy their desire for bloodshed. Toohoolhoolzote and Yellow Bull took seventeen warriors and returned to the Salmon River area with Wahlitis and his companions. They hunted down Samuel Benedict and murdered him. This triggered a two day killing spree in which between fourteen and seventeen settlers were slain.

Still unaware of the danger, Joseph and his family finished butchering their cattle. They packed the beef onto twelve horses and began their return to the main Nez Perce camp. Joseph was eager for news of his wife and new baby.

As they traveled along discussing their move to the reservation, they saw a horse and rider moving rapidly toward them for the direction of Tepahlewam. Soon they were close enough to recognize the rider as Two Moons. Ollokot said, "He must have news to tell us."

As soon as Two Moons reached Joseph and the others, he shouted excitedly, "War has broken out! Three white men were killed yesterday!"

The words struck Joseph like a physical blow. Signaling for Ollokot to follow him, he set out immediately for camp leaving his daughter and Wetatonmi to follow with the pack horses.

Joseph's hurried return to his people was briefly interrupted when he arrived at the lodge where his wife had recently given birth. The chief paused long enough to learn that the child was a healthy girl and his wife was recovering. Watching the baby peacefully sleeping in her mother's arms, Joseph was filled with conflicting emotions—hope for the future of this new life and despair for the proud past his people had left behind.

Chapter 16
A Battle in White Bird's Canyon

The Nez Perce camp was filled with activity when Joseph and Ollokot arrived. The people were hurrying to take down their tepees, gather their possessions, and move to a place of safety.

Looking Glass had already taken his Asotin band of Nez Perces to his home on the South Fork of the Clearwater River. His people had not been involved in the bloodshed and he wanted to keep them away from any possible violence. The chief believed that General Howard would not disturb his village of peaceful Indians. Husishusis Kute and the Palouses had gone with Looking Glass to avoid involvement in the war that was developing.

Joseph and Ollokot tried to persuade the remaining non-treaty bands to stay at Tepahlewam. The brothers said that surely General Howard would not blame the entire tribe for the actions of a few hot-headed young men. Running away would only make the Indians look guilty. They needed to remain, face the general, and explain what had happened.

White Bird's young men spoke out angrily against the advice of the Wallamwatkin leaders. These warriors were tired of hearing about peace. They were furious and wanted to strike back at their white tormentors. They accused Joseph and Ollokot of being cowards who were afraid to stand against the enemies of their people. They managed to convince everyone except the Wallamwatkins to continue packing and leave at once to escape the soldiers. Their destination was a place on Cottonwood Creek not far from the village of Looking Glass. The chiefs sent scouts back to watch for General Howard on all the trails and roads behind them. Before leaving Tepahlewam, they assigned about 35 warriors to remain with Joseph and his people in case the Wallamwatkins turned traitor and failed to stand by their Nez Perce brethren. The nontreaties could not afford to loose the support of Joseph whose band included the largest number of fighting men. White Bird and the other chiefs were prepared to use force if necessary to prevent the defection of the Wallamwatkins.

Joseph and his band remained at Tepahlewam overnight. They hoped General Howard would send someone to ask for an explanation of the recent hostility. Joseph still believed there was a chance to stop the war if he could tell what had really happened.

After the departure of the other nontreaty Indians, the Wallamwatkins nervously returned to their tepees to await the arrival of the soldiers. At about 10:00 p.m. as the Indians were settling down to get what rest they could, a shot was fired and a bullet tore through the wall of Joseph's lodge. Luckily no one was injured. The Nez Perces seized their weapons and rushed outside in time to see several white men riding away from the camp.

Unable to pursue his attackers in the darkness, Joseph posted guards about the area and met with Ollokot to decide what to do.

By the following morning, June 15, the brothers had made up their minds. They would join the nontreaties at Cottonwood Creek. Joseph later explained this decision when he said:

> . . . I saw that the war could not then be prevented. I counseled peace from the beginning. I knew we were too weak to fight the United States . . .
>
> There were bad men among my people who had quarreled with white men, and they talked of their wrongs until they roused up the bad hearts in the council. Still I could not believe they would begin a war. I know my young men did a great wrong, but I ask, who was first to blame? They had been insulted a thousand times; their fathers and brothers had been killed; . . . and, added to all this, they were homeless and desperate.
>
> I would have given my own life if I could have undone the killing of white men by my people. I blame my young men and I blame the white men. I blame General Howard for not giving my people time to get their stock away from Wallowa. I do not acknowledge that he had the right to order me to leave Wallowa at any time. I deny that either my father or myself ever sold that land. It may never again be our home, but my father sleeps there, and I love it as I love my mother. I left there, hoping to avoid bloodshed.

The arrival of the Wallamwatkins at Cottonwood Creek was a cause for joy among the nontreaty bands. Joseph and Ollokot explained that they could not desert their people in this time of need. Joseph said, "I can hardly go back. The white people will blame me, telling me that my young men have killed the white men, and the blame will come on me."

The other chiefs gave Joseph and his people a detailed report of the raiding that had occurred in the Salmon River and Mount Idaho area. When it was told that an Indian had been killed in these encounters, Joseph's nephew, Yellow Wolf, decided to avenge the death. He and

Chief White Bird

a group of Wallamwatkins attacked and killed another settler in retribution for the tribesman they had lost.

After Yellow Wolf's raid, the Nez Perces became concerned about their continued safety in Cottonwood Creek.

Their fears were justified when, on June 16, scouts warned them of the approach of Captain David Perry and a force of about one hundred soldiers from Fort Lapwai. The chiefs decided to move their people to a more defensible position in White Bird Canyon.

The nontreaties traveled to the floor of the canyon and pitched their lodges near the mouth of White Bird Creek. Steep, rocky walls hid the Nez Perces from view as they nervously awaited the arrival of the U.S. Military.

News of the hostile nontreaty Indians had spread quickly among the settlers of Mount Idaho and the Salmon River area. Mount Idaho was a principal white settlement located on the southern border of the Camas Prairie. It was sixty miles southeast of Fort Lapwai and a few miles south of Grangeville. When the raiding began, townspeople built barricades and organized a volunteer militia to protect their families. Farmers abandoned their crops and ranchers left their stock to seek the safety of Mount Idaho.

Settlers wrote letters to Idaho's territorial governor, Mason Brayman, pleading for help. The governor responded by supplying arms and ammunition for the volunteers defending the town.

L. P. Brown, secretary of the volunteers at Mount Idaho, sent news of the Indian attacks to Captain David Perry, commander of Fort Lapwai. Brown asked the soldiers to help the settlers by forcing the Nez Perces onto the reservation as quickly as possible.

General Howard had returned to Fort Lapwai on June 14 to see if the nontreaty Indians were obeying his orders. When he learned of the problems at Mount Idaho, he sent troops to investigate. The soldiers met two Indians who explained that only a few young warriors had caused all the trouble. With this information, Howard at first believed the attacks were isolated incidents of personal revenge. However, he soon began to think otherwise when settlers repeatedly stated, "One thing is certain, we are in the midst of an Indian war."

On June 15, Howard sent 99 soldiers of the First Cavalry under Captain Perry assisted by Captain Joel Trimble to protect the settlers of Mount Idaho and Grangeville. He also ordered reinforcements from Walla Walla and the Grande Ronde Valley in order to be prepared for any turn of events. By this time the general was convinced that all nontreaty Indians had been involved in the violence.

Captain Perry and his men left Fort Lapwai at 8:00 p.m. on June 15. They traveled all night through a downpour of rain to the Camas Prairie and arrived at Grangeville near evening the next day. The townspeople were overjoyed to see the soldiers and welcomed them into their homes to rest.

Soon after his arrival in Grangeville, Captain Perry met a settler named Arthur Chapman. This man was married to a Umatilla woman and was well known to the Nez Perce people. Chapman said he had been visited at his home by a young reservation Indian on June 14. This boy had recently been with Joseph's people and learned about the outbreak of hostility. He had warned Chapman of the danger to all white settlers in the area. Chapman claimed that the Indians were cowardly rascals who could be easily beaten if enough weapons were available. He urged the captain to strike back and put down the Nez Perce rebellion immediately.

The other settlers also advised Perry to act quickly. They had observed the nontreaties moving in force into White Bird Canyon. They said that from their present location, the Indians were likely to cross the Salmon River and escape eastward into the rugged mountains over the buffalo trail.

After consulting with the townspeople, Perry became convinced of a relatively easy victory over the Nez Perces. He decided to travel at once to White Bird Canyon and launch a surprise attack against the hostiles before they could cross the river. Though the soldiers were exhausted by their seventy mile forced march from Lapwai, the captain allowed only a few hours rest in Grangeville. Guided by Chapman and a group of eleven volunteers, Perry and his men were soon riding toward the Indian camp about sixteen miles away.

It was 10:00 p.m. and the weary men rode through the darkness in relative silence. They spoke little and passed the time thinking of the surprise attack their captain had planned for dawn. One trooper struck a match to light his pipe. As the match burst into flame, the howl of a coyote startled the soldiers from their thoughts. The sound seemed eerie and somewhat unnatural as it pierced the quiet of the night. Soon, however, it was forgotten and the tired men resumed their private visions of battle.

About midnight, the soldiers and volunteers reached the summit of White Bird Hill. Captain Perry ordered them to dismount and allowed them a brief rest before dawn. Though exhausted, many of the men were too excited to sleep. They crouched in the darkness whispering about the coming attack or lie on the uncomfortable ground gazing up at the stars overhead. Some were confident they could easily whip the Indians while others hoped their commanding officer had not underestimated the strength of the enemy they faced.

The strange howl of the coyote, which had only momentarily disturbed the soldiers, was of far greater importance to the Indians. The sound had been made by a Nez Perce scout alerting his people to the presence of soldiers in the area. Joseph posted guards to watch the summit of White Bird Hill and report on the movement of Perry's men. Next, he ordered the Nez Perce women to begin taking down their tepees and making preparations for a quick departure from the canyon.

The Nez Perces had about 150 fighting men. However, many of them were suffering from the effects of the whiskey brought back by their raiders and were too sick to ride into battle. Therefore, the Indians prepared to defend themselves with only 50 or 60 warriors. A few of these possessed modern rifles, but most were armed with bows and arrows, shotguns, and old, muzzle-loading rifles. The warriors concealed themselves behind boulders, bushes, and the rock ridges that formed the walls of the canyon. When the women had finished packing, they prepared to support the men by guarding the herd of horses and providing fresh war ponies during the battle.

Shortly before dawn on the morning of June 17, Captain Perry roused his men from their uneasy rest and ordered them to form a line of march. The cavalry, riding four abreast, was divided into three groups. The first group, containing only eight men, was led by Lieutenant Edward R. Theller. These soldiers rode about 100 yards ahead of the others and served as an advance scouting guard. If they sighted Indians, they were to halt immediately and report to Captain Perry, who followed with the second group of men. Perry's cavalry was accompanied by Chapman and the citizen volunteers. About forty or fifty yards behind Perry rode Captain Trimble and the final company of troops. The men were uneasy as they rode down the long, treeless draw that led to the floor of the canyon. Their eyes repeatedly scanned the hills and ridges on either side of the draw. These areas provided excellent hiding places from which Indians could easily launch a surprise attack.

Concealed behind a large boulder, Joseph and Ollokot watched the approach of the soldiers. The brothers still maintained a faint hope that war could be avoided. Joseph said, "Maybe there are some Nez Perces with them and they will tell us if the soldiers are coming with good hearts."

In a final overture for peace, the Nez Perce chiefs organized a small group of warriors into a truce commission. These men, led by Vicious Weasel, carried a white flag to meet Captain Perry and determine his intentions. Joseph borrowed a spyglass from one of his people and carefully watched the progress of the peace emissaries as they set out to intercept the soldiers.

The cavalry continued its descent into the canyon. As Lieutenant Theller and his advance guard reached the top of a ridge, they saw a small group of Indians advancing toward them. Following orders, Theller immediately stopped and sent word back to Captain Perry. The captain hurridly formed his troops into a line and moved forward at a trot. Accompanied by the citizen volunteers, the soldiers traveled around a small hill and were suddenly confronted by several Nez Perce warriors carrying a white flag of peace.

Arthur Chapman rode slightly ahead of the other volunteers. When the Indians made their unexpected appearance before the startled troops, Chapman foolishly raised his rifle and fired twice sending bullets whizzing past the peace commission. Vicious Weasel and the others turned their horses and began to ride away. As they fled, an elderly member of the group named Fire Body paused long enough to return a single shot with which he killed one of Captain Perry's trumpeters. With this brief exchange of fire, the first battle ever fought between the Nez Perce people and the United States Army had begun.

As Vicious Weasel and his men made their way to safety, Nez Perce warriors opened fire on the cavalry. The area exploded into activity as Indians appeared from their hiding places to take aim and fire at the soldiers.

Perry hurried to extend his battle line above the draw leading into the canyon. While shooting back at his attackers, he ordered the citizen volunteers to take cover on a rocky knoll to his left. Captain Trimble advanced and took up a fighting position on Perry's right. Perry's men quickly dismounted and herded their horses into a nearby field. Trimble, however, made the mistake of leaving his men on their horses. This made them excellent targets for Indians who shot several of them from their saddles. Most of the horses had never been in battle before. They soon became so terrified and difficult to control the soldiers were forced to dismount.

The Indians had no pre-determined battle strategy. They relied on their experience and keen perception to seize control of the situation. Most of the soldiers were new recruits who were as yet untried in battle. In the attack, they became stunned and disoriented by the deafening confusion around them. Indians whooping, rifles blasting, soldiers shouting, and horses stampeding combined with choking smoke and dust to throw the inexperienced cavalry into chaos.

Two Moons led a group of 16 mounted warriors to attack the citizen volunteers as they sought cover in the small hills on Perry's left. At the same time, Ollokot and another group of Indians launched an attack on Trimble's already disorganized ranks.

In the forefront of Two Moons' attack rode three young warriors wearing long red coats made from blankets and

Arthur Chapman opened fire on the Nez Perce peace commission.

shouting their defiance of the white men. Two of these, Wahlitis and Red Moccasin Top, were fanatically deter- mined to protect their people because their rash actions had helped bring about the war. The third young man was a friend of the other two named Strong Eagle. The trio so distinguished themselves with their bravery they came to be known as the "Three Red Coats."

Two Moon's men shot two of the citizen volunteers. The others fled in terror back up the draw. This exposed Per- ry's left flank to attack by the Nez Perces.

On Perry's right, Captain Trimble's men struggled to repulse Ollokot's charge. The Indians concealed them- selves among a large group of ponies and drove the herd directly through the line of troops. Having passed the battle line, the Nez Perces opened fire on the soldiers from the rear. Bullets and arrows appeared to rain down on the cavalry from all directions.

Looking to his left, Captain Perry saw the citizens retreat and the Indians gain possession of their area. This placed the captain in a dangerous crossfire between two groups of warriors. On the right, Trimble's men were also weakening under heavy fire from the Indians. Perry decided to retreat to the safety of a ridge back down the draw. However, he had lost his bugle and could not sound recall. He rode his horse back and forth shouting the order to retreat. Perry managed to communicate with Trimble, but his own men, unable to hear their leader's orders, became confused and paniced. The new recruits were as yet unable to handle the stress of battle. They ran for their horses and began to flee from the canyon. Soon, Trimble's men also broke ranks and joined the other soldiers in a general rout.

While the officers ordered and finally pleaded with their men to reform ranks and retreat in an orderly manner, the Indians pressed their advantage by rushing forward to attack.

Lieutenant Theller, who had led the advance guard into the canyon, now found himself at the rear of the cavalry as the soldiers made their hasty retreat. Theller and eighteen men desperately tried to overtake the main body of troops led by Captain Perry. In their haste, they mistakenly ran into a cul-de-sac where they were surrounded and trapped by the Indians. The tiny group of soldiers bravely defended their position until the last man lie dead.

The troops continued their dash for safety. Perry and Trimble continued their attempts at organization, but orderly fighting was now impossible. Occasionally, a small group of men managed to make a stand, but these were

The Battle of White Bird Canyon was a terrible defeat for the U.S. Army.

soon forced on by the Indians who, sensing victory, continued their forceful pursuit.

The soldiers were unable to make any kind of coordinated defense until they had left the canyon and arrived at an abandoned ranch about four miles from Mount Idaho. There Perry and his men tied their horses to some fence posts and took cover behind a group of large rocks. The Indians soon arrived and attempted to take the soldiers' horses. To prevent this, Perry ordered his men to make a dash for the safety of Mount Idaho. Along the way, the troops managed to form a skirmish line and keep the Indians at bay. As they neared Mount Idaho, a group of volunteers rode out to reinforce Perry's battered command. The Indians gradually gave up and returned in triumph to the canyon. Perry led his remaining troops to Mount Idaho and immediately sent a report of his defeat to General Howard at Fort Lapwai.

Next to the Custer massacre of 1876, the Battle of White Bird Canyon has been called the greatest defeat ever suffered by the U.S. Army at the hands of Native Americans. When the fighting was over, thirty-three soldiers and one officer lay dead. The Indians claim that none of their people were killed and only two were wounded. Captain Perry and General Howard learned what it means to underestimate the competency of an enemy. They developed a new sense of respect for Indian warfare and realized the Nez Perces were very worthy opponants. Like the Battle at Little Bighorn, Perry's defeat was an embarrassment to the U.S. Military. General Howard was determined not to make the same mistakes again. News of the battle spread rapidly throughout the United States. These reports focused the eyes of the nation on the drama unfolding in the Pacific Northwest along with Chief Joseph and his small group of rebels.

Chapter 17
Attack and Counterattack

The proud Nez Perce warriors returned to White Bird Canyon to celebrate their great victory over the white men. They collected 63 rifles and many pistols from the battlefield, but did not scalp or mutilate the bodies of the dead soldiers in any way. That night the walls of the canyon echoed with the throbbing drums and the rhythmic chanting of a Nez Perce celebration dance. The rock formations glowed with life as bright flames from the many campfires cast eerie shadows of moving bodies over their rough surfaces. The people gave thanks to the Great Spirit and their Wyakins for protecting them in this glorious battle against their enemies.

While the tribal members savored their moment of superiority, the chiefs remained in council facing the reality of the situation. General Howard would soon arrive with more troops to renew his attack on the Nez Perce people. The nontreaties must leave the canyon as soon as possible and prepare to defend themselves. But where should they go? Three routes of escape were discussed. The first led south into the rugged Seven Devils country where the Indians could conceal themselves in the fortress-like mountains and resist capture for a long time. The second route continued east over the trail to the buffalo country. The third path recrossed the Snake River and returned the nontreaties to their former home in the Wallowa Valley.

As the leaders discussed the advantages and disadvantages of each of these proposals, two important warriors, Rainbow and Five Wounds, approached the council with an idea. They suggested that the Nez Perces cross the swollen Salmon River and encourage the soldiers to follow them. The troops would have difficulty moving their heavy equipment and supplies across the swiftly flowing water. This would slow them down and allow the Indians, who had more experience fording rivers quickly, to travel upstream and recross the Salmon for an escape into the buffalo country. The council liked the plan at once and unanimously chose to accept it. Within a short time, the nontreaties were organized and moving in force toward Horseshoe Bend to cross the Salmon for the first time and await the arrival of the military.

General Howard was determined to capture the nontreaty Nez Perces and put an end to the hostilities as quickly as possible. He left Fort Lapwai on June 22 and traveled to White Bird Canyon with 400 troops, 100 volunteers, and two Gatling guns. The general left the fort under the protection of Captain Perry and his men who had recently returned from their terrible defeat by the Indians.

The soldiers reached the White Bird battlefield on June 26. They located the bodies of their dead comrades scattered about the canyon floor. The remains of Lieutenant Theller were wrapped in blankets and sent back to Fort Lapwai. The other casualties from Perry's command were buried where they fell. The sight of the corpses, stripped of their uniforms and weapons, filled General Howard's men with anger and they swore vengeance against Joseph and the nontreaties.

While the burial detail completed its grim task, Howard's scouts were sent to locate the fleeing Nez Perces. The scouts soon returned to report the hostiles had crossed to the west bank of the Salmon River. The general feared Joseph would return to the Wallowa Valley and attack the settlers who were now unprotected. To prevent this, he ordered an immediate pursuit of the Indians.

By June 28 the soldiers had arrived near the mouth of White Bird Creek where it empties into the Salmon River. As Howard and his men approached the riverbank, Nez Perce warriors appeared from their hiding places across the river and began to yell challenges and insults at the Americans. The Indians dared the troops to chase them and fired a few shots at those who were nearest the river. When Howard's soldiers returned the fire with their more powerful weapons, the nontreaties rode away laughing and taunting their white opponents.

Unknown to General Howard, whose attention had been successfully diverted by the Nez Perce warriors, the main force of Indians were at that time preparing to recross back to the north bank of the Salmon at Craig's Ferry about fifteen or twenty miles away.

While the general was deciding how best to transport his men and supplies across the turbulent river, he received a report that Looking Glass had been furnishing the hostiles with reinforcements and planned to join in the war himself in the near future. Since this chief had seemed to want peace, Howard had left him alone and attended to more urgent matters. Now, however, each new threat must be dealt with forcefully. Joseph must not be allowed to gain strength from an additional supply of fighting men. Not bothering to check the validity of this rumor, which would have proven false, the general immediately dispatched Captain Stephen G. Whipple to lead a company of cavalry and a small group of volunteers to arrest Looking Glass and his people and "turn all persons over, for safe-keeping, to the volunteer organization at Mount Idaho."

After four days of planning, the soldiers still had a great deal of difficulty crossing the swollen, rapids-filled Salmon River. The swift-flowing current tore their first raft of rough-hewn logs loose from its moorings and washed it away downstream. Finally, the men succeeded in stringing a heavy rope across the 250 feet of swirling water. This enabled them to ferry all their men, arms, ammunition, and supplies to the opposite bank of the river. The horses and mules were forced to swim the distance. One trooper observed that, "Some of them were turned over and over, and others were carried away down the stream, but I think all got over."

On Sunday, July 1, as General Howard completed his struggle to cross the Salmon River, Captain Whipple and his men arrived at the camp of Looking Glass and the Asotin Nez Perces. The soldiers were accompanied by some twenty citizen volunteers who had joined them from Mount Idaho.

The Indians were peacefully living in their own territory on the bank of Clear Creek, a tributary of the Clearwater northeast of Mount Idaho. The Asotins took great pride in their prosperous village with its herds of horses and cattle and gardens of corn, potatoes, squash, and other vegetables. The band contained about 40 men and 120 women and children. Although a few of the young warriors had been induced to join the ranks of the hostile non-treaties, Looking Glass had managed to keep the majority of his people away from the violence that surrounded him.

Whipple hoped for a surprise early morning attack on the Asotins. However, he misjudged the distance and arrived on a hill overlooking the village well after the sun had risen. The captain ordered his men and the citizen volunteers to leave their horses and proceed in a skirmish line down the hill toward the village which was located on the opposite side of the creek.

The Indians were lazily enjoying the warmth of the summer morning. A few individuals moved slowly about the camp, but most remained lounging inside their tepees. Looking Glass was in his lodge having breakfast with a group of friends. Suddenly the tranquility of the day was shattered when someone noticed the line of soldiers approaching the village. Looking Glass was immediately informed of the danger. The chief quickly dispatched a warrior named Peopeo Tholekt (Bird Alighting) to meet the troops and tell them the Asotins were peaceful and represented no threat to the white men.

Peopeo Tholekt had little chance to speak. When he reached Whipple and his men, one of the citizen volunteers pointed a gun at the Indian and demanded to know if he was Chief Looking Glass. When Peopeo Tholekt explained that he was not the chief, another volunteer said the soldiers would speak only to Looking Glass and ordered the Nez Perce messenger to go get him at once.

Looking Glass had watched the white men's treatment of his envoy. When Peopeo Tholekt informed him of the volunteer's request, the chief became suspicious and decided not to attend a meeting. Instead, he sent Peopeo Tholekt and another warrior to the soldiers carrying a white flag of peace. Again the volunteers demanded to know which one of the Indians was Looking Glass. Peopeo Tholekt said the chief had chosen to remain in camp, but was willing to have the leader of the soldiers visit him in his

Peopeo Tholekt

lodge. Captain Whipple and several of his men agreed to accompany the Nez Perces to their village. When they had crossed the creek and drawn near to the chief's tepee, Peopeo Tholekt hurried ahead to inform Looking Glass of their arrival. As the messenger disappeared into the lodge of his leader, the village was startled by a shot. One of Whipple's volunteers had recognized a Nez Perce he disliked and decided to open fire on him. The Indian fell with a wound in his ankle.

Immediately the village was thrown into a panic. The terrified Asotins fled in all directions. Some escaped on horses, others took cover in nearby bushes.

Whipple's troops hurridly advanced to join their leader in the village. In their attack, a seventeen-year-old Nez Perce boy was killed and several warriors were wounded. One woman seized her infant child and ran blindly into the Clearwater River to avoid capture. Caught in the swift current, both mother and child were drowned. Leaving their casualties behind, the rest of Looking Glass' people managed to escape their attackers.

Unable to accomplish his mission of capturing the Asotin Nez Perces, Captain Whipple vented his anger on their village. He ordered his men to destroy everything the Indians had left behind. The soldiers trampled the gardens and rounded up the cattle and horses to be sent to Mount Idaho. Next, they attempted to burn the tepees and erase the last traces of life in the camp. When the leather lodge coverings refused to ignite, Whipple's men used their bayonets to stab and slash the homes of their Nez Perce enemies.

When the senseless attack was over, Whipple and his men left for Mount Idaho with the Asotins' horses. After the soldiers had gone, the angry Nez Perces returned to their ruined village in stunned silence. They buried their

The soldiers destroyed Looking Glass' village.

dead and searched through the wreckage for what few possessions could be salvaged. Looking Glass' people had paid a terrible price for their last attempt at peace. The furious chief placed his feet firmly upon the path of war and resolved to make the white men pay for their ruthless display of cruelty.

When Captain Whipple and his men reached Mount Idaho, they received a message from General Howard ordering them to proceed at once to Cottonwood House, a ranch owned by a settler named B. B. Norton. The ranch, located thirteen miles northwest of Grangeville, had been used as a stage depot and tavern. Built on high prairie land between forested foothills, the area could be easily defended by soldiers in the event of an attack. For this reason, General Howard had selected Cottonwood House as the place to rendezvous with soldiers from Fort Lapwai and receive a fresh supply of arms and ammunition. Soon after crossing to the south bank of the Salmon River, Howard had sent word for Captain Perry and a group of twenty men to escort the ammunition train from Lapwai to Cottonwood. The general sent Captain Whipple to the ranch for added protection in case the Indians recrossed the Salmon and headed in that direction. He wanted to be sure the firearms transported by Perry did not fall into enemy hands.

Captain Whipple arrived at the ranch on July 2 ahead of Perry and the ammunition train. The next day, Whipple sent citizen volunteers Blewett and Foster to explore the land around Craig's Ferry and look for signs of Indians in the area. Just as General Howard had feared, the nontreaties had recrossed the Salmon and were traveling directly toward Cottonwood House. When the volunteers had traveled about twelve miles from the ranch, they suddenly encountered a Nez Perce war party. The hostiles immediately opened fire and shot Blewett from his saddle. Foster managed to escape and return to Captain Whipple with his report.

Fearing Perry and the ammunition train would be attacked, Whipple decided to provide an escort for the soldiers from Fort Lapwai. The captain sent Foster along with Lieutenant Sevier M. Rains and ten men to scout the area where Blewett was killed and determine the strength of the enemy. Shortly after their departure, Whipple followed them with his cavalry.

The Nez Perces knew their attack on Whipple's scouts would draw more soldiers to the area. Led by Five Wounds, Rainbow, and Two Moons, the nontreaties prepared a trap for their enemies. The warriors concealed themselves on both sides of the road from Cottonwood House. When

199

Rains and his men arrived, the Indians opened fire and forced them to take cover behind a large boulder.

Captain Whipple heard the sounds of battle as he followed about two miles behind Rains. Rushing forward with his men, he discovered his scouts trying desperately to defend themselves against a force of well-entrenched hostiles. Realizing he was not prepared to confront a large number of Indians, Whipple was forced to watch helplessly as Rains and his men were massacred by the Nez Perces.

Concerned for the safety of his men, Captain Whipple led the soldiers to a safer location a short distance away on the east side of a ravine. He ordered them to dismount and quickly form a line of skirmish.

When Rains and his scouts lay dead, the Indians approached Whipple's line of defense. However, they were careful to stay out of range of the white men's guns. As darkness fell, the Nez Perces gave up the attack and Whipple made camp for the night.

On the morning of July 4, Captain Perry arrived with the ammunition train and joined Whipple near the ravine. As senior officer, Perry assumed command of the troops in the area. He decided to continue on to Cottonwood House immediately and wait for General Howard.

The Indians were not seen again by the soldiers until noon. Then the Nez Perces appeared in force and surrounded the ranch. For the remainder of the day the hostiles attempted to drive Perry's troops from the rifle pits they had dug for protection.

The attack continued on July 5 and the soldiers bravely defended their position. Two of Perry's messengers managed to penetrate the Indians' line of attack and ride for help to General Howard who was still on the other side of the Salmon River. The general had followed the Nez Perces to Craig's Ferry. He had begun construction of a raft to transport his men and supplies back to the north side of the river.

That same day the settlers of Mount Idaho became involved in the battle at Cottonwood House. After waiting for two days with no word from Captain Whipple, the settlers finally learned of the attack on the soldiers. Captain D. B. Randall and seventeen citizen volunteers left Mount Idaho to help the besieged troops fight off their attackers.

When Captain Randall and his men were about three miles from Cottonwood, they were attacked by a large force of about 132 Indians. The hostiles suddenly appeared in front of the volunteers and blocked their path to the ranch. As soon as he saw the Nez Perces, Randall ordered his men to halt for a few seconds and then charge directly at the enemy lines. The volunteers rode at full speed toward the startled nontreaties shouting and firing their guns as rapidly as they could. This tactic worked at first causing the surprised Indians to give way long enough for the much smaller force of white men to gallop past them. However, the warriors soon recovered from the unexpected turn of events and hurried to pursue Randall and his men.

The volunteers, heavily outnumbered by Nez Perce warriors, were forced to take cover and make a stand. There followed a battle which lasted from about 11:00 until midafternoon during which the settlers from Mount Idaho, who have become known as the "Brave Seventeen", fought desperately for their lives. Captain Randall and a volunteer named Ben Evans were killed in the fighting and two other men were wounded. Two of the Indians were also shot and one of them later died from his injuries.

Captain Perry and his troops observed the fighting from the safety of their barracades at Cottonwood House. Finally, two of Randall's men managed to reach the ranch. They begged Perry to send help to their endangered comrades. The captain refused. He was afraid of suffering another embarrassment like his recent defeat at White Bird Canyon. He was also worried the Indians might gain possession of the arms and ammunition his men had transported from Fort Lapwai. Perry held firmly to his decision even when Captain Whipple pleaded for permission to ride to the settlers' defense. At last, a group of 25 citizen volunteers led by Sergeant Simpson decided to disobey Perry and attempt to save the Mount Idaho volunteers. Fearing these men would be killed, Captain Perry was forced to change his orders and allow his troops to take part in the battle.

Faced with the combined forces of soldiers and citizen volunteers, the Indians finally withdrew to join their people who were now headed toward the Clearwater River. When the Nez Perces had departed, Perry's men escorted the surviving members of the Brave Seventeen back to Cottonwood House.

Captain Perry was afraid to pursue the nontreaties with his small number of troops. He decided to travel to Grangeville and await further orders from General Howard.

Chapter 18

A Battle at the Clearwater River

The Salmon River was extremely swift and dangerous at Craig's Ferry. On July 6, General Howard's men completed construction of a raft to transport them back to the north bank of the river. They had built the craft using planks from the nearby cabin of a friendly Nez Perce scout named Luke Billy. The finished raft was a clumsy affair that proved impossible to control in the strong current of the river. Howard wrote that the attempt to cross ". . . lost us our raft which tumbled down the rapids at a swift rate, with all on board, for three or four miles."

With all hope lost for a safe crossing at Craig's Ferry, the general and his men were forced to return to the mouth of White Bird Creek where they crossed the river, and retraced their steps back to Grangeville. They arrived at the settlement on July 9 and were joined by Captain Perry and the soldiers from Cottonwood House. The combined number of regulars and citizen volunteers under General Howard was now over 500 men.

The general did not stay long in Grangeville. A group of settlers had discovered the location of the Nez Perce encampment. Their report encouraged Howard to continue his pursuit immediately before the Indians could cause more trouble. Guided by Arthur Chapman, who had fired on the Nez Perce peace commission at White Bird Canyon, the troops were on the move again by July 11 hoping to provoke a decicive encounter with the hostiles.

With a four-day lead on the soldiers, the Nez Perces had traveled north from Cottonwood House and camped by the South Fork of the Clearwater River. Though fully aware of the seriousness of their situation, the Indians displayed no outward signs of urgency or desperation. Their recent victories at White Bird Canyon and Cottonwood House had convinced them of their ability to defend themselves against the white man's army. Exhausted from their traveling and fighting with the soldiers, the nontreaties gratefully took the opportunity to rest and plan their next course of action.

Soon after their arrival at the Clearwater, the hostiles were joined by Looking Glass and his Asotin band of Nez Perces. Enraged by the vicious attack on his peaceful village, Looking Glass vividly described the events which now forced him to seek an active part in the war. He said:

> The white captain talked of peace even as the bullets of his soldiers began to fall upon our village like clouds of summer flies. For the women and the old ones it was very bad. We fought as well as we could and then we ran away, leaving everything behind us. The white soldiers pierced everything with their long knives. They burned everything. They trampled the gardens of vegetables and melons and cut all the young apple trees we planted some time ago. I tell you, my brothers, they acted like mad dogs. It is for this that I am here among you, now ready to fight the white soldiers. I will not forget this day.

The chiefs welcomed the Asotin leader and his people to their camp. However, the larger number of people and their combined herd of between 2,500 and 3,500 horses tested the ability of the chiefs to provide leadership and protection. Joseph, White Bird, Toohoolhoolzote, and Husishusis Kute soon met in council to make plans and unify the efforts of their individual bands.

General Howard caught up with the Nez Perce fugitives on July 11. The nontreaties were still peacefully encamped in the deep ravine where Cottonwood Creek empties into the South Fork of the Clearwater. Unaware of the danger that approached them, the Indians calmly went about their daily activities. Women prepared meals for their families, children played happily along the riverbank, young men raced their ponies, and tribal elders reclined lazily in the warm summer sun.

In the early afternoon, the tranquil summer day exploded with a barrage of howitzer fire over the quiet village. The startled Nez Perces began dashing about collecting guns and ammunition. One group of warriors immediately drove the horse herd up the Clearwater away from the danger. A second group prepared to defend the camp while a third group of about 24 men led by Toohoolhoolzote charged up the river on horseback and clambered up the wooded side of the ravine. These Indians managed to get between Howard's troops and the rim of the bluff overlooking the encampment. Hiding behind rocks, trees, and bushes, the warriors opened fire on their attackers.

The soldiers quickly formed a battle line to face Toohoolhoolzote and his men. The old chief soon received reinforcements from Rainbow, Five Wounds, and Ollokot who had assessed the situation and led their warriors to the heart of the action. Though there were still fewer than 80 Nez Perces engaged in the battle, the strength of their defense led General Howard to greatly overestimate their

The Nez Perces attempted to establish a peaceful camp near the Clearwater River.

numbers. Believing he now faced a large force of well-armed hostiles, the general refrained from ordering a direct charge of his cavalry upon the enemy lines. Instead, he ordered his men to dig rifle pits and construct barricades from saddles and supply boxes to engage in a pitched battle against the nontreaties.

The battle lines were widely separated and firing was largely ineffective for both sides. The Indians shouted taunts at the soldiers and a few warriors appeared on war horses to flaunt their bravery before the enemy entrenchments.

Water soon became a problem for the soldiers. They sweltered in their uncomfortable wool uniforms as the hot July sun beat down upon them. The Indians controlled all the water in the area. Their battle line lay between Howard's men and the river and they had also gained control of the only spring on the plateau. Nez Perce women supplied the warriors with fresh, cool drinks from the river while the soldiers dampened their parched lips with a few drops of rationed water from their rapidly diminishing supply.

The temperature cooled down at night, but this only meant a different kind of suffering for the troops. The high mountain air became cold and a heavy dew dampened the ground and chilled the men as they huddled behind their barricades. Still desperate for water, a few soldiers managed to slip past the Nez Perce guards and reach the spring. They returned with several buckets of water for their thirsty comrades.

Though they had managed to gain the upper hand, the Indians were impatient to end the confrontation with the white man's army. Eager to be on their way, they urged the chiefs to abandon the attack and allow them to quietly slip away in the darkness. Joseph, Ollokot, White Bird, and the other leaders begged their warriors to remain a while longer and strike a heavier, more crippling blow at the enemy. During the night, both Indians and soldiers worked to reinforce their barricades for the continued fighting at dawn.

Despite the wishes of their leaders, some Nez Perces decided to leave the battle line and return to their families in the ravine. They were more concerned with helping their people escape than killing a large number of soldiers. Claiming their right of free choice, these warriors silently withdrew leaving a much weaker line of defense for the hostiles.

By morning, General Howard was determined to seize control of the spring and provide water for his men. He ordered a direct charge on the Nez Perce barricades that guarded the valuable source of water. Howard's sudden, swift attack surprised the Indians and caused them to flee from the area. The victorious troops eagerly filled their canteens and brewed fresh coffee for a welcome breakfast of hardtack and bacon.

Despite their thinning ranks, the Nez Perces continued to oppose the soldiers. The fighting continued until early afternoon when a supply train escorted by a troop of cavalry was seen approaching Howard's men from the south. A group of warriors quickly mounted their ponies and set off to prevent the supplies from reaching their destination.

The general also took quick action and dispatched Captain Miller and his infantry to protect the packtrain from the hostiles. The race was on for possession of the valuable supplies.

The men of the packtrain soon became aware of the rapidly approaching Indians. Fearing for their lives, the drivers frantically whipped their mules and drove the wagons across the plain at top speed. Clouds of thick dust filled the air as soldiers and Indians converged on the packtrain.

Luckily for Howard's men, Captain Miller managed to gain control of the situation and drive the Nez Perces away from the supplies. This victory revitalized the soldiers and gave them renewed courage.

As Captain Miller escorted the supply train back to Howard's barricades, he suddenly launched a surprise attack on the enemy's line of battle. The captain repeatedly charged the entrenched warriors who had difficulty fighting back because of their reduced numbers. At last Miller succeeded in breaking through the Nez Perce defences and turning the battle in favor of the army.

Seizing the opportunity to defeat the hostiles, General Howard ordered his men to attack in force all along the enemy lines. The Indians were unable to hold their position against the advance of the army. They fled down the sides of the ravine in a desperate attempt to save themselves and their families.

The warriors soon reached the village under a hail of bullets from the pursuing soldiers. Joseph immediately began to gather the women, children, and old people and direct them to a place of safety. The village was in total confusion as the terrified people ran from their homes. Some of them left clothing, blankets, cooking utensils, and food behind. The troops took what souvenirs they wanted and set fire to the rest of the camp.

In the confusion, Joseph's wife, Toma Alwawinmi, and new baby were left behind in the flaming village. The chief had mistakenly assumed his family had escaped with the other women and children. As the soldiers made their way among the deserted tepees, Toma clutched her child and frantically tried to mount a frightened horse. The animal refused to stand still and struggled to break free of the woman's desperate grip. Fearing her baby would be hurt by the thrashing hoofs, Toma gave up and released the horse who immediately galloped away.

As the last of the Indians made their way out of the camp, Joseph's nephew, Yellow Wolf, decided to make one last search for survivors. He soon discovered Toma standing helplessly in the choking dust and smoke from the burning tepees. Yellow Wolf quickly lifted the woman and her baby up onto his war horse and carried them to safety.

The nontreaties managed to get away with most of their horses and many of their personal possessions. Once outside the camp, the chiefs quickly organized their people and began a retreat down the Clearwater toward the Kamiah Valley.

Toma and her child were left unprotected in the devastated campsite.

The Battle of the Clearwater had claimed four Nez Perce lives. The Indians had killed thirteen of Howard's soldiers and wounded twenty-seven others.

General Howard sent a wire to his superior, General Irwin McDowell, commander of the Division of the Pacific in San Francisco, claiming a victory over the Nez Perces at the Clearwater. However, the actual outcome of the battle was more of a draw with the Indians escaping from their captured village and the general suffering the greater loss of men. Perhaps Howard could have achieved a real victory if he had pursued the hostiles immediately after his occupation of their encampment. However, darkness was approaching and the general decided to wait until the next morning to follow the Indians. This gave the nontreaties the opportunity to retreat across the Clearwater and by July 15 reach their ancient tribal camas-gathering grounds on the Weippe Prairie.

Realizing the army could soon be upon them again, the chiefs immediately went into council to decide the best means of escape. Looking Glass suggested they should travel across the mountains into the land of the Crow Indians. A few years before, the Nez Perces had helped the Crows defend themselves when they were attacked by enemy warriors. Looking Glass believed the Crows would now return the favor and allow the nontreaties to take refuge from the Americans in their territory. If this was not the case, the Nez Perces could always continue on into Canada and join forces with Sitting Bull and the Sioux Indians who had fought in the Battle at the Little Bighorn. Looking Glass was certain that, as time passed, the trouble in Idaho would be forgotten and the nontreaty bands could return in peace to their ancestral homeland.

The other chiefs liked Looking Glass' ideas and decided to follow his advice. At nearly 45 years of age, Looking Glass had earned respect as a natural leader. He had frequently visited the buffalo country and was well-acquainted with the Lolo Trail over which the hostiles now must travel. He also had many influential friends among the Bannock, Flathead, and Crow tribes. For all these reasons, the council selected Looking Glass to become war chief of the combined nontreaty bands. They believed he could provide the necessary leadership to direct their warriors in battle and guide their people to a place of safety.

At the same meeting, the chiefs designated Joseph as their peace chief. He became responsible for the safety of all non-fighting individuals, the security of the camp including all supplies and personal possessions, and the guardianship of the large, valuable herd of horses.

Though leadership roles were assigned to Looking Glass and Joseph, all final decisions continued to be made by the tribal council. The chiefs ruled by persuasion and held their position of authority only as long as others voluntarily followed them. Joseph has frequently been called the principal leader and mastermind of the Nez Perce forces. This error is in large part due to General Howard's reporting of events throughout the war. Howard knew Joseph better than he knew the other chiefs. Therefore, in describing his encounters with the Indians, he tended to refer to the Nez Perces as "Joseph's people" and identify the Wallamwatkin chieftain as their sole leader. Joseph had also received a great deal of publicity before the war and the settlers viewed him as the foremost representative of his tribe. Though his influence was actually of much greater importance after the war, when he was left alone to gather and care for the scattered survivors of his defeated people, the dignified and humane Chief Joseph will always be the symbol of the Nez Perce fight for freedom.

As the council meeting drew to a close, the hostiles were joined by another band of nontreaty Nez Perces. This group of 17 warriors and 28 women and children, was led by an elderly chief named Red Heart. For the past year, they had been in the buffalo country and were unaware of the outbreak of war. Looking Glass explained the situation and warned Red Heart of the danger he faced if he returned to the Nez Perce homeland. Red Heart refused to believe the white men would harm his people. With his tiny number of warriors and only three rifles, the chief thought he could not possibly be considered a threat to General Howard's soldiers. Red Heart was eager to return

Hin-mut-too-yah-lat-kekht, also known as Chief Joseph.

home after his long journey and wanted no part of the current conflict.

Looking Glass argued that he too had wanted to remain at peace with the white settlers. Yet his village had been destroyed and his people driven from their land. The soldiers looked upon all nontreaty Indians as enemies and saw no difference between those who had participated in the war and those who had not. Looking Glass begged Red Heart and his people to remain with the other Nez Perces and join the exodus to safety.

Despite the opposition of the newly selected war chief, Red Heart remained firm in his decision to return home. The chief appeared so confident of having made the correct choice, he gave new hope for peace to a few of Looking Glass' people. Three Feathers and several other members of the Asotin band decided to travel back with Red Heart and live a peaceful life among the treaty Indians. Looking Glass, Joseph, White Bird, and the other chiefs looked on in concern and frustration as the tiny group of Indians left the camp and started on their journey toward Kamiah.

When they reached the Clearwater, Red Heart and his followers were taken as prisoners of war by General Howard. Despite their explanation that they were not affiliated with the warring bands and wanted only to return home, the Indians were immediately herded to the Kamiah subagency where their horses and supplies were taken away from them. Then, on foot, they were cruelly forced to march sixty miles to Fort Lapwai where they were loaded onto a steamboat and sent to Fort Vancouver. There they were imprisoned until April, 1877.

Howard's report listed Chief Red Heart and his people as hostile Nez Perces and labeled their capture a victory for his troops. Perhaps the confinement of these innocent Indians helped the general to overcome some of the embarrassment he felt concerning his failure to defeat the nontreaty bands. With the eyes of the nation focused upon his pursuit of the Nez Perces, Howard was undoubtedly eager to display his battle prowess and maintain his image as a competent officer. Though the white men may have been fooled by the capture of Chief Red Heart, the Nez Perces knew the truth and considered this to be one of Howard's most unjust actions toward their people.

Chapter 19
Over the Lolo Trail to the Bitterroot Valley

On July 16, the Nez Perces broke camp and began traveling up the wooded foothills of the Bitterroots toward the Lolo Trail to Montana. With 200 men, almost 550 women and children, and over 2,000 horses, the passage over the rugged mountain range would become the most difficult part of their journey.

After the capture of Chief Red Heart and his followers, General Howard hurried after the remaining Nez Perces. However, he arrived at the Weippe Prairie too late to prevent the nontreaties from reaching the Lolo Trail. When he learned the Indians were on their way to Montana, the general was forced to halt. The hostiles had passed out of his military jurisdiction and he had no authority to follow them. Howard wrote that, "This really ended the campaign within the limits of my department."

The general notified his superiors of the situation and waited for further orders. The pause gave Howard a welcome chance to rest and consider the position in which he found himself. In the days since the beginning of the Nez Perce War, the general had fought an inner battle just as difficult as the overt military campaign he waged. Howard's strict sense of duty demanded that he crush the Nez Perce rebellion while his personal Christian beliefs sought humane treatment for an oppressed people. The conflict of these two aspects of his personality continued to plague the general and prevent him from finding rest or peace. Adding to his problems, the newspaper accounts of the war were severely critical of him for his failure to capture the hostiles. Though he wished to redeem himself and prove these criticisms false, the general had grown extremely weary and the idea of withdrawing from the campaign may not have been entirely unattractive.

General Howard's sense of duty overruled his moral convictions when he received orders to continue his pursuit. The Commanding General of the Army, William Tecumseh Sherman, gave Howard the authority to follow the Indians regardless of military district boundaries. Sherman considered the troops at Howard's command to be the most effective forces available to supress the Nez Perce hostilities. Once again, General Howard put aside his personal feelings for the nontreaty bands and devoted himself to carrying out his government's wishes.

The general immediately began to develop a plan to capture the hostiles. He knew little about the Lolo Trail, but reports said it was extremely rugged and dangerous. Despite this, Howard decided to lead his men directly over the trail in an attempt to overtake the Indians. Before leaving, he sent Colonel Frank Wheaton north to cross the Bitterroots on the Mullan Trail which connected Fort Walla Walla in Washington with Fort Benton in Montana. Howard told Colonel Wheaton to warn other northwest tribes to stay out of the war. When he reached Montana, Wheaton was to proceed to Missoula over the Clark Fork route. Hopefully this would place the Nez Perces in a trap formed by the forces of Howard to the south and Wheaton to the north.

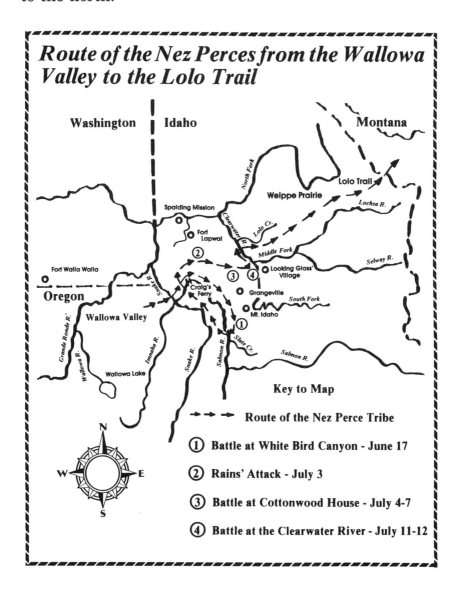

Route of the Nez Perces from the Wallowa Valley to the Lolo Trail

Washington | Idaho | Montana

North Fork

Lolo Trail

Welppe Prairie

Lochsa R.

Spalding Mission

Fort Lapwai

Clearwater R.

Lolo Cr.

Middle Fork

Selway R.

Fort Walla Walla

Looking Glass' Village

Oregon

Craig's Ferry

Grangeville

South Fork

Wallowa Valley

Mt. Idaho

Snake R.

Grande Ronde R.

Wallowa R.

Imnaha R.

Snake R.

Salmon R.

State Cr.

Salmon R.

Wallowa Lake

N
W E
S

Key to Map

- - - → Route of the Nez Perce Tribe

① Battle at White Bird Canyon - June 17

② Rains' Attack - July 3

③ Battle at Cottonwood House - July 4-7

④ Battle at the Clearwater River - July 11-12

To help ensure the capture of the nontreaties, the general set a third force in motion against them. A new army post was under construction at Missoula, Montana. Captain Charles C. Rawn and a small detachment of troops had arrived there a month before to provide supervision and protection. Howard notified Rawn to block the eastern exit of the Lolo Trail so the Indians could not escape into the Bitterroot Valley. Howard wrote to the captain, "If you simply bother them and keep them back until I can close in, their destruction or surrender will be sure."

With Rawn busy guarding the Lolo Trail, Colonel John Gibbon traveled from Fort Shaw in northern Montana to Missoula where he was assigned to protect the fort and the settlements from possible Nez Perce attacks. As news of the war spread among the settlers, so did feelings of fear and anger. Reports that a large force of hostile Indians was moving into the area generated images of destruction and death. Townspeople feared for themselves and their families. They began to gather together and prepare their defenses.

While General Howard was organizing his pursuit, the Nez Perces were hurrying ahead over the mountains. Traveling on the 150-mile Lolo Trail was extremely difficult. The passage was steep and went through thick forests with almost no grazing for the horses. Rocks, mud, thick underbrush, and fallen logs made every step perilous.

The journey was especially exhausting for the children and the old people. They struggled to keep pace and not slow down the progress of their people who were covering about 16 miles each day. A number of the tribal elders realized it was impossible for them to keep up the strenuous forced march. They were terrified that General Howard's troops would overtake their people and capture or kill their families. They desperately wanted the children to have a chance to live a full life as they had done. Because of this, some of the old people chose to leave the trail and remain behind to die. They willingly gave their lives for the continuance of the tribe. Leaving their families, they wandered alone into the wilderness and selected a quiet place to wait for death to find them. The remaining Nez Perces, grieving for their loss, hurried ahead so these courageous people would not have died in vain.

The nontreaties moved over the hazardous mountain pass in a highly organized manner. The chiefs selected a group of warriors to travel ahead and clear the trail of fallen logs and large rocks. Young women followed, removing branches, smaller rocks, and brush. The narrow path could then be traveled more safely by the main body of Indians with their baggage and horses. At the end of the procession, a final group of men replaced all the logs, rocks, and brush to hide the trail and create barriers which made the pass almost impossible for Howard's soldiers to use.

At 5 a.m. on the morning of July 30, General Howard resumed his campaign against the Nez Perces. Reinforced by troops from Boise, Idaho, the general led his two-mile-long column of 700 men onto the Lolo Trail. Among the troops were twenty Bannock Indian scouts led by a fiery young man named Buffalo Horn. Though intent on helping his American friends capture the Nez Perce enemies of his people, Buffalo Horn was destined to wage his own war against the white men in 1878 when settlers began destroying the Bannock's precious camas fields in southern Idaho.

By the time General Howard's soldiers entered the western opening of the Lolo Trial, the nontreaty bands had completed the nine-day journey to the trail's end. There they discovered Captain Rawn and his men had constructed a barricade of logs about three feet high to block their passage into Montana.

On July 24, Captain Rawn had hurried from Fort Missoula to the mouth of Lolo Creek with five officers and

To help their families travel more quickly, some of the old people remained to die on the Lolo Trail.

thirty enlisted men. He was met by a group of citizens who pleaded with him not to attack the hostiles and unleash the anger of the Indians against the people of Montana. The settlers were afraid the Nez Perces might defeat Captain Rawn and lay waste the Bitterroot Valley. When the captain refused to return to Missoula, 200 settlers decided to join with the soldiers and increase their chance of victory over the Indians.

Captain Rawn selected a narrow spot in a valley about six miles from the mouth of Lolo Creek. There he began felling trees to barricade the trail and trap the Nez Perces for General Howard.

The Indians arrived at the end of the trail on July 26. When they discovered the blockade, they camped to study the situation and plan the best way to bypass the danger.

A direct attack on the enemy was out of the question. Many Nez Perce lives would be lost as the white men opened fire from the safety of their log fortifications. The chiefs decided to attempt a meeting with the officer in charge to explain their peaceful intent and desire to avoid bloodshed.

On July 27, Looking Glass, White Bird, and Joseph met with Captain Rawn. The chiefs promised they would not harm anyone in the Bitterroot Valley if the soldiers left them alone. The Indians only wanted to escape the hostilities in Idaho and live in peace among the friendly people of Montana.

Captain Rawn said he could not withdraw his troops unless the Nez Perces gave up all their guns, ammunition, and horses. He knew the Indians would never agree to this request. However, he hoped the negotiations would stall the nontreaties long enough for General Howard or Colonel Gibbon to arrive with a force to defeat them.

The council continued for two days. Angered by the demands of Captain Rawn, the chiefs chose Looking Glass to be their sole representative at the second session. The war chief was better known to the people of Montana and might have greater influence at the bargaining table.

Looking Glass met with Captain Rawn and his interpreter in an open area out of rifle range of both Indians and soldiers. The captain refused to accept any form of compromise and the meeting continued without progress. Finally, Looking Glass ended the frustrating discussion by promising to present Rawn's conditions for passage to his people for their consideration.

While the Indians' promise to remain peaceful had no effect on the soldiers, it did have a decided impact on the 200 citizen volunteers who supported Captain Rawn. They had begged the captain not to attack the Nez Perces and

Traveling over the rugged Lolo Trail was extremely difficult for the Nez Perce families.

were only present because he had refused to honor their request. When they learned that their families were not in danger of attack, the settlers decided to abandon their positions at the barricade and go home. This so depleted the forces of Captain Rawn, he could not hope to hold the area against passage of the nontreaty bands.

Unaware of the captain's dilemma, the Nez Perces remained determined to enter the valley. On July 28, they moved into the steep hills to the north of the trail and began to march around the white man's barricades. One soldier later reported:

> About ten o'clock we heard singing, apparently above our heads. Upon looking up we discovered the Indians passing along the side of the cliff, where we thought a goat could not pass, much less an entire tribe of Indians with all their impe-

dimentia. The entire band dropped into the valley beyond us and then proceeded up the Bitterroot.

The tiny force of soldiers watched helplessly as the Nez Perces moved bravely past their blockade. A brief exchange of rifle fire commenced, but the Indians kept going and were soon lost from view. Captain Rawn could do nothing but lead his discouraged men back to Fort Missoula and await new orders from Colonel Gibbon or General Howard. The ineffective log barricade he left behind, which the Indians laughingly called a "corral", came to be known jokingly among the settlers as "Fort Fizzle."

The Nez Perces' triumph at Fort Fizzle and their peaceful entry into Montana gave them confidence and led them to believe they had reached a place of safety. General Howard was far behind and the settlers had deserted Captain Rawn.. Perhaps the weary nontreaty bands could rest at last among the friendly people of the Bitterroot Valley.

The Nez Perces spent their first night in Montana camped about eight miles above the mouth of Lolo Creek. There they were joined by three Indians who had served as scouts for Colonel Nelson Miles in the Sioux country of the Yellowstone. These newcomers, two treaty Nez Perces and a Yakima, had left Miles to return home when they learned about the trouble in Idaho. On their way to the Lolo Trail, they had met Eagle From the Light, a Nez Perce chief who had settled among the Flathead Indians in Montana. Eagle From the Light said he was afraid the nontreaty bands would not be safe if they decided to stay in the Bitterroot Valley. He asked the three travelers to locate the hostiles and warn them of the danger. He suggested the Nez Perces hurry to Canada by the shortest route and not count on help from the tribes in the buffalo country.

White Bird, Toohoolhoolzote, and several of the other leaders thought Eagle From the Light had sent good advice. Joseph listened with mixed emotions. He realized the seriousness of the situation; yet his heart ached for his beloved Wallowa Valley. He shuddered to think his people might die in a land so far away from their sacred Mother Earth. He nurtured the hope that one day their path would lead home.

Looking Glass finally persuaded the other chiefs to follow their original plan and remain in the valley. He assured them they would find safety among the Crow Indians, who had always been friends of the Nez Perces. He said Montana would be a good place to live. There would be plenty of buffalo and many good areas for the nontreaties to camp. It would be foolish to continue to run when the war was over. Looking Glass said it was time to rest and allow the wounds of battle to heal. He would lead his hungry people south to Big Hole, a favorite tribal campsite, from where they could hunt buffalo and regain their strength and spirit.

The Nez Perces continued their journey south at a leisurely pace. Instead of the usual thirty to fifty miles a day, they now traveled only twelve or fourteen. Listening to the advice of Looking Glass, they had come to believe they had left their problems far behind with the soldiers in Idaho. Many Montana settlers feared the nontreaty bands. They watched them pass through their county from the safety of barricaded cabins. The Indians, however, remained friendly and even purchased supplies from local merchants who charged them extremely high prices for such things as flour, sugar, tobacco, and coffee.

About this time, the nontreaties were joined by a group of ten or twelve Indians who were also on their way to the buffalo country. Among these was a half-French, half-Nez

Perce hunter known to the Indians as Lean Elk and to the white men as Poker Joe. A short, intelligent man with a loud voice, Poker Joe was considered by the Indians to be a capable leader. He frequently enjoyed visiting frontier towns where he earned his nickname playing cards in the white men's saloons.

Poker Joe had been traveling to Idaho to spend time with his Nez Perce relatives when news of the war reached him. He decided to remain in Montana to avoid the danger. A short time later, he cut his leg in a careless accident with a hunting knife. The wound caused much attention from the settlers in the Bitterroot Valley. They accused Poker Joe of being involved with the hostile Nez Perces. They refused to believe he had not been injured in one of the battles of the war. The white men's persistent accusations angered Poker Joe and he decided to locate the nontreaties and help them if he could. His thorough knowledge of Montana and the ways of the white man made him a welcome addition to the Nez Perce manpower.

Chapter 20

A Battle in the Big Hole Valley

The nontreaties continued their journey through Ross Hole and passed over the Continental Divide near present-day Gibbons Pass. Then they traveled to the head of Trail Creek, which they followed into the Big Hole Valley. By August 7, the Nez Perces were raising their tepees in their favorite campsite on the level prairie beside the Big Hole River. The beautiful area contained lush grassland where the Indians' ponies could eat their fill. The water abounded in fish and the nearby hills were rich in antelope and other game. Looking Glass decided to remain encamped several days to give his exhausted people a chance to refresh themselves.

Most of the Nez Perces were grateful for the chance to lay aside their problems for a short time. However, some warriors criticized the war chief's decision. They said the nontreaties should keep moving to make certain General Howard's troops could not overtake them. Looking Glass scoffed at these criticisms. He said these men were overcautious. They worried needlessly about things that would not happen. The war was over. Why punish the people more by forcing them to flee from an enemy that was no longer there? Looking Glass' will once again prevailed and the camp began to settle into the normal routine of tribal life.

During the day, the people worked to repair the damages caused by the war. They cut and dried new poles to replace those lost in the Battle of the Clearwater. The women dug camas roots and the men hunted and fished to provide a banquet for their hungry families. As these activities progressed, the mood of the Nez Perces became festive. The dark clouds of fear and anger began to lift and bright hopes for an improved future pierced their gloomy outlook. The nontreaties began to celebrate. On August 8, they danced and sang far into the night. Looking Glass felt so secure in the comfortable valley he saw no need to post guards about the camp or pickets to watch the horses. Fortune once again seemed to smile on the Nez Perce people.

Amidst the joyful tribal chants and dances, a subtle warning of danger went unheeded. In the shadows surrounding the flickering campfires, some young boys noticed two strangers wrapped in blankets silently watching their people. The youths realized the visitors were white men, but failed to report their presence to the chiefs. They thought the observers were probably just interested local settlers who had come to view the festivities. Clinging to their new sense of joy, the boys forced unpleasant thoughts about the white men from their minds. They rejoined the merrymaking which continued until well after midnight. Then, as the glow of the campfires faded, the weary Nez Perces wandered lazily back to their lodges to enjoy one of the few peaceful nights since the war began.

Contrary to the beliefs of Looking Glass, the soldiers had not given up their pursuit of the Nez Perces. Colonel Gibbon left Fort Missoula on August 4 with 17 officers and

146 enlisted men. His weapons soon included a mountain howitzer which he obtained from Fort Owen along the way. An honored veteran of the Civil War, Gibbon was a determined, experienced officer who had led a column of 450 men against the Sioux in 1876. His men had buried the dead after the Battle at the Little Bighorn. The colonel now directed all his skill and energy into the Nez Perce campaign hoping to bring about an early end to the hostilities. Before leaving Missoula, Gibbon had sent a message to General Howard on the Lolo Trail. The message stated that the colonel intended to overtake and capture the non-treaty bands as quickly as possible.

By August 7, Colonel Gibbon and his men were near Ross Hole, only one day's travel behind the hostiles. That evening, Lieutenant James H. Bradley volunteered to lead a scouting party to determine the exact location of the Nez Perces and make their capture easier by stampeding their horses if he could. After a difficult march through the darkness over fallen trees, the scouts camped beside the trail for breakfast. After the meal, Bradley and two of his men continued forward and soon heard the sound of axes being used to chop down timber. Bradley climbed a tall tree and saw some Indian women cutting new lodge poles for their tepees. Beyond, he saw the Nez Perce camp stretched out in a V-shape along the east bank of the river. Bradley and his companions hurried back to the other scouts and sent a messenger to Gibbon with news of their discovery.

After receiving the report of his scouts, Colonel Gibbon quickly moved his troops forward. By evening they reached Bradley's camp located only six miles from the Nez Perce village. Gibbon and his men rested until about 11:00 p.m. and then continued their advance in the darkness. Wishing to travel as quietly as possible, the colonel

Colonel John Gibbon

left his supply train, horses, and howitzer behind in camp. He also left some of his soldiers to bring the howitzer and a supply of ammunition to him later the following morning.

The troops marched silently through the night until they arrived on a slope directly above the Indian camp. There they found themselves in the midst of a herd of Nez Perce ponies. A few of the animals whinnied when they noticed the intruders, but there were no other signs of alarm and the Indians had posted no guards to notice the disturbance. The soldiers remained quiet and the horses soon wandered off to continue their grazing farther up the hill.

Colonel Gibbon and his men crept through the brush until they were within 150 yards of the Nez Perce encampment. It was two o'clock in the morning of August 9. The soldiers listened to the occasional barking of village dogs and watched the flickering Indian campfires as they settled down to await Gibbon's order to attack at dawn.

Waiting proved to be a difficult task for Gibbon's troops. Lying on the hard ground without blankets, they were chilled by the cold mountain air. They were forced to remain very still lest they be discovered and ruin their chance for a successful surprise attack.

Shortly after the soldiers had taken their position near the camp, several Indian women emerged from their lodges. The white men remained quiet almost fearing to breathe as the women threw fresh fuel on the campfires and engaged in a brief conversation. Much to the relief of Gibbon's men, the chill air soon forced these early risers to return to the warmth of the blankets inside their tepees.

About 3:00, another woman stepped outside and went to fetch water from the river. Once again the soldiers feared discovery. This time, however, the mounting tension caused one man to shift his position and make a slight rustling sound in the brush. The noise was immediately noticed by the Indian woman who turned and ran back inside to tell her husband. Unfortunately for the Nez Perces, the drowsy warrior dismissed his wife's concern and told her to go back to sleep. The nontreaties had ignored their last warning of the disaster that was about to befall them.

As dawn approached, the soldiers arranged themselves in a line of battle and began their advance on the sleeping village. As they neared the river, an old Nez Perce man riding a horse suddenly appeared before them. The man's name was Natalekin and he was on his way to check on the grazing herd of Indian ponies. Gibbon's men were startled by Natalekin's presence, but they recovered in time to shoot both the horse and its rider before the Indian could shout the alarm. As Natalekin fell dead from his horse, Colonel Gibbon launched his attack on the Nez Perces. The soldiers waded waist-deep through the river and came out firing upon the village. Roused abruptly from their peaceful slumber, the Indians ran screaming from their lodges as bullets rained down upon them.

The soldiers were not interested in taking prisoners. They began shooting and clubbing their way through the encampment. Some deliberately shot women and children as the terrified people fled from their attackers.

When the rifle fire began, Wahlitis and his wife were asleep in their tepee. Wahlitis was the young warrior who had helped start the war by avenging the death of his father, Eagle Robe. Startled by the explosions, the young couple hurried outside to find their village in total chaos. Wahlitis seized his gun and took cover with his wife behind a fallen tree where he began firing at the soldiers. Colonel Gibbon's men fired back and Wahlitis' wife was wounded. Seeing the fear and pain on the young woman's face, Wahlitis was reminded of all the suffering he and his people had endured because of the white men. Filled with anger and hatred, he rose up to take careful aim at his enemies. At that moment, he was spotted by Captain William Logan, who immediately opened fire and killed him instantly. Despite her wound, Wahlitis' wife managed to get her husband's gun and kill Captain Logan. Seconds later, the soldiers opened fire on the woman. Her lifeless body fell across that of her dead husband. So was forged the final link in Wahlitis' chain of vengeance.

Heavy fighting continued as the desperate Nez Perces attempted to rally their forces and defend themselves. White Bird pleaded with his warriors to hold their ground. Above the din of battle he shouted:

> Why are we retreating? . . . Shall we run into the mountains and let these white dogs kill our women and children before our eyes? It is better that we should be killed fighting. Now is our time to fight. . . . Fight! Shoot them down! We can shoot as well as any of these soldiers.

Many of the warriors had taken cover along the riverbank where they found protection among a thick stand of willow trees and dense clumps of brush. Frantically they called upon the magic powers of their Wyakins and sought to gain the strength to repel their enemies.

Gibbon's men now attempted to set fire to the village. The tepees, wet with frost, at first resisted the flames. However, the soldiers persisted and were finally able to ignite them. Tongues of fire consumed the lodges and sent thick smoke billowing through the devestated campsite.

Time and again Joseph entered this nightmarish scene in his attempt to rescue the helpless women, children, and old people. Unarmed, the chief darted in and out among the burning lodges searching for those who were hurt or

Wahlitis and his wife were among the first to be killed in the Battle at Big Hole.

lost in the deadly confusion of battle. Joseph's wife had been wounded. However, despite his desire to remain at her side, he drove himself to attend to his duties as peace chief. The welfare of his people must come first. The Nez Perce tribe must survive!

Gradually the warriors recovered from the shock of Gibbon's assault. They began to listen to their leaders and unify their efforts for defense. From their hiding places along the riverbank, they began firing at the soldiers in the village. The Nez Perce counterattack soon became strong enough to throw Gibbon's men into confusion. The colonel was wounded in the leg and his horse was shot from under him. Sensing the growing panic of his troops,

Gibbon ordered them to leave the village and retreat to the safety of a nearby hillside.

By 8:00 a.m., the soldiers had reached the wooded slope and begun to dig entrenchments behind fallen trees and boulders. The battle had reversed itself and the Nez Perces had gained the upper hand. The warriors rounded up their horses and herded them down river away from the danger. The Indians reoccupied the village and began to lay siege to Gibbon's men.

On his way through the smoldering campsite, the great warrior, Two Moons, discovered the body of his best friend, Rainbow. A wise man and fierce warrior whose advice was often sought in council, Rainbow had predicted his own death. Some time before the attack at Big Hole he had said:

> I have the promise given that in any battle I engage in after sunrise, I shall not be killed. I can face the point of the gun. My body no thicker than a hair, the enemies can never hit me, but if I have any battle or fighting before sunrise, I shall be killed.

Rainbow had died early in the battle before the sun was fully up.

Two Moons wept over the body of his friend and said:

> My brother has passed away. I too will now go . . . and I shall lie beside my brother warmate. He is no more, and I shall see that I follow him.

Two Moons did indeed follow Rainbow in death. Shortly after the nontreaties reoccupied their village, the grief-stricken warrior made a solitary charge on the soldiers' entrenchments. Under a hail of bullets, Two Moons willingly gave his life on the Big Hole battlefield.

237

The Nez Perce campsite was filled with sorrow as tribal members returned and located the bodies of their families and loved ones scattered about the area. Colonel Gibbon later wrote, "Few of us will soon forget the wail of mingled grief, rage, and horror which came from the camp ... when the Indians recognized their slaughtered warriors, women, and children."

The Nez Perces were determined to flee from the valley as quickly as possible. The warriors kept Colonel Gibbon and his men pinned down behind their barricades while Joseph and White Bird supervised the removal of the camp. Some of the Indians hurried to bury their dead as others frantically began tearing down tepees which had not been destroyed in the attack. Many things had to be left behind. By noon the main body of Nez Perces were headed south leaving clothing, buffalo robes, food, and many personal possessions scattered about in the charred remains of their former campsite.

While their families escaped with the wounded, the warriors fired steadily at Colonel Gibbon and his troops. Toohoolhoolzote and Ollokot led a group of sixty skilled marksmen to contain the soldiers until the Nez Perces had left the valley. Looking Glass also participated in the attack eventhough he no longer held much power as a leader. The Nez Perces held him responsible for their present situation. They believed his decision to travel slowly had allowed Colonel Gibbon to overtake them. Looking Glass was now in disgrace and unable to command the respect of his people as their war chief.

At noon, the Indians discovered a group of six soldiers transporting Gibbon's howitzer and a supply of ammunition to the besieged troops. Thirty warriors rode out to intercept the dangerous weapon before it could reach its destination. The tiny group of soldiers managed to fire the

Peopeo Tholekt and a group of Nez Perce warriors captured Gibbon's howitzer and a supply of ammunition.

howitzer twice before the hostiles were upon them. The Indians killed one soldier and wounded two others in their charge. The surviving white men fled from the area leaving the cannon and 2,000 rifle cartridges in the possession of the Nez Perces. Peopeo Tholekt wanted to use the howitzer against Colonel Gibbon and his men. However, when the Indians attempted to move the weapon, its wheels became stuck and they were unable to take it with them. Peopeo Tholekt then decided to dismantle the howitzer to prevent the soldiers from recovering it. The Indians tore the barrel from the weapon and Poker Joe rolled it over a bluff into some bushes. Then, with the rifle ammunition from the supply train, the warriors hurried to rejoin their people.

The attack on Colonel Gibbon continued all day. The troops, weakened by lack of food and water, fought to maintain their rapidly weakening position against the strength of the Nez Perce sharpshooters. Toward evening, the Indians decided to drive their enemies into the open with fire as Gibbon had recently done in the attack on their village. The warriors set fire to the tall, dry grass and soon hot flames were licking up the hillside toward the soldiers' barricades. Clouds of smoke engulfed the area making it difficult to see or breathe. Miraculously, when the fire was only yards away from the white men, the wind changed direction sending the blaze back over the blackened ground behind it where the flames soon expired from lack of fuel.

During the night, most of the Nez Perce warriors withdrew to follow after their families. Ollokot and a dozen marksmen remained to keep the soldiers from pursuing their people. These Indians repeatedly fired their rifles into the darkness to remind Gibbon's men they were still under siege. The white men spent a cold, uncomfortable night huddled behind their barricades. They had no blankets and were afraid that fires would make them easy targets for enemy sharpshooters.

In the early morning of August 10, a messenger arrived from General Howard. This man said that the general was "coming on, as fast as possible by forced marches, with 200 cavalrymen, to give the needed reinforcement." The news was welcomed by the soldiers. They faced their attackers with renewed courage until noon when Ollokot decided it was time to rejoin his people. After a final salute of riflefire, Joseph's brother and his warriors withdrew leaving Gibbon's men to count their casualties and attend to their wounded.

The Battle of Big Hole ended with neither side able to claim a decisive victory. Colonel Gibbon's plan of surprise had succeeded at the extremely high price of thirty-one men killed and thirty-eight men wounded. Seven of the seventeen officers involved were among the casualties. The Nez Perces had managed to turn the tide of battle and escape. Yet, they too had suffered great loses. Between sixty and ninety Indians lay dead. Most of them were women and children. Twelve of the best warriors had been slain and others would later die from their injuries. The surviving nontreaties were filled with scorn and hatred for the white soldiers who had ruthlessly slaughtered their women and children. Joseph later said, "The Nez Perces never make war on women and children; we could have killed a great many . . . while the war lasted, but we would feel ashamed to do so cowardly an act."

Chapter 21

Running and Raiding

Ollokot and his warriors soon caught up with the fleeing nontreaty bands where they had camped at Lake Creek about twelve miles from the Big Hole battlefield. Ollokot found the tribal leaders gathered in council to decide who should replace Looking Glass as war chief of the Nez Perces. Looking Glass' poor decisions had caused a lack of confidence in his leadership. A new chief was needed to take command and raise the sagging morale of the battle-weary fugitives. The person selected must have a thorough knowledge of the land ahead as well as an understanding of the enemy who followed closely behind. The only man who possessed these qualifications was Poker Joe, the half-breed who had recently joined in the exodus. Poker Joe knew every trail in Montana including the route which led across the Canadian border to Sitting Bull. He had also spent a great deal of time in the white men's settlements where he had gained an insight into the Americans' perceptions of Native Americans and their attitudes toward them. He knew the U.S. Army would not easily give up its pursuit of the Nez Perces and had disagreed with Looking Glass' decision to travel at a slower pace in the Bitterroot Valley.

Poker Joe agreed to become the new war chief if the Nez Perces would accept him on his own terms. He insisted that his orders be followed without question. The other chiefs must be willing to put aside their individual rights to disagree and bend to the will of the new war leader. All white men were to be considered enemies. Instead of peacefully bypassing the ranches of settlers in the valley, the Indians would now begin taking the Americans' horses and scattering or killing their livestock. The Nez Perces would leave nothing behind them that could be of use to General Howard and his troops. In addition to this, the nontreaties must now travel much more quickly. They would be on the trail by sunrise each day and continue their march until darkness forced them to stop. There would be only a single brief rest period during the hottest part of the afternoon. Having clearly stated these terms, Poker Joe left the council to make its decision.

The chiefs deliberated only a short time. Joseph and Ollokot both strongly supported Poker Joe and the other leaders could offer no effective alternatives. In the end, the decision was unanimous. The Nez Perces pinned their desperate hopes for survival on their new war chief, Poker Joe.

While the Nez Perces made their change of leadership, General Howard arrived at Big Hole to assume command of the forces moving against them. When Howard learned that Colonel Gibbon was in pursuit of the hostiles, he had hurried into the valley with twenty soldiers and seventeen Bannock scouts. His main body of troops followed about a day's march behind him. Arriving at the Big Hole battleground on the morning of August 12, the general discovered a wounded Colonel Gibbon and his soldiers still reeling from the force of the Nez Perce counterattack. After describing his assault on the Indian encampment, Gibbon wearily shook his head and inquired, "Who would have believed that those Indians would have rallied after such a surprise, and made such a fight?"

By evening, the main column of Howard's troops had arrived at the battleground. The general's doctors helped care for the wounded soldiers throughout the night until they could be transported to safety in the morning. On August 13, Colonel Gibbon and the survivors of Big Hole started for the settlement of Deer Lodge where they could recover from the battle and receive medical attention. Three of Gibbon's officers and fifty of his men were well enough to continue on with General Howard's forces when later that day they resumed their pursuit of the Nez Perces.

Poker Joe was not as certain of receiving help from the Crow Indians as Looking Glass had been. After leaving the camp at Lake Creek, the newly-selected war chief led the nontreaties south toward the land of the Shoshonis.

On August 12, the Nez Perces reached Montana's Horse Prairie. Colonel Gibbon's messengers had already spread the alarm and the terrified settlers were preparing to face a possible attack. A Nez Perce scouting party led by Yellow Wolf cautiously approached the Montague-Winters ranch where seven white men stood guard over their property and livestock. After learning of the danger, these settlers had sent their women and children to nearby Bannack City for protection and made ready to stand their ground if the Indians should appear on their land. As Yellow Wolf's warriors reached the house, a man named William Flynn fired his shotgun at them. This action signaled an attack in which Flynn and two other white men were killed. The Nez Perces ransacked the cabin hoping to find bandaging material for their people who had been injured at Big Hole. Then, taking the ranchers' horses, they continued about five miles up the valley where they discovered two more white men working in a hayfield. The warriors killed one of these and the other escaped to spread word of the incidents throughout the area.

Word of these attacks soon reached the nearby settlements of Bannack City, Montana and Junction, Idaho. Barricades were quickly erected. Riders hurried about the countryside warning everyone to take cover and protect themselves. When the alarm reached Salmon City at the junction of the Salmon and Lemhi rivers, fortifications were hastily built. Then, Colonel George L. Shoup, a prominent citizen of the little town who later became governor of Idaho, led a group of men to the nearby Lemhi Shoshoni reservation. They visited the friendly Chief Tendoy and secured his promise not to help the hostile nontreaties.

The Nez Perces arrived at Junction beside the Lemhi River on the morning of August 13. The Indians assured those in the barricaded town that they meant no harm. Poker Joe was aware that Chief Tendoy was a trusted friend of the white men. He hoped he could persuade the Lemhi chief to intercede with the Americans on behalf of the hostiles and help bring an end to the war. White Bird was chosen to meet with Tendoy in council as spokesman for his people. The Nez Perces were given a cool reception on the Shoshoni reservation. Tendoy said the nontreaties were unwelcome visitors and could expect no comfort or assistance from him. He strongly urged them to leave immediately and continue their journey east.

The Nez Perces were disappointed by Tendoy's refusal to help them. The Shoshoni chief had made his position very clear and Poker Joe realized that further entreaties would

246

Yellow Wolf

be useless. He decided to strike camp and leave the area as quickly as possible. By noon, the hostiles were moving in a southeasterly direction up the Lemhi Valley. As the Indians departed, the settlers of Junction breathed a sigh of relief. They quickly sent a messenger to Bannack City to report their narrow escape and notify friends of their safety.

As the Nez Perces left Junction, General Howard led his men from the Big Hole battlefield. He had not traveled far when news reached him of the Indians' attacks on Horse Prairie and their westward march toward Idaho. When this information was circulated, two treaty Nez Perces, who were serving the army as horse herders, offered advice to the general. These Indians, Captain John and Old George, both had daughters who were traveling with the nontreaty bands. They told Howard that Joseph's people would almost certainly circle back eastward toward the Clark Fork of the Yellowstone River and the buffalo country. If the soldiers hurried south and followed the stage route over Monida Pass, they could block Targhee Pass and intercept the hostiles before they entered Yellowstone National Park. This strategy pleased General Howard. Altering his plans to follow the Indians west, he instead moved south to place himself in front of the nontreaties after they circled back toward the park.

While the general put his new plan into action, the Nez Perces continued their hurried march up the Lemhi Valley. Crossing present-day Gilmore Divide, they started down Birch Creek toward the eastern end of the Snake River Plains. There, on the afternoon of August 15, a scouting party encountered a freight train of four wagons and a trailer hauling liquor and supplies to Salmon City, Idaho. The Indians approached the wagons as the six white men and their two Chinese passengers were camped for their noon meal. The meeting was friendly until the hostiles said they wanted the eight horses belonging to the freighters. As they argued over the animals, the warriors noticed the barrels of liquor in the wagons. They seized the barrels, broke them open, and began drinking the whiskey. As the Nez Perces drank, they became more violent. They forced the Chinese passengers to get down on all fours and pretend to be horses. When the white men refused to endure a similar humiliation, the Indians opened fire and killed five of them. One of the warriors was also mortally wounded by a stray Nez Perce bullet. During the shooting, Albert Lyon, a horse herder who had joined the train for companionship, managed to escape. After hiding in the willows that lined the stream, he made his way to Salmon City with a report of the incident.

The Nez Perce chiefs were angry when they learned of this attack. They understood their young men's bitterness and desire for revenge after the Battle at Big Hole. However, they could not condone the senseless slaughter of innocent people by drunken Indians. They poured the remaining whiskey on the ground and burned the wagons. Then, as Howard's advisors had predicted, they hurried their people on toward Targhee Pass and the west entrance of Yellowstone Park.

The attacks at Horse Prairie and Birch Creek caused many of the settlers in the area to panic. They sent messengers to General Howard begging for protection. The general remained convinced that the hostiles would double back toward Yellowstone National Park. Reports of the violence in Idaho reached him as he was preparing to bypass Monida Pass and lead his troops directly across Montana to Targhee Pass. Despite his better judgment, Howard could not refuse to answer the call for help. He agreed to continue south along the route from Bannack

City to Monida Pass. This would lead him closer to the site of the recent attack at Birch Creek and the last reported sighting of the Indians. Not wishing to completely abandon his original plan, the general sent Lieutenant George Bacon and fifty cavalrymen east over the shorter route to Targhee Pass. Their orders were to take control of the area and delay the Nez Perces at the entrance to Yellowstone Park until the main body of troops could overtake them. In his hurry to make this decision, Howard did not stop to consider how so few soldiers could hope to stand against the entire combined force of the nontreaty bands. Lieutenant Bacon and his men were riding into a very dangerous situation.

On the morning of August 18, General Howard and his troops traveled south across Monida Pass. With them were fifty cavalrymen from Fort Ellis, Montana and a group of fifty-five volunteers from Virginia City. After riding all day, the soldiers made camp near Dry Creek. In the evening, Chief Buffalo Horn and his Bannock scouts joined them. They had discovered the Nez Perce encampment only about fifteen or eighteen miles away in the Camas Meadows. Howard was now just a single day's ride from his quarry.

The soldiers realized just how near the hostiles were when the bodies of two Nez Perce women were found lying beside the creek. The Battle of Big Hole had continued to claim innocent victims. These women had apparently been injured in the fighting and found themselves too weak to keep up with their people. Struggling to help each other, they had become separated from the others and met a lonely death in this isolated place. Perhaps the sight of their lifeless bodies helped Howard's men to understand Joseph's comment that those who made war on women and children should "feel ashamed to do so cowardly an act."

On August 19, Howard continued his pursuit into the Camas Meadows. That evening the opposing forces were camped only a few miles apart. Buffalo Horn urged the general to attack. However, the soldiers were exhausted and Howard decided to allow them time to rest before engaging in another major battle. They were now in a beautiful area filled with lush grass, shady trees, and a clear stream teeming with fish. The men swam, fished, and hunted grouse. They became so comfortable the general had to sternly remind them to take the normal security precautions before retiring for the night. The soldiers arranged their tents in a circle. They tied their horses to picket lines and their team animals to wagons. Then, they hobbled the mules from the packtrain and posted guards about the area.

While Buffalo Horn and his warriors were busy determining the location of the hostiles for General Howard, Nez Perce scouts were carefully watching the approach of the soldiers. When Poker Joe learned about the nearby military encampment in the Camas Meadows, he immediately called a council of the chiefs. Looking Glass suggested a surprise raid on the army's horse herd. Such an attack would avoid bloodshed while delivering a crippling blow to Howard's men. The council was impressed with this idea and decided to conduct the maneuver that very night. The warriors were divided into three groups led by Ollokot, Looking Glass, and Toohoolhoolzote.

Riding silently through the darkness, the raiders arrived at Howard's camp at about 3:30 in the morning. One group stood watch over the soldiers' tents while the others located the livestock. A few warriors dismounted and crept forward to cut the animals loose while the rest waited to stampede them away. As they were doing this, a sentry noticed the disturbance and called out, "Who goes there?"

This unexpected challenge startled the Indians and one of them, a young man named Otskai (Going Out), fired his rifle. The shot awakened the soldiers who stumbled from their tents groping about in the darkness for their guns and ammunition.

When their presence was discovered, the Nez Perces immediately charged into the herd yelling and waving buffalo robes. They rounded up as many animals as they could and drove them away from the camp. By the time Howard's men were mounted and ready for pursuit, the Indians were far ahead.

As daylight arrived, the warriors, who had been congratulating themselves on the success of their mission, were disappointed to see they had not been as effective as they had hoped. Instead of stealing their enemy's horses as they had planned, they had driven off 200 mules from the general's packtrain. The darkness of the night and the early discovery had caused them to make this mistake. The raiders took some comfort from the knowledge that they had at least made it more difficult for the troops to transport their supplies and ammunition. This would slow them down and give the Nez Perces time to hurry ahead.

The startled soldiers quickly recovered. As the bugler sounded "Boots and Saddles", nearly a hundred cavalrymen under the command of Captain Randolph Norwood rode out to recover their stolen animals.

The Indians were now about five miles ahead of their pursuers. When they learned the soldiers were chasing them, they decided to prepare a trap. Several warriors continued driving the mules toward the Nez Perce camp while the others took cover behind rocks to await the cavalry.

When the soldiers arrived, they suddenly found themselves under heavy fire from the entrenched Nez Perces. The assault was so fierce that Captain Norwood soon gave the order to retreat and the troops hurried to the protection of a nearby grove of cottonwood trees. Norwood needed information about the strength and location of the attackers. Sergeant Hugh McCafferty bravely volunteered to climb a tree and make these observations. McCafferty watched the movements of the Nez Perce warriors and sent word to the captain via another man stationed at the base of the tree.

The fighting occurred only about eight miles from the soldiers' main camp. A report soon reached General Howard and he hurried forward with reinforcements and a howitzer. Seeing the approach of more soldiers and their powerful cannon, the raiders soon gave up and withdrew from their attack. Howard arrived to find six of his men were dead and three more were wounded. None of the Indians had been killed and only a few had received slight injuries. The general sent his casualties to Virginia City and returned to camp with the remainder of his men. The soldiers had lost their chance to overtake the nontreaties and prevent their entrance into Yellowstone Park.

On the night after the attack, General Howard and his men camped among the trees near Henry's Lake. Indians were rumored to be nearby and the soldiers feared another sudden attack. As the men tried to overcome their uneasiness and get some rest, Captain S. G. Fisher arrived with thirty Bannock scouts from the Fort Hall Indian Reservation. These were welcomed by Chief Buffalo Horn who asked General Howard for permission to hold a ceremonial dance. The general agreed and soon the sound of drums and chanting filled the night.

Emboldened by the excitement of the dancing, Buffalo Horn accused Howard's three Nez Perce scouts and herders of being spies for the hostile nontreaty bands. The chief said these traitors should be killed before they could

Chief Buffalo Horn accused Howard's Nez Perce scouts of being spies for the nontreaty bands.

be of any further use to the enemy. General Howard found it difficult to believe that the friendly treaty Nez Perces were involved in treachery and deceit. Both Captain John and Old George had demonstrated their loyalty by providing information about their people and serving the general as advisors during the pursuit. However, when Buffalo Horn persisted with his accusations, Howard summoned the Nez Perce scouts and confronted them with the charges. All three men vigorously denied having committed any form of disloyalty and reaffirmed their friendship and support for the Americans. Their apparent sincerity reassured the general and he dismissed the attempt of the Bannock chief to incriminate them.

None of the soldiers were able to rest that night. The noise from the Bannock celebration and their own fears of a second attack made it impossible for the men to settle down. Since nobody was able to sleep, Howard decided to break camp. By 2:00 in the morning, the troops were packed up and moving toward Henry's Lake on their way to Targhee Pass.

Failing in his own attempt to block the path of the Nez Perces, General Howard still hoped that Lieutenant Bacon would succeed in stopping the hostiles at Targhee Pass. However, this plan was also doomed to prove unsuccessful. Bacon had arrived at the pass the day before the raid at the Camas Meadows. He found no Indians in the area and decided the chiefs had probably chosen another route into the park. Impatient to rejoin the main body of soldiers, Bacon led his men back toward General Howard. On his return, the lieutenant chose not to follow the main trail from the pass and so missed both the Nez Perces and the general's pursuing force. The entrance into Yellowstone was now clear for the passage of the nontreaty bands.

Soon after the departure of Bacon and his men, the main force of Nez Perces arrived and made camp at Henry's Lake. When the raiding party caught up with them, the chiefs were disappointed to see mules instead of horses being driven before their warriors. Joseph said he was tired of being so closely pursued by General Howard and hoped the attack would "set him afoot" and slow him down. Stealing the mules would hinder the soldiers' progress, but not as greatly as the theft of their horses would have done.

The Nez Perces had taken little time to rest since the terrible attack at Big Hole. Now, as they camped beside beautiful Henry's Lake, they began to feel the effects of their strenuous retreat. Joseph and several other chiefs asked Poker Joe if they could declare a day of rest and give their exhausted people a chance to recover. Poker Joe firmly refused to permit any form of delay. The soldiers were still close behind and the Nez Perces were in extreme danger. Stopping now for any reason was unthinkable. Poker Joe's sarcastic reply to the chiefs' request was, "Do you people enjoy digging graves?"

Urged on by their determined war chief, the Indians crossed Targhee Pass on August 22 and entered Yellowstone Park the following day. Poker Joe chose a difficult, little-known route through the park to confuse General Howard and delay his pursuit. The Nez Perces traveled east over a treacherous mountain trail toward Yellowstone Lake. As they made their way through the heavily wooded slopes, even Poker Joe became somewhat unsure of the direction in which to travel.

As Nez Perce scouts explored the trail ahead, they heard the sound of someone chopping wood. The woodcutter turned out to be John Shively, an old prospector on his way from the Black Hills to the gold fields of Montana. Shively was frightened when he found himself helplessly surrounded by the Nez Perces. However, the warriors only wanted information about the park and made no move to harm the old man. When the prospector said he knew the route east to the land of the Crow Indians, the scouts decided he should talk to their chiefs. They took him to Poker Joe who demanded his services as a guide. Shively spent the next week traveling with the hostiles. During that time, he was treated with courtesy and respect. The prospector marveled at the Nez Perces' ability to travel swiftly and safely over difficult mountain trails. With little rest or nourishment, the fugitives labored twelve to fourteen hours each day transporting hundreds of people and herding thousands of animals over pathways so narrow that two horses could barely walk abreast. The Indians bore their burdens in silence and the white man never heard a complaining word while he was with them. When Shively was no longer needed, Poker Joe released him.

The old man departed on August 31 filled with stories about the Nez Perces that would later appear in newspapers throughout the country. None the worse for his stay with the hostiles, Shively seemed to have actually enjoyed the experience.

In contrast to Shively, General Howard was not having positive feelings about his involvement with the Nez Perces. The soldiers arrived at Henry's Lake on August 22, about a day after the Indians had departed. There had been no word from Lieutenant Bacon and the general now realized his plan to blockade Targhee Pass had failed. The hostiles would already be traveling through Yellowstone Park endangering tourists and bringing criticism upon Howard for his failure to stop them. Adding to the general's misery was the deteriorating condition of his command. The soldiers lacked food, clothing, medicine, and blankets. They had lost a large number of mules in the raid at the Camas Meadows and the remaining animals were exhausted from overwork. Howard's chief medical officer, Doctor C. T. Alexander, requested a four-day stop at Henry's Lake to rest the men and replenish their supplies. Howard knew he must grant the doctor's request even though he would have preferred to hurry after the Indians.

When the camp had been established, General Howard and an escort traveled sixty miles to Virginia City to purchase the needed horses and supplies. The general also sent Captain Norwood, Captain Cushing, and two companies of cavalry to Fort Ellis with the soldiers' worn-out horses and mules.

While in Virginia City, Howard telegraphed Fort Ellis to order military supplies and make reports to his superior officers. William T. Sherman, Commanding General of the Army, was at Fort Shaw in northern Montana. Howard telegraphed him a message asking the whereabouts of

257

Colonel Nelson A. Miles and Colonel Samuel D. Sturgis. Howard thought that if these officers were near the Yellowstone River, they might be able to prevent the Nez Perces from entering the territory of the Crow Indians.

General Sherman was becoming impatient with the progress of the Nez Perce campaign. Reports of the war had become national news and Howard had been severely criticized for his delay in capturing the hostiles. The "Idaho Semi-Weekly World" had said, ". . . of one thing we feel confident, General Howard ought to be relieved and someone else placed in command of the forces." Statements such as this made Sherman uneasy and caused him to question Howard's ability to successfully end the war. Sherman also feared the lengthy campaign might encourage other Indians to rebel against the U.S. Government. The Sioux and Cheyenne tribes had recently been subdued at great military expense and officials hoped to avoid another costly venture against the Nez Perces. When Howard stated that he and his men had grown weary from the long pursuit and were in need of reinforcements, Sherman replied, "If you are tired, give the command to some young, energetic officer and let him follow them . . ." Upset by this lack of confidence, Howard was quick to explain:

> . . . I never flag. It was the command, including the most energetic young officers, that were worn out and weary by a most extraordinary march. You need not fear for the campaign . . . nor doubt my pluck and energy.

Sherman wired back a reply saying he was glad to hear that General Howard was "so plucky." The message went on to assure Howard that action had been taken by the Department of Dakota to assist him by surrounding Yellowstone Park in an effort to capture the Nez Perces. To the north, Lieutenant Gustavus C. Doane led two compan-

Colonel Nelson A. Miles

ies of cavalry and a group of Crow Indian scouts to block the park's exit at Mammoth Hot Springs. To the east, Colonel Samuel D. Sturgis led six companies of cavalry to guard the Clark Fork River route while Major Hart commanded five companies of cavalry and a hundred scouts to patrol the Shoshone River exit near present-day Cody, Wyoming. Colonel Miles was currently stationed at Fort Keogh far to the northeast at the mouth of the Tongue River. However, he was prepared to enter the campaign with a large number of troops whenever he was needed. Having set these forces in motion, General Sherman felt confident that Howard now had the support necessary to bring about an end to the war.

The criticism leveled against General Howard did have one positive effect. When the men serving the general learned about the unfavorable opinions of their leader, they rallied to support him and prove the critics wrong. Howard later wrote that his officers and soldiers said, "We will go with you to death." The general concluded, "It was worthwhile to bear a little chagrin in order to awaken such a loyal spirit." With their new-found esprit de corps, General Howard's 200 cavalry, 300 infantry, 50 scouts, and 50 Montana volunteers left Henry's Lake and crossed Targhee Pass on the morning of August 27.

Chapter 22
A Terrifying Trip Through Geyser Land

While General Howard was in Virginia City telegraphing ahead for reinforcements, the Nez Perces were hurrying through Yellowstone Park. The day after they captured John Shively, the hostiles discovered more white men in their path.

In 1872, Yellowstone became the first of the national parks to be established by the U.S. Congress. By 1877, it was already a popular tourist attraction. Though still mostly undeveloped wilderness with few roads, bridges, or designated camping areas, the park was filled with hundreds of visitors each year. In the summer of 1877, Frank Carpenter, a citizen of Helena, Montana, organized a group of his friends and relatives to explore the wonders of what he called "geyser land." The party included Albert Oldham, William Dingee, A. J. Arnold, Charles Mann, Carpenter's two sisters, Ida and Emma, and Emma's husband, George Cowan. Another man named Henry Meyers went along to take charge of the travelers' wagons and horses.

On the evening of August 23, the carefree group of sightseers were peacefully encamped in the Lower Geyser Basin. They had recently heard rumors about the Nez Perce War and had decided to remain in the park only two or three more days and then return home. That night, as they relaxed in their comfortable camp, they were completely unaware that hostile warriors were observing their every move. Yellow Wolf and five Nez Perce scouts had discovered the tourists and couldn't decide what to do with them. All white men were now considered to be enemies. Yellow Wolf wanted to kill these people, but Henry Tabador, a half-breed interpreter, said the chiefs should decide their fate. Finally, the Indians agreed to visit the campers and see if they were friends or enemies.

The next morning, the scouting party walked into the white men's camp as Carpenter and the others were preparing breakfast. Though frightened by the unexpected visitors, William Dingee managed to smile and shake Yellow Wolf's hand. This simple act of friendship probably saved the lives of everyone in the party. After the warm reception, Yellow Wolf decided the tourists might not be dangerous and should be allowed to live.

Tabador told Carpenter the Indians were hungry and wanted something to eat. At this point, George Cowan stepped in and said they had no food to spare. Cowan was worried about the safety of his wife and wanted the Nez Perces out of the area as soon as possible. Because of his concern, Cowan had made a serious mistake. The tone of the meeting now became more hostile. One of Yellow Wolf's men walked toward the edge of the camp and began to whistle. Cowan, fearing this was a signal for more Indians to attack, pointed a gun at the warrior and ordered him to stop. Sensing events were getting out of control, Carpenter said he wanted to visit the Nez Perce chiefs and ask their permission to leave the park in safety. While Yellow Wolf was considering this request, Carpenter's friends quickly finished preparing breakfast and fed the hungry Indians. The meal had to be served without coffee because one of the nervous tourists dropped the container and spilled all of the ground coffee beans. The food seemed to calm everyone down and Yellow Wolf finally agreed to escort Carpenter's party to Chief Looking Glass.

As the tourists loaded their wagons and harnessed their teams of horses, Yellow Wolf warned them that his people were divided in their opinions about the Americans. Some remained extremely bitter after the Battle at Big Hole. They wanted to kill every white man they encountered. Others directed most of their hatred at the soldiers and realized that all white men should not be blamed for the terrible actions of a few. If Carpenter and the others were to survive, they must hold their tempers and watch their actions carefully. They must not provide any excuse for the more violent members of the tribe to attack them.

When the tourists had packed their belongings into the wagons, the Nez Perce scouts led the way to the main body of Indians. Carpenter noted with admiration that the long column of men, women, children, and animals stretched over three miles of the rugged Yellowstone landscape. As the white men approached with their escort of scouts, thirty or forty warriors rode out to meet them. These Indians gathered around the captives to investigate the contents of their wagons and admire their fine teams of horses. Tabador attempted to hold them back but his efforts were largely unsuccessful. The interpreter was greatly relieved when a messenger arrived with orders to take the white men to Looking Glass at once.

The remainder of the journey was difficult and unpleasant. The area through which they traveled was filled with fallen trees many of which blocked the passage of the wagons. Hot-blooded young warriors repeatedly charged to-

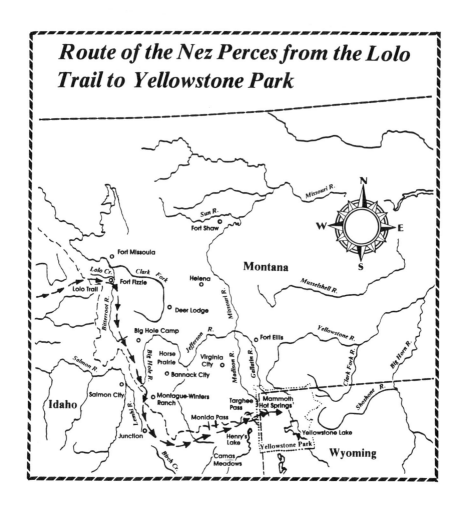

Route of the Nez Perces from the Lolo Trail to Yellowstone Park

ward the prisoners yelling their fierce war whoops, waving their rifles, and attempting to lasso the white men's horses. Finally, the large number of logs on the ground stopped passage of the wagons altogether. The tourists were forced to abandon them and ride their horses the rest of the way. As soon as the teams were unhitched, the Indians plundered the wagons taking everything of value and damaging the vehicles beyond repair.

Despite the many threats hurled at them, the captives arrived safely at their destination. Carpenter later described Looking Glass as:

...a man of medium height, and is apparently forty-five years of age, his hair is streaked with grey. He has a wide, flat face, almost square, with a small mouth running from ear to ear ... The ornament worn by him, that was most conspicuous, was a tin looking-glass, which he wore about his neck and suspended in front ... He wore nothing on his head and had only two or three feathers plaited in his black hair.

The chief informed the white men that he did not have the authority to decide their fate. They would have to present their request for freedom to Poker Joe, the new war chief of the combined nontreaty bands. They would be taken to meet this leader when the Indians stopped to rest and eat their noon meal.

Poker Joe received the tourists in a reserved, businesslike manner. The white men took some comfort from the presence of John Shively in the camp. The old prospector appeared unharmed and gave the captives hope for similar treatment.

The war chief explained that the Nez Perces were traveling to the buffalo country and meant no harm to the people of Montana. He angrily described the events at Big Hole and the relentless pursuit of his people by General Howard. He said that he needed guns, ammunition, and blankets and asked what the white men had to trade for their freedom. Carpenter's party had nothing left of value except their horses. Poker Joe demanded these animals in exchange for worn-out Indian ponies. Remembering the warning of Yellow Wolf, the tourists sadly agreed to the unfair trade.

Poker Joe decided to release the captives in small groups rather than allowing everyone to leave at once. Not wishing to kill the innocent people himself, perhaps he thought their chances for survival in the wilderness were less if they were unable to help or support each other. First to be set free were A. J. Arnold and William Dingee. Poker Joe placed these two men on old broken-down horses and allowed them to ride off through the dense timber. Some angry young warriors fired several shots at the departing white men who hurried away in the direction of Henry's Lake.

The shots fired after the release of Arnold and Dingee frightened the other tourists. They began to fear that Poker Joe was playing some terrible game and planned to kill them all as they attempted to leave the camp. Carpenter thought perhaps another chief might offer them protection. He remembered that Chief Joseph had once been a friend of many white men. Carpenter asked Poker Joe for permission to visit the Wallamwatkin leader.

The request was granted. However, some of the tourists' worst fears became a reality on the way to the peace chief's camp. The captives had not traveled far with their armed Nez Perce escort when the warriors called a halt and took the bridles and saddles off the white men's horses. As soon as they were remounted, one of the Indians turned and shot George Cowan in the thigh. The terrified man jumped from his horse and attempted to hide in the brush beside the trail. As Cowan fled for his life, another Indian took aim and shot Albert Oldham in the left cheek. The bullet passed through his mouth and came out under his right jaw. Falling from his horse, Oldham rolled into a small ravine and drew a revolver he had hidden in his clothing. With only three bullets in the gun, the injured man took careful aim at his attackers. However, the gun misfired and the weapon proved useless. This was lucky for the other tourists because if Oldham had opened fire, the angry warriors would have killed them all. Failing in his attempt to strike back at the Nez Perces, Oldham managed to conceal himself in the underbrush where he remained for thirty-six hours suffering from his wounds.

After their shooting spree, the attention of the Indians was once again drawn to George Cowan who lie bleeding beside the trail. The remaining captives had gathered around the fallen man and his wife, Emma, cradled his head in her lap. Emma's sister, Ida, though nearly hysterical with fear, pushed her way through the ring of tourists and Indians and threw herself down beside her brother-in-law. The warriors did not know what to do with the injured white man. One of them decided to end his suffering by killing him. Though Emma desperately begged for her husband's life, the Indian drew his revolver and shot Cowan in the forehead. Then, with their thirst for vengeance temporarily quenched, the warriors delivered the remaining prisoners to Chief Joseph.

The peace chief was outraged when he discovered the senseless cruelty of his young men. Though Joseph also harbored violent feelings of anger and bitterness after the tragedy at Big Hole, he refused to condone the mistreatment of innocent people. Carpenter noted the Indians' respect for the chief's authority. In a later description of Joseph, he wrote, ". . . He talked but little, but I noticed that when he spoke to the Indians, there was no hesitancy about obeying him."

It was late in the day when the tourists arrived and Joseph offered them the safety of his camp for the night. That evening, the chief appeared visibly upset by the actions of his young warriors. He sat brooding by the fire silently staring into the flames.

The captives were given blankets, but the horrible events of the day made it impossible for them to sleep. Clutching her blanket around her, Emma Cowan got up to

Toma asked the reason for Mrs. Cowan's great sorrow.

sit with Joseph beside the fire. Tears streamed down her face as she thought about her husband lying dead in the cold, dark night. In a short while, Toma, the chief's wife, brought her baby to join the somber little group. She sat beside Mrs. Cowan and offered to let the grieving woman hold the sleeping infant. Emma carefully cradled the new life in her arms and appeared to derive some comfort from the child's peaceful innocence. A faint smile flickered across Joseph's face as he watched the white woman and his little daughter. To him they represented the innocent members of both cultures, Indian and white, who suffered most from the destruction of war.

Toma wanted to know the cause of Mrs. Cowan's great sorrow. Emma's brother, Frank, explained that his sister's husband had been killed that afternoon by vengeful Nez Perce warriors. Toma understood the heartbreak of losing a loved one and her eyes filled with tears of sympathy as she sat quietly beside the widow.

The next day, Joseph held a council to decide what to do with the captives. He was afraid that, if he released them, they would be killed by the young warriors whose behavior was sometimes out of control. Poker Joe offered to take the tourists across the Yellowstone River and place them on the path to safety away from the main body of Indians. Joseph liked this idea and the other chiefs were also in agreement. Without further discussion, Carpenter and the others were given worn-out Indian ponies and told to follow Poker Joe.

The war chief led his former prisoners across the river and placed them on a well-defined trail leading out of the park. He said that if they traveled all day and all night without stopping, they would reach the safety of a white settlement within two days. He asked them to tell the other white men that the Nez Perces wanted only a peaceful journey to the buffalo country. They were not interested in harming the settlers of Montana or continuing a war with the U.S. Government. Before leaving, Poker Joe gave the tourists some food for their journey. Then, turning his horse, the war chief proudly rode back to his people.

After all they had been through, Carpenter and the others did not completely trust Poker Joe. Emma wanted to return for the body of her husband, but she was stopped by her brother. George Cowan was beyond help and his companions must now look after their own safety. As soon as Poker Joe was out of sight, the little group of tourists left the main trail and traveled under cover of the timber. Watching closely for signs of Indians, they traveled quietly through the trees toward the northeastern exit of the park.

While Frank Carpenter and the others made their escape from the Indians, the miraculous story of George Cowan was continuing to unfold. Cowan had remained unconscious for two hours after he was shot and left for dead by the Nez Perce scouting party. When he awoke, he was extremely thirsty. In great pain and unable to walk, the severely injured man began to slowly crawl about in search of water. As he made his way onto the trail, he suddenly became aware of being watched by an Indian on horseback. Cowan desperately tried to crawl back into the brush, but before he could escape, the warrior shot him in the hip, the bullet passing out through his abdomen. Cowan lay motionless and once again he was presumed dead. The Indian rode away without bothering to examine his victim.

Bleeding profusely from his three gunshot wounds, the remarkable Cowan clung stubbornly to life. He now began a three-day ordeal in which he crawled nine miles back to the place where the Indians had plundered his party's wagons.

The warriors had taken everything and there was nothing left to do but continue on to the old campsite in the Lower Geyser Basin. Cowan remembered that some coffee had been spilled there on the morning of his capture. Perhaps if he could find and boil it, the warm liquid would make him feel better. With this thought in mind, Cowan dragged his aching body back to the deserted camp. He managed to locate the coffee and prepare it in an old tin can with water from the shallow Firehole River.

The strong brew did have a soothing effect on the injured man. However, he was now too weak from loss of blood to continue beyond the camp. It seemed that he would die in this place and never know what happened to his wife and friends.

Despite the apparent hopelessness of the situation, luck remained on the side of George Cowan. Just when things seemed darkest, two scouts from General Howard's command rode into camp. They built a fire and wrapped the wounded man in warm blankets. Then they fed him and made him as comfortable as they could. Because of Cowan's serious condition, the soldiers were unable to transport him to their camp. They said he would have to remain where he was until the general and his troops arrived the next day. Cowan told his rescuers that the Indians had captured his wife and the other people traveling with him. He thought they must certainly be dead by now. Howard's men said they would continue on ahead and attempt to locate the rest of Cowan's party. Then they rode off leaving the exhausted man beside the fire.

Once again alone, Cowan ate some more of the food the soldiers had left for him and settled down to try and sleep. During the night, he was awakened by an intense heat and discovered the wind had fanned his small fire into a roaring blaze. The flames quickly spread to the dry grass upon which he lie. Though extremely stiff and sore, Cowan managed to drag himself away from the inferno toward the water of the nearby Firehole River. He managed to reach safety, but not before his legs and hands were badly burned. Cowan remained in the water until the fire burned itself out. Then he crept back to his charred campsite and huddled wet and shivering until General Howard found him the next morning.

The army doctors tended Cowan's wounds and he was transported to a ranch not far from Mammoth Hot Springs. There he was reunited with his wife who was astonished and overjoyed by his survival.

Cowan also learned that A. J. Arnold, William Dingee, and Albert Oldham had been rescued by the soldiers. Incredibly, all of the tourists in Frank Carpenter's party had survived their ordeal with the Nez Perce Indians. Cowan eventually recovered completely from his injuries and made several more trips to Yellowstone Park.

The Nez Perce chiefs attempted to keep firm control of their warriors. However, as the long column of Indians stretched out several miles along the trail, it was difficult for the leaders to remain in close contact with all of their men. Small groups of warriors rampaged throughout the countryside on both sides of the main body of Indians. These unauthorized forays provided excellent opportunities for the tribe's volatile young men to vent their anger on many hapless victims. Perhaps the raiders were able to justify this behavior using the mixed message they received from their leaders.

Since Poker Joe's rise to power, there had been two distinctly different points of view concerning the retreat. The new war chief said all white men were enemies of the Nez Perces and would help the soldiers in any way they could. It was therefore necessary for the Indians to attack white settlements and remove or destroy anything that might be of use to the military. In contrast to this opinion, was the belief of Joseph and some other chiefs that unprovoked killing was not necessary. They said their people should not harm innocent settlers and should only strive for a safe passage to the buffalo country. How unfortunate it was that the Nez Perces' desperation led them into this state of confusion wherein they became guilty of the same cruelty they despised in their enemies.

Soon after Frank Carpenter and his party encountered the hostile nontreaty warriors, another group of white men felt the force of the Indians' hatred. On August 13, a party of sightseers left Radersburg, Montana to visit Yellowstone Park. Though they had heard about the Nez Perce uprising, they thought their chances of meeting Indians in the park were very slim. The group included a music teacher by the name of Richard Dietrich and his friends, Andrew J. Weikert, Frederick Pfister, Joseph Roberts, Charles Kenck, Jack Stewart, August Foller, Leslie Wilke, and Leonard Duncan. The men enlisted the services of a black man named Ben Stone to do the cooking for them.

By August 25, the vacationers had traveled past Mammoth Hot Springs on their way to view the Upper and Lower Falls. As they rode over the rough terrain leading their pack animals, they saw, in the distance, a large group of Indians following along the riverbank. Fearing the warriors were members of a Nez Perce war party, the white men immediately looked for a place to camp and stay out of sight. They selected a secluded spot in the dense timber near Otter Creek. The camp would have been easy to defend, but the inexperienced tourists did not disperse to guard and protect the area. Instead, they huddled together hoping to escape detection by roving groups of hostiles.

The camp remained secure all morning. In the afternoon, Andrew Weikert and Leslie Wilkie decided to look around and see if the Indians had left the area. Near Alum Creek they saw a colt they believed had wandered away from the Nez Perce herd. The two men considered capturing the young horse, but decided it would be too much trouble. As they turned to ride away, Weikert spied an Indian concealed behind some fallen trees. Fearing an attack, he alerted his companion and the two white men wheeled their horses about and fled.

As soon as their presence was discovered, the warriors opened fire, but the riders crouched low over their horses and the bullets only managed to wound Weikert in the shoulder. The white men hurried back to warn the others of the danger.

Meanwhile, while Weikert and Wilke were away, Nez Perce raiders attacked the camp at Otter Creek. The Indians opened fire as Ben Stone was lighting the evening campfire and the other men were relaxing and calming down from their eventful morning. At the first sound of gunfire, the white men scattered in all directions looking for places of refuge. Duncan escaped through the trees and made his way back to Mammoth Hot Springs. Roberts and Foller hurried west and followed the Madison River to Virginia City. Pfister headed for the Yellowstone River and Dietrich hid in the tall grass beside Otter Creek. Stone also fled up the creek and managed to find a place of concealment. Kenck and Stewart were not as fortunate as the others. These men were closely pursued by the raiders as they attempted to escape from the camp. Unable to outdistance the warriors, Kenck was killed and Stewart was wounded in the side and in the leg. The injured man fell to the ground and the hostiles quickly surrounded him. As they were about to end his life, Stewart began to plead for mercy. For some unknown reason, the warriors decided to take pity on the terrified man and agreed to let him live.

Having driven the white men away, the Indians plundered the camp. They took food, blankets, tents, saddles, and anything else they thought might be useful. Then they set fire to the rest and galloped off to return to their people.

Soon after the attack, Weikert and Wilke returned to the devastated campsite. They were unable to locate their friends and thought perhaps everyone had escaped. They decided to return to Mammoth Hot Springs and report the incident to the military. On the way, they were joined by Stewart and Stone who were headed in the same direction. Dietrich, Duncan, and Pfister also arrived safely at the hot springs.

Jack Stewart begged the Nez Perce warriors for his life.

The distressed campers converged on a small Mammoth hotel and store operated by Jim McCartney. Stewart reported that Kenck had been killed but nobody knew what had happened to Roberts and Foller. Dietrich felt responsible for the safety of Joe Roberts. He had promised the young man's mother he would take good care of her son. Therefore, when the other campers returned home, Dietrich, Stone, and Weikert decided to remain and search for the two missing men.

On the morning of August 31, Weikert and McCartney returned to Otter Creek to bury the body of Charles Kenck and attempt to find Roberts and Foller. Dietrich and Stone stayed at the hotel in case their two lost friends arrived back there.

The next day, while Weikert and McCartney were away, a Nez Perce raiding party arrived at the hotel. Dietrich apparently heard the sound of horses and thought his friends had returned. He opened the door to welcome them and was killed instantly by a bullet through the heart. Unlike Dietrich, Stone took no careless chances. When the Indians first appeared, he ran out the back door of the hotel and climbed a tree in nearby Clematis Gulch. There he remained concealed among the branches until the danger had passed.

Almost immediately after the Indians had vandalized and left the hotel, a company of soldiers arrived. They found the body of Dietrich lying on the porch and carried it inside the building. Then they searched the area for survivors and rescued the frightened Ben Stone. The black man told them that two of his companions had ridden out to Otter Creek, but the troops were in a hurry to pursue the Indians and could not take time to wait for them. Stone decided to remain with the soldiers and hoped his friends survived to join him later.

While Stone was being rescued at the hotel, Weikert and McCartney were having an encounter of their own with the Nez Perces. The two men had arrived at Otter Creek and buried Kenck's body. Then, since there was no sign of Roberts or Foller in the area, they decided to return to Mammoth immediately. About eighteen miles from the hotel, they encountered a group of hostile warriors. The Indians immediately opened fire and Weikert's horse was killed. The shots frightened McCartney's horse and it began to buck. McCartney's saddle slipped loose and he was thrown to the ground. Forced to escape on foot, the white men raced away from the trail and concealed themselves in the dense underbrush. The Indians were not interested in searching about for the tourists. Satisfied with the new horse and two saddles, they withdrew from the area waving their rifles and shouting their fierce war cries.

When they one again felt safe, Weikert and McCartney crept from their hiding places and returned to Mammoth Hot Springs. There they found Dietrich's body inside the ransacked hotel. There was no sign of Stone so they decided to continue on to a ranch near the Gardiner River. It was almost dark when the two men began their seven mile walk to safety. Along the way, they happened upon the campsite of the soldiers who had rescued Ben Stone. They were reunited with their friend and the three men returned home together. The trio had a pleasant surprise waiting for them when they discovered that Roberts and Foller had also survived their disastrous vacation in Yellowstone Park.

Chapter 23

Failure and Frustration for Colonel Sturgis

Reports of violence in the national park brought more public criticism of General Howard for his failure to capture the hostiles. However, the general was by now too occupied with the physical problems of the campaign to pay much attention to what people said or wrote. The terrain of Yellowstone Park was extremely rough and presented many difficulties for the soldiers with their wagonloads of supplies and ammunition.

Since entering the park on August 27, Howard and his troops had followed slowly in the wake of the nontreaty bands. Captain S. G. Fisher and his Bannock Scouts rode ahead and closely monitered the movements of the Indians and reported their whereabouts to Howard. The main body of troops found their progress hindered by the slow movement of their cumbersome supply wagons. Roads for these vehicles had to be constructed through the dense timber of the undeveloped park. To accomplish this, Captain W. F. Spurgin traveled between the soldiers and the wagons with his infantry and fifty volunteer frontiersmen from Idaho. These men laborously constructed a narrow roadway through the wilderness for the general's wagons and supply train.

The soldiers followed the Nez Perces through the Lower Geyser Basin east toward the Yellowstone River. On September 1, they encountered a discharged soldier from Fort Ellis named Irwin. This man had recently been held prisoner by the hostiles for a few days and provided valuable information about their location and future plans. Irwin suggested a way for the soldiers to close the gap between themselves and the Nez Perces. He said that, instead of following the Indians directly east, the troops should travel north and cross the Yellowstone River at Baronett Bridge. Having taken this shorter route, General Howard could then intercept the Nez Perces when they eventually turned north at the Clark Fork River. The general liked this suggestion. He knew that Colonel Samuel Sturgis and his force of 360 men already blocked the Clark Fork Canyon in anticipation of the Indians' arrival. If Howard could move closer to the hostile bands, he could trap them between his own soldiers and those of Colonel Sturgis.

Having adopted this new line of march, Howard's troops were soon traveling north on the west bank of the Yellowstone River toward Baronett Bridge. Not wishing to lose close contact with the Nez Perces, the general ordered Captain Fisher and his Bannock scouts to continue west on the heels of the nontreaties and keep him informed of their movements.

The Bannocks were becoming tired of the long chase over the rough park trails. They occasionally were close enough to fire a few shots at the hostiles, but were hesitant to ride into battle against their ancient enemies. A few days after leaving the main body of troops, most of the Bannocks decided to return home. They deserted Captain Fisher and headed back toward the west exit of the park.

The departing scouts met General Howard as he traveled north. The Bannocks decided to take some of the soldiers' horses as payment for their services to the military. They drove off forty animals from Captain Spurgin's road-building crew.

General Howard was quick to take action against the thieves. He captured ten of the Bannocks and placed them under heavy guard. Chief Buffalo Horn soon came to the defense of his warriors. He said the Indians had not tried to steal from the soldiers. The horses must have wandered off from the main herd. Howard replied that the chief might be correct, but the prisoners would not be released until all of the missing animals were found. Within a short time, the Bannocks returned twenty of the horses claiming that was all they could find wandering in the hills. The general thanked the warriors for their help, but insisted on holding the scouts until all of his property had been returned. That night, the Bannocks brought back the remaining horses, ransomed their friends, and continued on their way home. Before they departed, Howard managed to persuade a few of them to return to Captain Fisher and continue their service as scouts. Though generally disappointed in the Bannocks, the general thought they still might prove useful and did not want to lose any part of his command at this critical time in the campaign.

The soldiers reached Baronett Bridge on September 5. They were disappointed to find that the rickety old bridge had been partially burned by Indians. The men faced another delay to repair the damage and make the structure safe for their crossing of the Yellowstone River. While this work was in progress, General Howard ordered a group of soldiers to sort through the wagons and remove all of the important supplies and equipment. The general had decided it was becoming far too difficult and time-consuming to continue making use of the wagons. The horses were exhausted from pulling them over the rough trails and the men were becoming tired of constructing roads and maneuvering the wagons up and down the steep walls of canyons and ravines. In crossing one ravine along the Yellowstone River, the weary soldiers had been forced to perform the back-breaking task of lowering the heavy vehicles on ropes six hundred feet down a steep wall of rock. Afraid he would encounter more such imposing obstacles to his progress, Howard decided to return the wagons to Fort Ellis and rely on the mules in his pack train to transport all of his supplies.

When repairs on the bridge were complete, General Howard and his troops hurried across the Yellowstone River and traveled east up the Lamar River. The general was eager to reach the Clark Fork Canyon and help Colonel Sturgis spring their trap as soon as the Nez Perces entered it.

Near the mouth of Clark Fork Canyon, Colonel Samuel D. Sturgis waited impatiently for word from General Howard. The Indians had successfully blocked communication between the two groups of soldiers and Sturgis had become concerned about his chances of capturing the hostiles. Being actively involved in this campaign was extremely important to the colonel. Having lost a son in the Battle at the Little Bighorn, he was eager for the chance to vent his hatred of Indians on the approaching nontreaty bands.

With no word from General Howard, Sturgis decided to learn for himself the whereabouts of the Nez Perces and the direction in which they were traveling. The Clark Fork Canyon was extremely narrow and the colonel thought perhaps the Indians had decided to leave the park by another route. Two other possibilities existed. One of these

Route of the Nez Perces from Yellowstone Park to the Yellowstone River

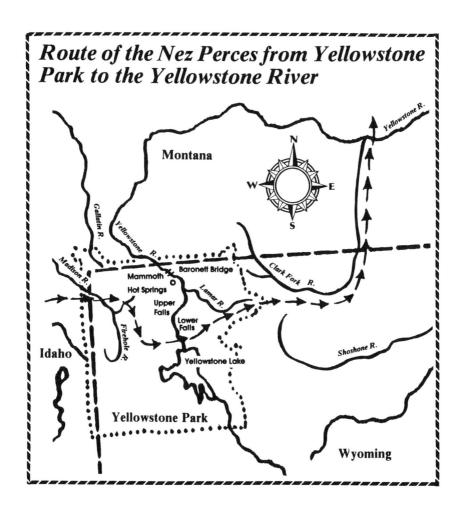

followed the Yellowstone River and the other followed the Shoshone River. On September 8, Sturgis sent scouts to locate the hostiles and prepared to lead his command in pursuit.

The scouts reported seeing the fleeing Nez Perces in the area of the Shoshone River. After locating the trail of the Indians, Sturgis' men had discovered a large herd of horses being driven along the riverbank by a group of young warriors. The Indians had been watering the animals and made no attempt to conceal their tracks as they continued on their way.

Sturgis decided to leave at once and intercept the hostiles at the Shoshone River. Arriving at his destination on September 10, the colonel soon discovered he had been outmaneuvered by the clever Nez Perces. There were numerous tracks of Indian ponies in the area, but no sign of the hostiles themselves anywhere. After making a quick evaluation of the situation, Sturgis' scouts discovered the Indians had only pretended to take the Shoshone River exit from the park. After traveling for a distance along the riverbank, they had milled their ponies about to confuse the direction of their tracks. Then, they had doubled back to their original path in the direction of the Clark Fork Canyon. Under cover of heavy timber, the Nez Perces had eluded the soldiers and exited the park through a canyon so narrow that, as Howard later wrote, "two horses abreast could hardly pass." This tunnel-like gorge opened into the Clark Fork Valley only a few miles from Sturgis' former campsite. The colonel was upset to realize he must have passed the hostiles as he traveled to the Shoshone River on a route that paralelled the canyon in which they made their escape. Worse yet, was the scouts' report that General Howard had also passed Sturgis in pursuit of the Indians and was still intent on springing the trap originally set by the two commands.

Colonel Sturgis was angered and humiliated by his failure to stop the Nez Perces. One of his men wrote:

> We knew our colonel was hopping mad that the savages had outwitted him, and . . . we heard the old veteran, with many an explosive adjective, declare that he would overtake the Indians before they crossed the Missouri River if he had to go afoot and alone.

Sturgis had little time to nurse his wounded ego. After learning the truth about his situation at the Shoshone

River, he quickly followed General Howard. Under the circumstances, the only thing to do was admit his mistake to the general and hope for the chance to redeem himself in the future.

When the Nez Perces reached the Clark Fork Valley, the chiefs decided it was time to approach the Crow Indians and ask for a safe place to live. Since Looking Glass claimed to have close allies among the Crows, the other leaders chose him to ride ahead and make the contact. Looking Glass visited both the Mountain Crows and the River Crows, but, even though he reminded them how the Nez Perces had taken their side against the Sioux Indians, both divisions of the tribe refused to help the hostiles. The Crows had made peace with the white men and did not want to risk being drawn into another war. The Mountain chiefs said they would remain neutral, but the River chiefs said they would take the side of the white men against their former Nez Perce friends. Looking Glass soon realized the only safe place for his people was in Canada with Sitting Bull and the Sioux Indians. Yellow Wolf expressed the disappointment and confusion the Nez Perces felt concerning the Crows when he said, "I do not understand how the Crows could think to help the soldiers. They were fighting against their best friends."

The Nez Perces left Yellowstone Park on September 9 and headed northeast along the Clark Fork River. Late the following day, General Howard and his troops made their exit from the park about fifty miles behind the hostiles. On September 11, Colonel Sturgis overtook the general and the two commands made camp in the Clark Fork Valley. Howard had been confident of his ability to trap the nontreaties and end the war that was causing him embarrassment and frustration. Now, as he listened to Sturgis' description of the elaborate Nez Perce deception that had spoiled his plans, the general was filled with bitter disappointment and renewed respect for his clever adversaries.

Howard was now afraid that the Indians would escape capture altogether and find safety out of his reach in Canada among the Sioux. To prevent this, the general sent two messengers north to Colonel Nelson A. Miles at Fort Keogh on the Tongue River. Howard explained how the Nez Perces had escaped from him and their probable route to Canada. He asked Colonel Miles to travel west across Montana, intercept the hostiles, and delay them until he could catch up and capture them.

General Howard knew he must move quickly if he hoped to keep up with the fleeing nontreaty bands. Since Sturgis' horses were in better condition than his own, Howard decided to send the colonel and his men ahead in pursuit of the hostiles. Though Howard's own officers were opposed to this idea, the general held firmly to his decision. He equipped Sturgis with two howitzers and additional cavalry and scouts. Sturgis was eager for the chance to make up for his mistakes at the Clark Fork Canyon. At dawn on a rainy September 12, he left Howard's camp with nearly 400 men on his second attempt to defeat Joseph's people.

Determined though he was to succeed, Sturgis' progress was immediately slowed by heavy rain and difficult traveling conditions. The trails were filled with thick, slippery mud and the streams were swollen and dangerous to ford. After covering nearly 60 miles without fresh signs of Indians, the wet, miserable soldiers began to lose confidence and Sturgis dreaded having to face another failure. On September 13, the disheartened troops crossed the Yellowstone River and camped about ten miles north of the place where the Clark Fork River empties into the Yellowstone. Sturgis hoped that a brief rest and a chance to dry their wet clothing would help lift the men's spirits and restore their positive outlook. Perhaps a better remedy for their condition would have been the knowledge that at that very time the Nez Perces were camped only a few miles away in a place called Canyon Creek.

After leaving Yellowstone Park, the Nez Perces had followed the Clark Fork River toward its junction with the Yellowstone. Along the way, they had killed several miners and raided the ranch of J. M. V. Cochran. The warriors had spared the lives of Cochran and his friends, but killed two trappers who had stopped at the ranch for a visit. Another group of raiders attacked the P. W. McAdow sawmill and took the horses and livestock. When the Indians reached the Yellowstone River, they captured a stagecoach at the ranch of Bill Brockway. Luckily, the passengers noticed the approaching hostiles in time to escape from the coach and hide before they were discovered. The excited warriors eagerly took possession of the abandoned stagecoach and recklessly rode it about scattering baggage and mail in all directions.

Soon after the Nez Perces arrived in Canyon Creek, they were spotted by Pawnee Tom, one of Sturgis' best scouts. Just when the soldiers most needed to hear good news, Pawnee Tom rode into their camp yelling, "Indians! Indians!" Within fifteen minutes Sturgis' men were mounted and ready to ride into battle.

While the troops prepared to attack, the Nez Perces struck camp and began moving toward the mouth of Canyon Creek. Indian scouts soon became aware of the danger and raced toward their people frantically waving bright red blankets in a signal that meant, "The soldiers are close!"

With Sturgis' men less than seven miles away, the Nez Perce chiefs hurried their women, children, and old people

Nez Perce warriors attacked miners and trappers along the Clark Fork River.

toward the safety of a canyon about three or four miles ahead. The warriors formed a rear guard to protect their retreating families from the rapidly advancing soldiers.

The lower valley of Canyon Creek was a broad sagebrush plain that gradually narrowed as it led north from the Yellowstone River. The upper valley eventually formed a canyon whose steep sides were protected by overhanging rocks and whose mouth could be easily defended by a small force of sharpshooters.

Driving their livestock before them, the Nez Perce women, children, and old people fled into the canyon. In their haste, they were forced to abandon some 400 worn-out horses that were too slow to keep pace with the rest of the herd. As the main body of Indians moved rapidly forward, warriors took defensive positions on bluffs at the canyon mouth to await the arrival of the soldiers.

Colonel Sturgis and his men arrived in time to see the hostiles moving into the canyon. Nez Perce warriors opened fire as soon as they saw their enemies. The troops responded with a shot from one of their howitzers that fell short of its intended mark. Sturgis ordered his forward cavalry to dismount and advance on the Indians in a skirmish line. This was a tactical mistake because it slowed the soldiers and allowed the nontreaties more time to escape. With most of his men on foot, Sturgis sent one group of mounted cavalry to cut the Indians off before they could travel too far into the canyon. These troops were soon forced to retreat under heavy Nez Perce fire. Two of the soldiers were killed and the rest dismounted and took cover in a nearby ravine.

The fighting continued all afternoon. The Nez Perces were only interested in escape. They did not want to prolong the battle any longer than necessary. As the main body of Indians moved deeper into the canyon, the warriors withdrew after them stopping at intervals to keep the soldiers at bay. As the canyon narrowed, fewer and fewer sharpshooters were needed to cover the retreat. One by one the warriors were able to leave the battle and join their families on the canyon floor. Yellow Wolf claimed that near the end of the encounter only one warrior remained hidden behind the rocks to hold the soldiers back.

As darkness descended, Colonel Sturgis decided to give up the chase for the night. His men were damp, cold, and exhausted. The recent rain and a raw, September wind chilled the air and the troops shivered in their wet, wool uniforms. They returned to the mouth of the canyon and made camp for the night.

Unlike their adversaries, the Nez Perces did not seek the warmth of a campfire on that cold, unpleasant evening. The chiefs kept them moving throughout the night.

When the soldiers stopped their pursuit, young warriors took the opportunity to block the trail and delay the advance of Sturgis in the morning. They filled the narrow areas in the trail behind their people with logs, brush, and boulders just as they had done while crossing the Lolo Trail. With all of these obstacles in their way, the soldiers could not have followed the hostiles in the darkness if they had tried. Toward morning on September 14, the Nez Perces emerged from the canyon and camped for a brief rest in the hilly area to the north.

That same morning, General Howard caught up with Colonel Sturgis in his camp at the mouth of the canyon. The general had learned about the fighting and hurried forward with his scouts and fifty men. Howard decided to wait for the remainder of his troops and supplies before continuing his advance. Once again he sent Sturgis ahead in rapid pursuit of the hostiles. The colonel sent Howard's Bannock scouts and his own Crow scouts to locate the Nez Perces and impede their progress until the soldiers could overtake them.

The hostiles broke camp early and continued north in the direction of the Musselshell River. The chiefs sent several scouts back to determine the location of the soldiers. These warriors soon discovered the army's Bannock and Crow scouts rapidly approaching from the south. The enemy scouts rode close behind the Nez Perce column and harassed the fugitives for two days. During that time they continually charged into the ranks of the nontreaties to steal horses and anything else of value. Ollokot and the other warriors were kept busy fending off these sudden attacks. Yellow Wolf estimated that as many as 100 Crows and Bannocks participated in the fighting. He said that, "Only when we were moving would they come after us. When we met them, they ran from us." The army scouts killed one Nez Perce warrior and two old men who had wandered away from the trail. The Crows managed to steal about forty horses. The nontreaties were forced to abandon several hundred more of their worn-out horses along the way bringing the total to nearly a thousand lost animals.

Despite their persistent assaults, the scouts were unable to slow the movement of the equally determined Nez Perces. Finally, the Crows decided to return home and the Bannocks set out to rejoin the soldiers. The Nez Perces were greatly relieved to be rid of their Indian attackers. The angry warriors yearned to take revenge for the cruel treatment they had endured. However, they saw the wisdom in their chiefs' refusal to enter into a time-consuming battle with the army's scouts. Escape was the important thing, and nothing must delay the Nez Perces until they reached their goal of safety. With this purpose in mind, the weary travelers resolutely continued northward. They crossed the Musselshell River on September 17 and moved through Judith Gap in the direction of the Missouri River.

Colonel Sturgis and his men lagged behind their Indian scouts. The Nez Perces had blocked the trail in many places and delays were frequent as the soldiers cleared fallen trees and boulders from their path. Sturgis became impatient with the slow progress through the canyon. His only hope for success rested on the effectiveness of the Crow and Bannock scouts. If they managed to stall the retreating Nez Perces, the soldiers might still be able to overtake them. Otherwise, the colonel must be prepared to face the complete failure of his mission.

The difficult week-long journey soon exhausted the already weary troops. Supplies were low and the hungry men were forced to kill several of their weaker horses for food. Sturgis lost all feelings of optimism when the Ban-

Ollokot

nock scouts returned and reported their failure to stop the nontreaties. To make matters worse, many of the soldiers' horses became ill with what one man called a "disease of the hoof." This forced the cavalry to dismount and continue painfully on foot over the rocky canyon floor. By the time the troops had traveled the hundred and fifty miles to the Musselshell River, the Nez Perces were far ahead of them. Angrily, Colonel Sturgis ordered his men to stop and make camp beside the river. Desperately in need of rest, supplies, and fresh horses, the colonel knew the soldiers could not hope to catch up with the Indians. He decided to abandon the chase and wait for the arrival of General Howard.

Chapter 24

"Our Chiefs Are Killed"

While Sturgis and his men were struggling through the canyon, the Nez Perces continued their flight north from the Musselshell River. Their recent harassment by the colonel's Crow scouts proved how unwelcome they were in their former Montana hunting grounds. Poker Joe said their last chance for freedom lay with Sitting Bull and the Sioux Indians. The nontreaties must continue their forced march and remain ahead of the soldiers. Alone and friendless, they could expect no comfort or assistance until they crossed the border into Canada.

On a brief rest stop near Judith Gap, Looking Glass began to reassert himself and challenge Poker Joe's authority. Looking Glass said his people should now be allowed to travel at a slower pace. They had repelled the Crow and Bannock scouts and outdistanced Colonel Sturgis and his men. The soldiers were far behind and General Howard had not been seen for many days. The women, children, and old people had been pushed to the point of exhaustion. They needed time to rest and regain their strength.

Poker Joe reminded Looking Glass that similar reasoning had allowed the army to overtake them at Big Hole.

He refused to take the chance of facing another such attack. The Nez Perces had been able to maintain their forced march thus far. Poker Joe was certain they could survive the rapid pace a while longer. With safety almost within their reach, it made no sense to slow down and risk capture. The other chiefs continued to support Poker Joe, even though, like their people, they were exhausted and Looking Glass' arguments were beginning to sound convincing.

With Canada about two hundred miles away, the non-treaties hurried on through Judith Basin. Along the way, they passed the camp of some once-friendly Crow Indians. The Nez Perces attacked their former allies, seized their food, and drove off many of their finest horses. Then they pushed on toward the Missouri River covering a distance of seventy-five miles in only thirty-six hours.

On September 23, the Nez Perces reached the Missouri at a favorite crossing place opposite the Cow Island Landing. This was also the stopping place for steamboats traveling up the river with supplies for Fort Benton and other white settlements. The Missouri was at its lowest ebb this time of year and was too shallow for navigation above the landing. Steamboats had been unloading their cargos at Cow Island where they were guarded by four civilians and a dozen soldiers until they could be taken overland to their destinations. There were presently nearly thirty tons of government freight and twenty tons of private supplies awaiting transport.

The guards at Cow Island Landing had been warned about the Nez Perce uprising. They had dug rifle pits and constructed earthen breastworks to protect themselves if they were attacked.

The Nez Perces traveled about two miles upriver from the landing. They crossed the Missouri and made camp near the mouth of Cow Creek. The hostiles were badly in need of supplies. However, the chiefs did not want to start more trouble. They warned their people not to fire first if the white men proved to be unfriendly. They then sent two warriors to begin bargaining for food.

At the first sign of Indians, the guards at Cow Island took cover behind their breastworks. When the two Nez Perce warriors approached these defenses, Sergeant William Moelchert went out to talk with them. The Indians explained their need for food and other supplies. They offered to pay for whatever they were given. Moelchert said he could not help the nontreaties. It was against his orders to sell the things stored at the landing. They were either the property of the U.S. Government or belonged to private citizens. There was nothing here to buy or sell.

The warriors pleaded for something to feed their hungry families. They said they would rather purchase what they needed than attack and take it by force. At the threat of violence, Moelchert relented somewhat and gave the Indians a side of bacon and half a sack of hardtack from his men's rations. This, he said, was all that he could spare.

The Nez Perces were angry and insulted by Moelchert's paltry handout. Toward sunset, some warriors fired a few shots at the landing. In the brief exchange that followed, two civilian guards and one Nez Perce warrior were wounded.

After dark, the hostiles managed to slip past the defenders and begin taking the supplies they needed. Some warriors found four barrels of whiskey and soon became drunk on the contents. These men made three unsuccessful attempts to capture the white men while their people continued to loot the storage area. When Joseph learned about the drinking, he ordered the barrels of whiskey to be emptied out on the ground. The angry peace chief threatened to shoot the drunken warriors if they remained out of control. He wanted to supply food for his hungry people not massacre all the white men at the landing.

The Indians took flour, sugar, bacon, coffee, beans, and other supplies as well as an assortment of pots and pans for cooking. When they were finished, they set fire to the remaining freight to prevent its use by their enemies. Yellow Wolf reported that, "It was a big fire!"

By ten o'clock the next morning, the Nez Perces were moving again toward the pass between the Little Rockies and the Bear Paw Mountains. After traveling only ten miles, they encountered a long, heavily-loaded freight train drawn by oxen. The warriors attacked immediately. They killed three of the teamsters and drove the others away. Then they began searching the wagons for anything they could use.

While the Nez Perces ransacked the freight train, they were spotted by Major Guido Ilges and his thirty-six volunteers from Fort Benton. Major Ilges had been searching the area for signs of Indians when he discovered the destruction at Cow Island Landing. He had followed the trail of the hostiles to their present location and now watched angrily as they looted the wagons. Ilges realized that his few men were far outnumbered by the Indians. This prevented him from launching an open attack. Instead, he decided to open fire on the Nez Perce families from the cover of a nearby hill.

When the warriors heard the shooting, they immediately set fire to the wagons and hurried to protect their people. They fired back at their attackers and managed to kill one of them. Fearing the loss of more men, Ilges soon retreated to the safety of Cow Island. The Indians did not pursue the white men. Seeking escape rather than vengeance, they continued rapidly on their way toward the mountains.

At noon, during a short rest stop, the Nez Perce chiefs went into council. Once again Looking Glass challenged Poker Joe's position as leader. Looking Glass said the rapid pace had now become unbearable for the older members of the tribe. A true chief would not make his people suffer in this way. Canada was less than a hundred miles away and General Howard was at least two full days to the south. Surely now the nontreaties could move more slowly. They needed longer rest breaks and more time to sleep at night. Looking Glass demanded to be reinstated as war chief so he could provide these things for his people.

Poker Joe was also becoming weary from the constant strain and pressure of the long retreat. Angered by Looking Glass' cutting remarks, he snapped back:

> All right, Looking Glass, you can lead. I am trying to save the people, doing my best to cross into Canada before the soldiers find us. You can take command, but I think we will be caught and killed.

In one of the greatest mistakes of the war, the other chiefs accepted the change of leadership. Perhaps they were too tired to argue or they really did share Looking Glass' optimistic view of their situation. Whatever the reason, they restored their old war chief to power and allowed him to slow the pace of their flight.

Perhaps the chiefs would have acted otherwise if they had known that, at that very moment, Colonel Nelson Miles was riding rapidly in their direction with 353 soldiers, 30 Cheyenne scouts, a Hotchkiss gun, and a twelve-pound Napoleon cannon. General Howard's messenger had reached Fort Keogh on September 17 and Miles had immediately assembled his forces. He had hurried west on

Looking Glass reclaimed his position as war chief as the Nez Perces approached the Bear Paw Mountains.

September 18 to intercept the hostiles before they could cross into Canada. General Howard had planned another trap for the Nez Perces and this time they were walking right into it.

Howard and Sturgis received word of Colonel Miles' activities on September 20 as they continued their march northward. With this information, Howard decided to advance more slowly and give Miles time to get into position to block the Indians' retreat. The general did not want to follow the Nez Perces too closely and force them to make a run for the Canadian border.

On September 25, Howard received two messages that caused him to move more rapidly. The first was from Major Ilges at Fort Benton. It described the Indians' raid on the supplies at Cow Island and their attack on the freight train a short time later. The second message said that Colonel Miles had crossed the Missouri near its junction with the Musselshell River and was hurrying to overtake the hostiles.

General Howard rapidly traveled north to the settlement of Carroll, Montana. There he left Colonel Sturgis and the main body of soldiers while he boarded the steamer Benton and traveled to Cow Island with his Indian scouts and a small escort of troops. The general hoped to reach Miles at the Bear Paw Mountains in time to witness the final outcome of the campaign.

Meanwhile, the Nez Perces were continuing their leisurely march through the grasslands toward Canada. The slower pace and frequent rests were a welcome relief after their hundred-day flight through thirteen hundred miles of rugged wilderness. Autumn was drawing to a close and the hunters now had time to look for buffalo to provide their families with a winter supply of meat. On September 29, their search was rewarded and several of the huge animals were killed. When Looking Glass learned about the successful hunt, he ordered his people to halt and make camp. A warrior named Wottolen challenged the wisdom of this decision. Looking Glass made fun of the young man saying his fears were groundless. The soldiers were far behind and the families needed food. With the safety of Canada only about two day's travel ahead, the Nez Perces could afford to relax and take advantage of their good fortune in locating the buffalo. He said times would soon improve for the favorite children of Mother Earth.

The Nez Perce camp was situated on the east side of Snake Creek near the northern slope of the Bear Paw Mountains. The site, which was only about forty-five miles from the Canadian border, was a broad, grassy, treeless plain flanked by low bluffs and traversed by deep ravines that one soldier said were "from two to six feet in depth and fringed with enough sage brush to hide the heads of their occupants." The Indians called the area Tsanim Alikos Pah (Place of Manure Fire) because of the abundance of buffalo chips which they used for fuel in the absence of timber. At this time of year, the plain was cold and lonely. A frigid arctic wind carried the promise of snow and forced the Indians to take shelter in the hollows beside the creek. The chiefs gathered their tired people together and settled down to build fires, cook buffalo meat, and prepare for the final move into Canada.

Concealed from the Indians by a range of mountains, Colonel Miles and his troops crossed the Missouri River and rapidly approached the Bear Paw campsite. Early on September 30, Cheyenne scouts discovered the trail of the hostiles and soon witnessed some Nez Perce hunters pursuing a herd of buffalo. The scouts immediately notified Colonel Miles who hurried forward and rode to within a mile or two of the camp. The soldiers could not see the Indians who were concealed in ravines along the creek. However, they were able to observe their large herd of horses grazing on the northeast side of the stream. Suddenly, there appeared to be a disturbance among the animals. The colonel feared his forces had been discovered and the hostiles were preparing to flee from the area. He took action immediately to stop them. Signaling his trumpeters to sound the attack, Miles led his men in a full charge toward the Nez Perce encampment.

Shortly before the early morning attack, Looking Glass' scouts had spotted the troops approaching them from the south. Frantically waving their red blankets, the scouts had charged back to camp shouting, "Soldiers! Soldiers!"

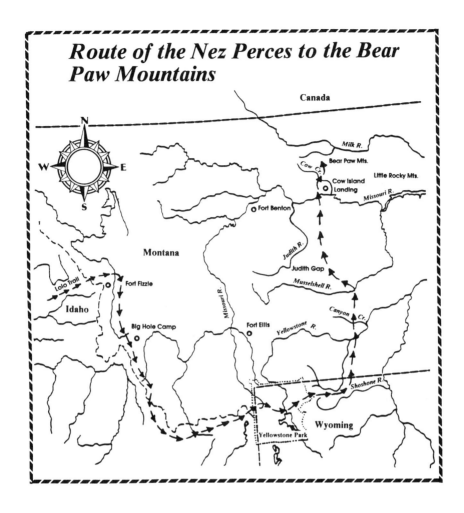

Route of the Nez Perces to the Bear Paw Mountains

Canada

N
W   E
S

Milk R.

Cow Cr.

Bear Paw Mts.

Little Rocky Mts.

Cow Island Landing

Missouri R.

Fort Benton

Montana

Judith R.

Judith Gap

Musselshell R.

Lolo Trail

Fort Fizzle

Idaho

Missouri R.

Big Hole Camp

Fort Ellis

Yellowstone R.

Canyon Cr.

Shoshone R.

Wyoming

Yellowstone Park

Many of the Indians were still eating breakfast when the alarm was given. Instantly, the peaceful village exploded into a nightmare of panic and confusion. Some of the people hurried to pack their most valuable possessions and flee north with their families. Others, like Joseph, hastened to gather the horses and drive them away from the danger. Warriors, led by Ollokot, Toohoolhoolzote, Poker Joe, and Looking Glass, seized their rifles and scurried up the slopes on the south and east sides of the camp. There, they crouched behind boulders to hold back the troops until their families could escape. From his place of concealment, Yellow Wolf heard "a rumble like stampeding buffaloes" and saw "hundreds of soldiers charging in two wide, circling wings" toward the camp "firing at everybody."

Colonel Miles' men swarmed through the ravines toward the terrified Indians. When the soldiers were about two hundred yards away, the warriors opened fire with all the force they could muster. Their fierce defense soon repelled Miles' gallant charge and forced the white men to retreat leaving their dead and wounded behind.

While one group of soldiers withdrew under heavy fire, another company of cavalry dashed directly into the Nez Perce herd of horses. Some of the Indians were already there frantically trying to save their valuable animals. Warriors sought their war ponies while women and children scrambled for mounts to carry them to safety.

Joseph and his twelve-year-old daughter, Walking in Crushed Snow, were trapped among the charging soldiers, stampeding horses, and panicing Indians. Fearing for the life of his child, Joseph thrust a length of rope into her hands and told her to capture a horse and flee. Walking in Crushed Snow obeyed her father and soon disappeared from view. The chief would not learn of her successful escape until sometime after the war.

Having provided one member of his family with a chance for freedom, Joseph's thoughts now turned to his wife and baby in the besieged camp. Silently praying for help from the Great Spirit, the peace chief boldly ran through the line of soldiers dodging bullets and challenging death every step of the way. He later said, "It seemed to me that there were guns on every side, before and behind me." Miraculously, Joseph managed to safely reach the door of his lodge. There he was met by his frightened wife who handed him his rifle and said, "Here is your gun! Fight!"

Joseph joined the warriors in their desperate attempt to save the remaining members of their tribe. They fought well and the soldiers suffered heavy losses. Captain Hale, Lieutenant Biddle, and twenty-two enlisted men were killed. Thirty-eight others were wounded. The troops were finally forced to withdraw from their attack. Colonel Miles ordered them to surround the area, dig rifle pits, and prepare to lay siege to the camp.

Despite their bravery and battle prowess, the Nez Perces also suffered tragic losses. As the first day of fighting at the Bear Paw Mountains drew to a close, between twenty and twenty-five Indian people lay dead and an untold number suffered from wounds. Among those lost in battle was Joseph's beloved brother, Ollokot. The fearless leader of the young warriors had been killed as he fought to hold back the soldiers from the rocks overlooking the village. Toohoolhoolzote died in the same attack as did Poker Joe, who was mistaken for a white man and shot by a Nez Perce warrior.

In addition to the loss of these brave men, the non-treaties were further crippled by the soldiers' capture of a large part of their horse herd. Without these valuable animals, the Indians could not hope to complete a successful exodus to Canada.

As darkness fell, the Nez Perce camp was filled with sadness and mourning. The cries of hungry, frightened children rose to join the eerie high-pitched death wail as families identified the bodies of their dead. Joseph worried about Walking in Crushed Snow and grieved for Ollokot whose lifeless body still lie on the battlefield. It seemed this cold, dark night of suffering and death would never end.

Toma handed Joseph his rifle and said, "Here is your gun! Fight!"

Yet, even in this darkest hour, the fight for survival must continue. Joseph sent messengers to seek help from Sitting Bull and his Sioux warriors in Canada. As the wind increased and snow began to fall, Nez Perce women, children, and old people frantically began to dig caves and tunnels as places of safety and shelter. Without food or rest, they dug in the cold ground with knives, frying pans, and anything else they could find. They labored throughout the night in frigid weather that soon attained the full force of a blizzard. Their efforts saved many lives and enabled their people to withstand Colonel Miles' siege which was to last five days.

The soldiers also spent a cold, uncomfortable night in their trenches. Their supply wagons had not arrived and the men had no tents to protect them from the howling wind and thick snow that swirled about them. Campfires drew enemy fire so the white men were forced to huddle miserably in their rifle pits and wait for dawn to arrive. Colonel Miles spent a sleepless night fearing that Sitting Bull would ride in to reinforce the ranks of the hostiles. The Sioux leader was said to have over 2,000 warriors at his command. A large force such as this could easily tip the balance of power in favor of the Indians and render the military helpless against them. Miles sent messengers to General Howard and Colonel Sturgis urging them to hurry forward with their extra manpower. The ambitious Miles wanted credit for ending the Nez Perce campaign. He was determined to capture the nontreaties before anyone could arrive to help them.

Chapter 25

"I Will Fight No More"

On the morning of October 1 there were five inches of new snow on the Bear Paw battlefield. Still concerned about the arrival of the Sioux, Colonel Miles decided to attempt to negotiate the surrender of the Nez Perces. He sent two messengers under a white flag to arrange a meeting with Chief Joseph. General Howard's comments and reports had mistakenly led the colonel to believe that Joseph was the primary war leader and spokesman for his people.

The Nez Perce leaders listened in silence to Miles' representatives. Then they held a council to decide what action should be taken. Looking Glass and White Bird were opposed to surrender on any terms. Joseph wanted the opportunity to talk to Colonel Miles and see what could be done to save his people. Looking Glass reminded the council that white men could not be trusted. Indian leaders who fought the Americans in the past had been arrested and hanged. It was much better to die fighting as a warrior than suffer the indignities of a prisoner of war. Despite this opposition, Joseph wanted to attend the meeting. He promised not to make agreements with the white soldier chief. He would only listen and report back to the council. Finally, the other chiefs agreed and Joseph set out to meet Colonel Miles with several warriors and the half-breed, Tom Hill, acting as interpreter.

The meeting was held in a place about halfway between the two opposing camps. Tom Hill rode ahead to tell the colonel that Joseph was willing to meet with him. When the chief and his warriors arrived, Miles welcomed them and said, "Come, let us sit down by the fire and talk this matter over."

Yellow Wolf and a group of warriors watched the proceedings from a safe distance. They held their rifles ready in case the white men attempted to harm their leader. Yellow Wolf said to himself, "Whenever they shoot Chief Joseph, I will shoot from here."

Colonel Miles offered the Indians food, blankets, and good treatment if they would give up their rifles and make an unconditional surrender. Joseph wanted to return home. However, Miles was unwilling to make any promises about where the hostiles would be sent after the war. Joseph said he would have to keep at least half of his rifles. These were needed to provide food for his people. Miles wanted all of the guns handed over at once. It was soon obvious that the two leaders could not agree and the proceedings rapidly broke down. Finally, Joseph decided it was time to leave. As he stood to go, he was seized by the soldiers and taken under guard to their camp. There, his hands and feet were bound and he was rolled in two blankets so he could not move. Then he was unceremoniously confined in an area where mules were kept for the night. In this shameless manner, Colonel Miles violated the flag of truce and humiliated the Nez Perce peace chief.

The warriors who were with Joseph were allowed to return to their people. When they arrived without the chief,

Looking Glass and White Bird were opposed to Joseph's meeting with Colonel Miles.

many of the young men wanted to attack at once. However, Yellow Wolf and Wottolen cautioned them to restrain their anger until a plan could be made to rescue Joseph. As they were engaging in this discussion, a solution to their dilemma rode right into camp.

Colonel Miles had ordered Lieutenant Lovell Jerome to reconnoiter the Nez Perce camp and see what the Indians were doing. Instead of remaining at a safe distance, Jerome used questionable judgment and rode directly into the midst of the hostiles. Yellow Wolf immediately grabbed the reins of the lieutenant's horse and pulled him from his saddle. The Nez Perces now had a hostage of their own to exchange for the freedom of Chief Joseph.

In contrast to the treatment of Joseph in the white men's camp, Lieutenant Jerome was very well cared for by his Nez Perce captors. In a message to his commanding officer he wrote:

> I had good supper and good bed. I had plenty of blankets. This morning I had a good breakfast. I am treated like I was at home. I hope you officers are treating Joseph as I am treated.

While Joseph was detained in Miles' camp, the soldiers' supply train arrived with food, blankets, medicine, and the Napoleon cannon. The firearm was difficult to use at first but soon the troops were exploding shells in the Nez Perce camp. The Indians were terrified and several of them were wounded by pieces of flying rock.

As the firing continued around him, Yellow Wolf made his way to Colonel Miles' camp to negotiate the release of his chief. Miles was angry when he learned about the capture of Lieutenant Jerome. His plan to weaken the Indians' position by capturing their chief would now have to be abandoned. His valuable hostage would have to be released to save the life of the lieutenant.

The colonel would not permit Joseph and Yellow Wolf to talk in private. However, he did allow them a brief meeting in his presence. When he learned about the Nez Perces' plan to rescue him, Joseph cautioned Yellow Wolf, "If they kill me you must not kill the officer. It will do no good to avenge my death by killing him."

The exchange of prisoners took place on the morning of October 2. The Indians spread a buffalo robe on the ground about halfway between the lines of battle. Joseph was escorted to this place by several soldiers carrying a white flag of truce. Looking Glass, White Bird, and several warriors brought Lieutenant Jerome to meet them. Joseph briefly shook hands with the lieutenant and the men returned to their own people.

As the fighting continued, the suffering in the Nez Perce camp increased. Wetatonmi, Ollokot's widow, said, "We slept only by naps, sitting in our pits; leaning forward or back against the dirt wall. Many of the warriors stayed in their rifle pits all the time." The old people suffered in silence while the children sobbed in their mothers' arms. Everyone was wet, cold, and hungry. Some people had been without food for days and water could be gotten only at night.

On the morning of the fifth day, the soldiers managed a direct hit with their cannon on the Nez Perce entrenchments. Four women, a little boy, and a twelve-year-old girl were buried when the walls of their shelter caved in around them. The Indians frantically began to dig them out. They managed to rescue everyone except the girl and her grandmother who were found dead. The Indians buried the bodies of the two victims in the ruins of their shelter.

General Howard arrived at the Bear Paw battlefield on the evening of October 4. Colonel Miles received him in a somewhat unfriendly manner fearing he now would assume command and take credit for capturing the Nez Perces. Miles' attitude improved when the general assured him he would not take charge until after the Indians surrendered. This event now must be planned and the two officers spent a great deal of time discussing it. They finally decided to send Howard's Nez Perce scouts, Captain John and Old George, as emissaries to the hostile camp. Both scouts had daughters among the nontreaties and this gave them the best chance of persuading the bands to surrender.

Captain John and Old George visited the Nez Perce campsite on the morning of October 5. They carried a white flag and were immediately taken to see Joseph.

General Howard arrived at the Bear Paw Mountains on October 4.

They told the chief that General Howard had arrived and would treat the Nez Perces honorably if they agreed to surrender. The hostiles would be given food and blankets and taken to a place beside the Tongue River to spend the winter. In the spring, they would be returned to the Northwest. The chiefs would not be executed for rebelling against the Americans. The scouts said, "You have fought well, but now is the time for rest and peace."

Joseph had little respect for the treaty Nez Perces. However, he listened politely to their words and sent them back safely to General Howard. When they were gone, he called a council meeting to decide what to do.

Both Looking Glass and White Bird refused to lay down their arms. White Bird was now in his seventies. He said

314

he would rather die than be confined on the white man's reservation. He was determined to escape into Canada and would take anyone with him who wished to go.

Looking Glass also refused to surrender. He still believed that Sitting Bull would arrive with his Sioux warriors to drive the soldiers away. He said to Joseph, "I am older than you. I have my experiences with a man of two faces and two tongues. If you surrender, you will be sorry. I will never surrender to a deceitful white chief."

Joseph worried about his people who were scattered throughout the area in isolated shelters and trenches. He said, "The women are suffering with cold, the children crying with the chilly dampness of the shelter pits. For myself I do not care. It is for them I am going to surrender."

Joseph decided to send his own wife and baby to Canada with White Bird. He would remain behind to care for those who were unable to escape. He said:

> I could not bear to see my wounded men and women suffer any longer; we had lost enough already. General (Joseph's mistake; Miles was a colonel.) Miles had promised that we might return to our country, with what stock we had left. I thought we could start again. I believed General Miles, or I never would have surrendered . . . I would have held him in check until my friends came to my assistance, and then neither the generals nor their soldiers would have left Bear Paw Mountain alive.

While Joseph made preparations to surrender, Looking Glass returned to his warriors in the trenches. Shortly after his arrival, his attention was drawn to an Indian riding toward him in the distance. Looking Glass immediately assumed the rider was a messenger sent from Sitting Bull to say that help was on the way. Filled with relief and joy, the chief sprang up to point out his discovery to the others. At that instant, a bullet struck him in the forehead and he fell dead before his horrified warriors. The distant rider was not a Sioux. He was one of Colonel Miles' Cheyenne scouts.

The war chief's death left Joseph and White Bird as the last remaining guardians of their people. The old order of Nez Perce culture was coming to an end. The great chiefs were dead and there was no one left to replace them. Soon White Bird would leave for Canada and Joseph would be completely alone to gather up the fragile remains of a once great and powerful people.

On October 5 at about 2:20 p.m., all firing ceased on the Bear Paw battlefield. A strange quiet settled over the area as if Mother Earth herself stood poised in hushed anticipation. The day was cold and snowy. Only a few dim rays of sunlight pierced the steel gray clouds that filled the sky. A raw winter wind blew across the battlefield chilling the Indians in their exposed trenches and causing the soldiers to wrap their woolen overcoats more tightly about them.

Two hours later, Chief Joseph rode from his camp toward a small gathering of soldiers waiting silently on the plain. The chief was accompanied by five warriors and the Palouse chief, Husishusis Kute, who walked beside Joseph's horse and conversed with the chief in a soft voice. Joseph sat straight in the saddle with his rifle resting across his knees. His head was bowed slightly as he listened to the words of his friend.

Looking neither right nor left, Joseph rode directly to the little group of soldiers that included General Howard, Colonel Miles, Lieutenants C. E. S. Wood, Oscar Long, and Guy Howard as well as an interpreter named Arthur Chapman. When the chief was directly before General Howard, he proudly swung down from his saddle and extended his arm in a broad gesture of salutation.

Joseph wore no special adornment for this important occasion. His long, black hair hung in thick braids on either side of a somber face that bore the mark of a bullet that had grazed his forehead. He wore buckskin leggings and a gray wool blanket which he had draped over one shoulder. When his eyes met those of General Howard, the chief offered his rifle as a token of submission. However, the general only smiled and waved his hand toward Colonel Miles who stepped forward to accept the weapon. Joseph solemnly gave up the gun and stepped back a few paces from the group. Then, he proudly faced his captors and spoke the famous words that have echoed the pain and suffering of the Nez Perce chief throughout history. With Arthur Chapman as interpreter and Lieutenant Wood as recorder, Joseph said:

Tell General Howard I know his heart. What he told me before, I have it in my heart. I am tired of fighting. Our chiefs are killed. Looking Glass is dead. Toohoolhoolzote is dead. The old men are all dead. It is the young men who say "yes" or "no." He who led the young men is dead. It is cold, and we have no blankets. The little children are freezing to death. My people, some of them, have run away to the hills, and have no blankets, no food. No one knows where they are—perhaps freezing to death. I want to have time to look for my children, and see how many I can find. Maybe I shall find them among the dead. Hear me, my chiefs! I am tired. My heart is sick and sad. From where the sun now stands I will fight no more forever.

So saying the chief drew his blanket over his head and turned his gaze toward the empty battlefield. The war was over and Joseph's shoulders sagged with the weight of sorrow and responsibility that lay heavily upon him.

For the rest of the afternoon Joseph's people straggled into Miles' camp from their hiding places in the ravines. They were tired, sick, wounded, cold, and starving. Yet, the

"From where the sun now stands I will fight no more forever."

soldiers could not fail to notice that their spirit had not been broken by their experiences. Even in defeat they maintained the sense of pride and dignity that befitted the favored children of Mother Earth. The white men had captured their bodies, but their spirits remained free to wander the land they loved.

Of the nearly 800 Nez Perces who left Idaho, 418 surrendered with Joseph. Of these, 87 were warriors, 184 were women, and 147 were children. About 233 others escaped to Canada with Chief White Bird. The last to leave was Joseph's nephew, Yellow Wolf. He promised to locate and care for the chief's family in exile. At least 120 Nez Perces had been killed. Of these, 65 were men and 55 were women and children. The soldiers suffered comparable losses with 180 killed and 150 wounded.

The remarkable flight of the Nez Perces carried them over 1,700 miles of wilderness in nearly four months of painful travel. They had fought over 2,000 American soldiers and volunteers in four major battles and many lesser skirmishes. Colonel Miles said: "The Nez Perces are the boldest men and best marksmen of any Indians I have ever encountered, and Chief Joseph is a man of more sagacity and intelligence than any Indian I have ever met." The colonel summed up his feelings about the campaign when he said, "The fight was the most fierce of any Indian engagement I have ever been in. The whole Nez Perce movement is unequalled in the history of Indian warfare."

When asked about the great military skill displayed by the Nez Perce leaders in their encounters with the military, Joseph stated simply, "The Great Spirit puts it in the heart and head of man to know how to defend himself." And defend themselves they did until the strength of their opponents overwhelmed them. On his trip to Washington, D.C. in 1879, Joseph explained his feelings about the white man's treatment of his people. He said:

> Whenever the white man treats the Indian as they treat each other, then we shall have no more wars. We shall be all alike—brothers of one father and one mother, with one sky above us and one country around us and one government for all. Then the Great Spirit Chief who rules above will smile upon this land, and send rain to wash out the bloody spots made by brothers' hands upon the face of the earth. For this time the Indian race are waiting and praying. I hope that no more groans of wounded men and women will ever go to the ear of the Great Spirit Chief above, and that all people may be one people.

Epilogue

The United States Government did not keep the promises made to Chief Joseph on the Bear Paw battlefield. After the Nez Perces surrendered, they were taken to Fort Keogh on the south bank of the Yellowstone River where they were to spend the winter. Both General Howard and Colonel Miles thought the nontreaty bands would be returned to Idaho when weather permitted in the spring. However, W. T. Sherman, Commanding General of the Army, had other ideas. Sherman believed in showing no mercy to a defeated enemy. During the Civil War, he had adopted the practice of crushing his adversaries so they could not rise up and fight him again. This policy, combined with his theory that "the only good Indian is a dead Indian", meant continued suffering for the Nez Perce tribe. Sherman wanted Joseph and his people permanently exiled from the Northwest so they could never again threaten the peaceful settlement of the area.

During the war, General Howard and Colonel Miles had grown to respect the Nez Perces and had developed a concern for their fair treatment. Their efforts on the Indians' behalf were ignored by Sherman who wanted his subordinates to support his harsh treatment of the hostiles. Miles was left alone in his crusade when General Howard stopped trying to help the nontreaties and endorsed the policies of Sherman.

Howard was angry when Miles failed to give him proper credit in his official report of the war. The general decided to make his part in the campaign known by publishing his own account of the conflict. Howard's aide, C. E. S. Wood, wrote the article which was featured in a Chicago newspaper. This action caused Howard to be criticized by his superior, General Philip Sheridan, who disapproved of the conflicting reports. Howard was aware that Sheridan was a strong supporter of Sherman's Indian policies. To regain the favor of his commanding officers, Howard turned his back on the defeated Nez Perces and joined the ranks of Sherman's movement against them.

On November 1, only ten days after the Nez Perces' arrival at Fort Keogh, they were transferred to Fort Lincoln until a place could be found for them in Indian Country (present-day Oklahoma). Fort Lincoln was located near Bismarck in Dakota Territory, a journey of 800 miles from Fort Keogh. The 418 Nez Perce prisoners were terrified at the thought of traveling so far from their native land. They were certain they would all be executed when they reached the distant fort.

Fourteen flatboats transported the sick and wounded down the Yellowstone and Missouri rivers while the remaining captives rode overland with an escort of soldiers led by Colonel Miles. The flatboats were so heavily overcrowded the water rose nearly level with the decks. No concern for the Indians' welfare was shown aboard the boats. One woman with a baby strapped to her back in a cradleboard leaned over to get drinking water from the river. As she bent forward, the binding slipped loose from the board and the child fell into the water. The woman immediately dove in to save her baby. Both mother and child were lost when the boatmen refused to stop for them. Incidents such as this increased the fear of the Nez Perce prisoners and they began to sing their protective chants as they approached Fort Lincoln.

Contrary to their expectations, Joseph and his people were warmly welcomed by the people of Fort Lincoln and Bismarck. The citizens had read about the courageous flight of the Nez Perces and admired the nontreaties for their "bravery and humanity." Joseph was honored with a banquet given by the ladies who lived in the area.

Colonel Miles continued to call for the fair treatment of the defeated Indians. In his report to the Secretary of War he stated:

> . . . I have the honor to recommend that ample provision be made for their civilization, and to enable them to become self-sustaining. They are sufficiently intelligent to appreciate the consideration which, in my opinion, is justly due them from the government.

In addition to his report, Miles urged General Sherman to allow Joseph and a delegation of Nez Perce leaders to travel to Washington and plead their case before the President. The colonel was very disappointed when his recommendations were ignored and the Indians were herded aboard a train and transferred to Fort Leavenworth.

The Nez Perces arrived at Leavenworth on November 27 and were assigned to a hot, malaria-ridden section of land in the swampy bottomland of the Missouri River. The area proved to be extremely unhealthy for the Indians who were used to the much cooler climate of their high moun-

323

tain plateau. Chief Joseph watched in agony as many of his people became sick and died. In describing this terrible time in his life he said:

> I cannot tell how much my heart suffered for my people while at Leavenworth. The Great Spirit who rules above seemed to be looking some other way, and did not see what was being done to my people.

In desperation the chief joined with seven other Nez Perce leaders in petitioning the government to help their tribesmen. Joseph pleaded for a return to Idaho or a transfer to a healthier climate. Both requests were denied by General Sherman.

In May, 1878, Congress appropriated $20,000 to send the Nez Perces to the Quawpaw Indian reservation in Kansas Territory. Thirty-one of the captives died before they could be moved in July. Over two-hundred were ill when they left Leavenworth and three more died on the way to their new home.

The climate on the Quawpaw reserve was also unsuitable for the Nez Perce people. They were unable to recover from the malaria they had contracted at Leavenworth, and shortly after their arrival, one fourth of them died of the disease.

In late July, the survivors were taken to a 7,000-acre section of land purchased from the Miami and Peoria Indians. The Commissioner of Indian Affairs, E. A. Hayt, hoped this would be a better place for the captives to live. However, the climate was still far too warm and the dry sagebrush plain was a poor substitute for the lush grassland of the Wallowa Valley. With poor sanitation and no medicine available, the nontreaties continued to die. By October, forty-seven more Nez Perces were dead.

Chief Joseph feared that all of his people would die if something were not done immediately. In January, 1879, he finally obtained permission to visit Washington and plead his case before President Hayes and other governmental officials. Accompanied by Yellow Bull and an interpreter named Arthur Chapman, the chief spoke to an assembly on January 14. He said:

> . . . I cannot understand how the government sends a man out to fight us, as it did General Miles, and then breaks his word. Such a government has something wrong about it . . . I do not understand why nothing is done for my people. I have heard talk and talk, but nothing is done . . . Words do not pay for my dead people. They do not pay for my country, now overrun by white men. They do not protect my father's grave . . . I am tired of talk that comes to nothing. It makes my heart sick when I remember all the good words and all the broken promises. There has been too much talking by men who had no right to talk. Too many misrepresentations have been made, too many misunderstandings have come up between the white men about the Indian . . .
>
> You might as well expect the rivers to run backward as that any man who was born free should be contented penned up and denied liberty to go where he pleases.
>
> I know that my race must change. We cannot hold our own with the white men as we are. We only ask an even chance to live as other men live. We ask to be recognized as men. We ask that the same law shall work alike on all men.

Joseph's speech made a favorable impression on his audience. However, no action was taken to return the Nez Perces to the Northwest. The government still feared trouble in Idaho if the nontreaties were returned to their former territory.

While Joseph made his eloquent appeal in Washington, Commissioner Hayt selected a new home for the Nez Perces on the Ponca reservation in Oklahoma. The captives were transferred there in June of 1879. The huge 90,735-acre area was more fertile. However, there were no

Chief Yellow Bull

rivers or mountains and the climate was still unhealthy for the Northwest Indians. Heavy fall rain and bitter winter cold caused more sickness and death. With poor shelter and almost no medicine, most newborn babies could not survive. Joseph continued to grieve for his people who desperately longed for their life-giving homeland.

Like their fellow tribesmen in Oklahoma, the Nez Perces who had fled to Canada with Chief White Bird were also becoming homesick for the Northwest. Some of the fugitives left their sanctuary in small groups and began the long journey home. Traveling secretly through forests and over mountains, they received little help from Indians or white men along the way. On the contrary, some of them were hunted down and killed while others lived for years hiding on one reservation after another. Those who managed to reach Lapwai faced a cool reception from the Christian Nez Perces who still considered them to be unwanted troublemakers.

In 1878, Yellow Wolf returned to Idaho with Chief Joseph's daughter, Walking in Crushed Snow. Yellow Wolf was arrested and taken under guard to join the other Nez Perce captives. At Lapwai, Walking in Crushed Snow met a man named George Moses. She married him on July 21, 1879 and took the name Sarah Moses. She lived with her husband on the reservation for the remainder of her life.

In 1881, Colonel Miles renewed his efforts to return the Nez Perces to Idaho. Supported by General Howard's former aide, C. E. S. Wood, the Indian Rights Association in Philadelphia, and the Presbyterian Church, Miles succeeded in making the plight of Joseph and his people a national issue.

In May, 1881, the government responded to the requests of the pro-Indian groups by returning twenty-nine of the Nez Perce captives to Lapwai. This action failed to satisfy

Colonel Miles and the others who refused to be pacified until all of the nontreaties were sent home.

After four years of determined work, the Indian sympathizers were finally successful. The remaining 268 Nez Perce survivors were returned to the Northwest in the spring of 1885. The Indians traveled home on the Union Pacific and Oregon Short Line railroads. When they arrived in Pocatello, Idaho, they were divided into two groups. Captain Frank Baldwin of the Columbia Military Department sent 118 of the nontreaties to the reservation at Lapwai. Joseph and the remaining Nez Perces were sent to the Colville reservation at Nespelem, Washington. The people of Idaho refused to accept the Wallamwatkin chief who they still mistakenly blamed for the war of 1877.

Joseph and his followers were treated as intruders by the Indians who already occupied the Colville reservation. It was necessary to call in troops from Fort Spokane to enforce the rights of the Nez Perces to their share of the land. Joseph considered his stay on the reservation to be temporary. He stubbornly continued his efforts to return to the Wallowa Valley. Finally, in 1899, the chief was allowed to visit his beloved valley for the first time since the war. He traveled about with a man named A. C. Smith hoping to purchase a section of land for his people. Joseph was received politely wherever he went, but no one would even consider selling land to the Nez Perces. The chief suffered bitter disappointment and sadly returned to Colville. However, he refused to give up the hope of returning home to the land of his fathers one day.

In 1900, Inspector General James McLaughlin from the Indian Bureau visited Joseph and discussed the Nez Perces' possible relocation to Idaho. McLaughlin accompanied the chief on a trip to the Wallowa in an effort to acquire land for a reservation.

While in the valley, Joseph paid a visit to the grave of his father, Tuekakas, venerable leader of the Wallam-watkin Nez Perces. Joseph's eyes filled with tears as he gazed at the gravesite. His father's last words echoed across the years: "Never sell the bones of your father and your mother." Would the old chief understand his son's failure to honor this final request? Would he forgive? How different things were before the white men arrived with their guns, missions, whiskey, diseases, fences, and neverending hunger for Indian land. Joseph longed for the old days when his proud, free people lived in peace and harmony with Mother Earth. How good it was to roam freely about the land with no thought to borders, settlements, forts, treaties, or other white man's restrictions about where Indians could and could not go. But those days were gone forever; and the Nez Perces had now become trespassers on the very land that had once given them life and strength.

Despite Joseph's persistence, his attempts to return to the Wallowa continued to meet with failure. The citizens of the valley stated in no uncertain terms that they would not tolerate the return of the Nez Perces.

In 1904, Joseph attended the commencement exercises of Carlisle Indian Industrial School in Pennsylvania. In a strange trick of fate, the Nez Perce chief was seated at the same banquet table as his former enemy, Major General Oliver Howard. Fortunately, the passage of time since the war had served to temper the emotions of the one-time combatants and the two men were actually able to toast each other. Joseph said:

Friends, I meet here my friend, General Howard. I used to be so anxious to meet him. I wanted to kill him in war . . . We are both old men, still we live and I am glad . . . Ever since the war I have made up my mind to be friendly to the whites and to everybody . . . I have lost many friends, and many men, women, and children, but I have no grievance against any of the white people, General Howard or anyone.

When he returned to Colville, Joseph seemed more resigned to his life on the reservation. The memory of his former days in the Wallowa lingered in his mind like a cherished dream. In his final days, the chief would often sit alone for hours silently staring into the flames of his campfire. While his captive body remained completely motionless, his mind was free to roam the familiar trails of his beloved Wallowa homeland. This is how Joseph was occupied when death came to him on September 21, 1904. Wrapped in his blanket, the lonely old man fell forward on his face before the flames of his fire. The agency doctor listed the cause of death as "a broken heart." So died the last of the great Nez Perce chiefs—a man of peace hopelessly shackled by the chains of war. His greatest wish can best be stated in his own words, taken from his Washington speech of 1879 in which he said:

If the white man wants to live in peace with the Indian . . . there need be no trouble. Treat all men alike. Give them all the same laws. Give them all an even chance to live and grow. All men were made by the same Great Spirit. They are brothers!

"All men were made by the same Great Spirit. They are brothers!"

Acknowledgements

Myrtle A. Fisher

Nola Mileck

Wendy E. Schurkey

Kathy Spence

Merle Wells, Ph.D.

Charlene Wicks

Nancy Williamson

Index

339

131, 138, 143, 150, 153; and
1877 meeting of Nez Perces
with General Howard, 155–
163; and the return of the Nez
Perces after the war, 327

Lawyer, Chief, 25–26, 39, 52, 55,
60, 76, 80–85, 94–98, 104,
106, 108–109, 111–113, 120,
131, 138

Lean Elk. See Poker Joe

Lee, Jason, 39

Lemhi River, 246

Lemhi Shoshoni, 246

Lemhi Valley, 12, 248

Lewis and Clark Expedition, 14–
17, 21, 23, 25–26, 82

Lewis, Joe, 63–64

Lewiston, Idaho, 165

Lindsley, A. L., 142

Little Rockey Mountains, 298

Logan, Captain William, 235

Lolo Creek, 221–222, 225

Lolo Pass. See Lolo Trail

Lolo Trail, 12, 15, 211, 217–218,
222, 225, 231, 290

Long, Oscar, 316

Looking Glass, Old Chief. See
Old Looking Glass

Looking Glass, Young Chief: 33;
becomes chief, 104; and 1874
council at Tepahlewam, 132;
and 1877 council with General
Howard, 155, 161, 163; and
1877 gathering at Tepahlewam, 166, 168; decides to remain out of war, 177–178; and
attack on his village, 193–
195, 197–198, 204; becomes
war chief, 211–212; and Chief
Red Heart, 214; and the end
of the Lolo Trail, 223; at Big
Hole, 226, 229–230, 238; loses
position as war chief, 243–
245; and the Raid at the
Camas Meadows, 251; and

Yellowstone Park, 263–265;
and the Crow Indians, 285;
challenges Poker Joe's authority, 295–296; becomes war
chief once again, 299; at the
Bear Paw Mountains, 301–
303, 309, 312, 314–315; death
of, 315

Lostine River, 120

Lower Geyser Basin, 261–262,
270, 280

Luke Billy, 203

Lyon, Albert, 249

Lyon, Caleb, 111

Madison River, 274

Mammoth Hot Springs, 259,
271, 273–274, 277

Man of the Morning, 26–27, 30,
37

Mandan Indians, 12

Mann, Charles, 261

Mason, Charles H., 91

McAdow, P. W., 287

McCafferty, Sergeant Hugh, 253

McCartney, Jim, 275–277

McDonanld, Finan, 18

McDowell, General Irwin, 210

McKenzie, Donald, 21

McLaughlin, Inspector General
James, 328

McLloyd, John L., 43

McLoughlin, Chief Factor Dr.
John, 35–36, 45–46

McNall, Ephriam, 144

McNall, Wells, 140–141, 143–
144, 147

Metat Waptass, Chief, 76, 89

Methodist Church, 39

Meyers, Henry, 261

Miami Indians, 324

Miles, Colonel Nelson A., 225,
258, 260, 286, 299–302, 304–
307, 309–313, 316–317, 319,
321–323, 327–328

Mill Creek, 99